MY BODY

Women Speak Out
about Their Health Care

MY BODY
Women Speak Out about Their Health Care

MARION CROOK, B.Sc.N., R.N.

Foreword by

Sari Tudiver, Ph.D.
and
Janice L. Nusbaum, R.N., M.N., M.B.A.

 **INSIGHT BOOKS**

PLENUM PRESS • NEW YORK AND LONDON

Library of Congress Cataloging-in-Publication Data

Crook, Marion.
    My body : women speak out about their health care / Marion Crook.
        p.   cm.
    Includes bibliographical references and index.
    ISBN 0-306-44943-9
    1. Women--Health and hygiene--Sociological aspects. 2. Women's
health services. 3. Women--Health and hygiene--Information
services.   I. Title.
RA564.85.C76 1995
610'.82--dc20   95-2401
                                                                    CIP

ISBN 0-306-44943-9

© 1995 Marion Crook
Insight Books is a Division of Plenum Publishing Corporation
233 Spring Street, New York, N.Y. 10013-1578

An Insight Book

10 9 8 7 6 5 4 3 2 1

Printed in the United States of America

Foreword

Sari Tudiver
Janice L. Nusbaum

As part of my job as Resource Coordinator at the Women's Health Clinic in Winnipeg, I speak with many of the women who call for health information. Inquiries such as "I need to know more about fibroids" can be handled easily by referring the woman to a useful book or articles. Other questions reveal the very complex decisions women are asked to make by their doctors, often without being provided enough information to evaluate their options.

For example, I recently spoke with a 48-year-old woman from a small town in Manitoba who had cancer of the lymphatic system 6 years earlier. The chemotherapy treatment she received resulted in an early menopause, but she was now clear of the cancer, feeling healthy and active with no uncomfortable symptoms. Her family physician had prescribed hormone replacement therapy "to help prevent heart disease." She felt very uneasy about taking hormones, given her history. She asked me: "What do we know about the long-term effects of hormone therapy on someone with my history of cancer?" We suggested she discuss this difficult and inadequately researched question with her cancer specialist, while making him aware of her current good health and fears of hormone use.

Other women have been told by their doctors that they need a hysterectomy, but whether they have their ovaries removed is up

v

to them. They are overwhelmed by the decision since they have little information to guide them. In any one week, women may ask about fertility drugs, prenatal genetic screening, chronic fatigue syndrome, drug therapies or surgeries for endometriosis, the signs of anorexia and other eating disorders in teens, side effects of the injectable contraceptive Depo-Provera, and how to get involved in a local support group for women with breast implants. For some of the women who call, English is not their first language. Sight-impaired women are looking for information on tape. We do the best we can, but our time and resources are limited.

In their search for clear information that will help them make informed decisions and, hopefully, be healthier, women encounter parallel, sometimes contradictory, trends in the health care system. For example, there is a well-established movement in both Canada and the United States to make childbirth more woman-centered and less medicalized and to accept trained midwives as the primary caregivers for women during pregnancy and normal childbirth. At the same time, prenatal screening tests to determine possible genetic problems in the fetus are offered routinely in many North American centers. Women and their partners are suddenly confronted with decisions that may require them to deal with genetic counselors, assess risk scores, and explore their attitudes and anxieties about abortion and disability. If a woman and her partner choose the path of "least technology," they may find themselves covering some rough terrain in order to decide what they are rejecting and why.

Women do not want to reject a test or treatment that may be of benefit, but they do not readily know how to differentiate what is going to be helpful or appropriate from what might be unnecessary or even harmful. In the face of hard-to-access scientific research, medical jargon, and aggressive marketing of drugs and technologies by the pharmaceutical industry, women are trying to find balanced and critical information they can understand, including information about alternative therapies. And once information has been gathered, women must try to reconcile what they know with what they feel. Many ask us: "Should I trust my intuitive or 'gut' feelings about what to do?" Reading Marion Crook's *My Body* should help enormously in this process.

To ask questions, gather information, and trust one's feelings requires that a woman has some confidence in herself. A woman's sense of self-esteem, and how she feels about her body, are largely shaped by her personal and family histories—whether as a child and young woman she learned to respect herself and was comfortable with how her body grew and matured or whether she was taunted, humiliated, and abused. The emotional baggage a woman carries from the past and the conditions of her present life determine whether she is able to take action. A woman in an abusive relationship may be threatened if she makes a phone call to a health center. A woman who feels her English is poor will be afraid to try. A woman who is tired, overworked, and living in poverty will not have the energy to do research or mobilize already meager resources.

Most medical encounters are too short and formal to explore or reveal the deeper issues of the past and a woman's current social environment of disease. Many women never find a voice to raise the questions or issues they are dealing with. They often say, "My doctor isn't a talker. I couldn't ask that." Their personal selves are kept separate from their care. This is especially true for deaf women who need interpreters to communicate with health providers and for women from ethnic groups where doctors are held in great esteem and where it is not considered appropriate to share such feelings.

As a result, providing basic health information may never result in changed behavior and better health if the profound emotional barriers women face are not addressed. I have heard many health professionals wonder about the low levels of breast-feeding among northern First Nations women. The nursing director of a clinic run by a tribal council in northern Manitoba could easily understand it. Herself a First Nations woman, many of her clients have confided that they don't breastfeed because they cannot bear to look at their bodies without shame, after years of being sexually and physically abused. Campaigns to promote breastfeeding will not succeed unless caregivers acknowledge the

roots of such pain and allow appropriate opportunities for healing. Where do women find the space to speak about who they are
in relation to the care they need?

In *My Body* Marion Crook has listened carefully and respectfully to the stories and insights of diverse women in Canada and
the United States concerning their health and needs for information and services. Her skills have been honed over the years
working as a nurse with families from different cultural backgrounds and in previous research interviewing young women
with eating disorders and teens who attempted suicide. What
emerges is a clearly written, practical, and insightful guide to new
ways of thinking about our selves and our bodies and what we all
need—women and men, laypersons and professionals—in order
to achieve what she calls a "healing environment."

Using plain language, Crook explores many of the assumptions and attitudes that guide the dominant North American health
care system, including the image that diseases must be "attacked."
She highlights some of the ways male-dominated institutions of
church and state in Europe and North America consolidated their
power over medicine and healing and displaced women practitioners, depriving them of access to formal learning in universities
and to a significant role in how science would be practiced. A
fragmented, highly specialized, doctor-centered system is the
norm, in which body parts are treated separately and an integrative
approach to care is rare. As Crook comments, this system reinforces
the view for many people that "health" is luck and healing an
external procedure given to them by someone else.

Despite many advances in treatments, Crook wisely notes
that we have little understanding of what illness expresses, why
some people need illness, how the body experiences and reflects
social and cultural pressures, and what truths this tells about our
past. For example, women are only now beginning to understand
the links between childhood abuse and later addictions. Women
have little faith in their ability to understand their bodies, one
outcome of a society that treats women with violence and denies
them equality, status, and respect. Approaches to healing from
other cultural traditions that stress the meaning and context of

illness for the individual and the community and that seek balance have been disparaged by mainstream medicine. Many of these non-Western views are consistent with the holistic, integrative approaches to health that women are seeking.

The book's basic arguments are refreshingly sound and the suggestions practical. We have unrealistic expectations of doctors, assuming their expertise is broad and holistic when it is limited. This is unfair to both women and physicians and unhealthy for society as a whole. Women need more than one source of health information and should seek out other care providers, such as community nurses, nurse practitioners, librarians, researchers, health educators, and laywomen mentors with experiences and skills. Crook proposes an apt image: A woman should be in the center of a web receiving information from a network of interconnected systems. The book is filled with many creative examples of community health centers, hospital-based programs, grassroots organizations, and women's health information networks in the United States and Canada that Crook visited as part of her research and with the insights of women who are attempting to put their visions of woman-centered care and health education into practice. Collaborative models where staff members, including doctors, and volunteers work together to provide a range of services in sensitive and cost-effective ways are possible. I know, because I work in such a center.

A major theme of *My Body* is the need to reassign responsibility for health and healing from the individual doctor to the patient and the community. This rethinking of how we deal with health and healing and how we can better use the many community resources we have should be required reading for those involved in health reform. It should not be mistaken for a conservative, "back-to-the-basics" approach. Crook recognizes how circumstances of poverty, low literacy, discrimination, and racism directed against First Nations peoples, immigrants, the elderly, and persons with disabilities produce emotional and physical ill health and limit access to information and services, especially for women. Powerful interest groups—the pharmaceutical industry, insurance companies, professional organizations of doctors, politicians, religious groups—all play key roles in shaping women's dependencies and reinforcing the status quo. These interest groups benefit from maintaining their power.

Crook warns the reader to beware of how governments and other insurers are promoting a view of "individual responsibility" and "community care" while cutting back on covering needed services and treatments. Cost-cutting measures to de-insure services will place added family responsibilities and stresses on many women. In contrast, Crook's call for a "healing environment" seeks to empower women and give them a greater voice in their health and healing. She urges individual women to make small changes in how they approach the medical system by knowing one's rights, persistently asking for information, and listening to one's body. But she recognizes that when a system does not provide health care as a right for all, it may be more difficult for some women to take action.

The book helps us reflect on the situations of women in both Canada and the United States, countries with two different health care systems and vast regional diversity. The Canadian system provides universal health coverage, and the principles of universality and accessibility to care are enshrined in the Canada Health Act. The U.S. system is a patchwork of private and public insurers, with excellent care for some and many people unable to secure the health care they need. Yet, as Crook points out, both countries have a doctor-centered model, rely largely on fee-for-service payment, and generally practice medicine in similar ways. Women in both countries have many of the same difficulties securing appropriate health information, being treated with respect by care providers, and finding services that meet their range of needs. In both countries, the rising costs of medical care are driven by high, unregulated drug prices; the introduction of new technologies and intervention, many of which have not been adequately assessed; doctors' fees; and administrative costs. Within each country, states and provinces are grappling with "health reform" efforts to achieve cost reductions that are politically acceptable to voters. Crook's discussion leads us to consider what true health reform might be in each country if health policies were directed to eliminating the root causes of poor health, including poverty and environmental hazards, and to creating a "healing environment."

Like a wise aunt sharing experiences, Marion Crook includes sound advice that can help the reader recognize and avoid quacks; seek out and research information from many different sources; choose health advisors, advocates, and interpreters; and have more effective doctor visits. There are insightful comments for parents on how to nurture positive attitudes in children so they become more confident in their abilities to take charge of their health. The book is worth reading for these sections alone.

Most of all, this is a book that generates energy and hope. It's about working for personal and social transformations in small increments, day by day, rooted in the present, remembering the past, envisioning the future. It's about finding new ways for women to come together and share information, stories, and dreams, whether around a kitchen table, a healing circle, or on the Internet. They will sharpen their skills to be cynical, analytic, persistent, funny, and sensitive—finding a voice they never heard before. Women know there are no easy answers, that information can never be complete, that the pharmaceutical industry is not easily challenged, and that some women will not heal. But they will continue to struggle to make the world better for themselves, their families, and others. Along the way, they will make history. *My Body* is an important contribution to that process. You're in for a treat.

Sari Tudiver, PhD
Resource Coordinator
Women's Health Clinic
Winnipeg, Manitoba, Canada

• •

My Body is a timely book for all women, and I recommend it to all health care providers. The perspectives presented need to be part of our awareness. Women are still considered to be the ones responsible for the health of their families: children's immunizations, husbands' low fat diet, grandma's side effects from high blood pressure medication, Uncle John's care in the nursing home, and their own overall care. All sorts of health care systems have to be known and used appropriately and prudently. Where is this information? Who knows what to ask? As public health nurses, we help many people through some of this maze. However, only 12% of the population may be reached. Volunteers, outreach workers, school-linked family resource and wellness centers, and community health fairs try to reach more people with health care information. All these efforts are aimed to increase personal responsibility for one's own health care. All these efforts are, however, frequently in vain. Ask the question: "Who owns the illness/disease?" The answer often starts out as: "My doctor (this)" or "My nurse (that)" or "My daughter (the other)." Answers such as these certainly make it sound like someone else owns the illness other than the person who lives with it. Women may socially be given the responsibility of the health of their families; however, they usually do not have the authority to go with the responsibility. The health care provider most often maintains the authority over the illness and consequently over the person who has the illness. Quite a dilemma! Information is power, and power can equate to authority. Might it be that the more health information women acquire the more power they have and the greater their authority over their own bodies?

My Body brings into clear view the difficulties women have getting reliable health information as well as being able to use it. There is another aspect the reader might keep in mind while reading: Where do men (non-medical) get their health information? Most likely from women . . . mothers . . . wives. Men today are more likely to be single parents than ever before. The responsibility for their children's health is a new role for many men.

Mr. C came into a walk-in immunization clinic to get his three children their booster shots. He gave the nurse all the past immunization history and current health status of all three children. When the nurse asked Mr. C to bring his children to the next room to get their shots, Mr. C. replied: "They are home. Aren't you going to give me the medicine to take home?" Mr. C's only experience with health care had been getting a prescription, going to the pharmacy, and taking the medicine home. His past experience shaped the way he gave information, asked for information, and expected service.

With *My Body: Women Speak Out about Their Health Care*, Marion Crook introduces the reader to what women experience in their quest for health information. The reader is enlightened to find that what kind of health information is looked for and asked for is shaped not only by the life experiences of the woman herself, but also by the history of women's acquisition of health information. The book examines the barriers that prevent women from getting what they need to know as these barriers relate to the wish for a more open system and hope that needs for information will be met.

My Body is written to help women understand the difference between what is the nature of the system and what is the nature of the women seeking health information. Marion Crook takes the reader by the hand and introduces women who were in search of health information since ancient days. The trials and tribulations women experienced through the ages are fascinating. I could not help but pause and reflect on personal experiences that have a ring of similarity. You may also ponder a discovery as "Well, no wonder . . ."

The reader is also provided an opportunity to "listen" to many women of all ages. Their experiences and hopes for easier access to the information they need are not unfamiliar. Again and again I paused to reflect: "That happened to her, too!! I know several of our clients that described the same experience."

The author guides the reader through a process that can enable women to experience being in charge of getting information needed to help them decide about treatment and goals for their health care. The reader is then taken on a kind of guided tour of some "systems" in place that are approaching that for which women hope and wish when seeking health care and information. The existence of these systems is indicative of everyone's need for a more "user-friendly" response to the need to know, understand, and be responsible for one's own health. Hope and wishes for more of these care delivery systems can come true when assisted by hard, dedicated work. This is every woman's job.

Marion Crook's views expressed toward the end of the book are illustrative of how the life experience of writing *My Body* has shaped what information she thinks women need to look and ask for. The impact of both her research into the history and interviewing so many people to write the book rings strong as she shares her thoughts and feelings. The reader has been brought through the same life experience as much as possible page after page. I could not help but nod in agreement and mumble to myself: "It's my body!"

Janice L. Nusbaum, RN, MN, MBA
Director, Public Health Nursing
Pima County Health Department
Tucson, Arizona, USA

Acknowledgments

I am grateful to the fifty-four women who sat down with me and gave me their time, information, opinions, and solutions. I promised them confidentiality so I will not list their names, but I acknowledge that their contributions are the basis of this book. I am grateful also to the following health care practitioners who spoke with me:

Kathyrn Grand, Liz Longmore, Raine Mackay, Hamda Umar, Rosario Taiavera, Silvia Vidal, Lynne Brown, Louise Hara, Sandi McIntyre, Tracy Pehar, Cheryl Collins, Judy Barlett, Barbara Wiktorwicz, Sari Tudiver, Arlene Hache, Faith Ann LeLievre, Lorraine Erickson, Mildred Wilkie, Irene Kakfrwi, Jody Erickson, Lynne Brooks, Eileen Fitzpatrick, Kate Hamilton, Winnie Fraser Mackay, Maureen Cochrane, Nancy Peterson, York Wong, Mary Glavin, Valerie Konopliff, Robin Barnett, Gary Poole, Sharon Jinkerson, Evelyn Voyageur, Wilma Doxtader, Madelleine Dion Stout, Mae Cohan, Steve Olson, Margaruite Johnston, Karin Jasper, Peng Jiu Ling, Bill Crook, Marjorie Schurman, Arlene Trustham, Diane Herbert, Jacqueline R. Scott, Lori Russell, Michele Johns, Gloria Lemay, Yvonne Stevenson, Kathie Cook, Sue Wright, Deanna Severence, David W. Southern, Millie Moran, Barb Gibson, Phyllis Morgan, Lisa Cobb, Amanda Olivo, Sarah Bacorn, Julie Weiss, Matthew Cushing, Clarice Foster, Shiela Casey, Cst. Boulderhigh, Gladys Pound, Angie Todd Dennis, Carolyn Wilken,

Janice L. Nusbaum, Marylyn Morris McEwen, Cheryl Ritenbaugh, Anne L. Wright, Chris Fox, Lauren Tancona, Jocelyn Withers, Elizabeth Santa Maria, Alma Puij, Rosalie Lopez, Tula McCarthy, Janice Crook, Brenda Mackay, T. Sukumaran, Maggie Amarualik, Tutili Oyokuluk, Meena Oyokuluk, Claudia Craig, Penny Jennett, Lynne Parton, Bronwyn Punch, Robyn Smith, Jim Kirkpatrick, Terry Russel, Bernie Seier, Jeanette Long, Connie Patio, Diane Herbert, Robin Smith Peck, Carol Mosier, Nancy Nelson, and Penny Nelson. I am also grateful to the Canada Council and the Van Dusen Fund.

Contents

Chapter 4

Walls around Us 47

Chapter 7

Alternative Practitioners: Complementary or Fringe Figures   93

Chapter 10

Chapter 11

Introduction

The Beginning

In 1991 I lived for a week with an Inuit family on northern Baffin Island, 450 miles north of the Arctic Circle. The warmth and friendliness of the people were almost a spiritual experience for me. They were curious but tolerant, accepting, and friendly. Many women of the community visited with me speaking either through an interpreter or in English. When the women realized that I was a nurse as well as a writer they asked questions about health. They revealed the misinformation they had been living with for years, misinformation that had caused heartache, pain, and a resignation that death was imminent. Because a health practitioner had given them incorrect information, their lives had been unnecessarily twisted and scarred. That unnecessary pain stayed with me, almost haunted me, until after meeting other women with similar problems in the south I was pushed into "doing something." I decided to find out how women got health information, what experience shaped the ways they looked for and asked for information, what they thought would be better, and what they thought would be wonderful.

The Method

The best way I knew to understand this problem was to go to women and ask them what their experiences were. I thought they would tell me, and they did. I advertised in the papers and went into communities to ask women what they wanted to know, how they asked for information, if they got it, and what they thought would improve the situation. I traveled across the country interviewing women who lived in suburban houses, communal homes, slum apartments, farmhouses, hunting tents, and high-rise apartments. With the help of The Canada Council and my publisher I was able to travel to areas as diverse as Yellowknife, Northwest Territories, Canada, and Wendover, Kentucky, USA. I talked to lay advisors in a clinic in Winnipeg, Manitoba, and a nurse practitioner from Madras, Oregon. I talked to government health officials, hospital directors and CEOs, public health administrators and staff nurses, nurse midwives, lay midwives, health resource center counselors, and drop-in clinic staff. A head nurse of a busy city hospital invited me to spend a day on her ward so I could see how women were treated there. I toured the patient-centered St. Charles Medical Center in Bend, Oregon, and the Planetree Hospital in The Dalles, Oregon. I talked to health aides who worked in the Hispanic community in Tucson, Arizona, as well as the public health nurses of Pima County. I talked to public relations officials of clinics and hospitals, staff nurses, and patients. It became a bigger project than I had first planned as new information opened the way to new ideas.

The Situation

I found that while women are angry, frustrated, and anxious to make changes, so are governments—perhaps not angry, but certainly willing to make changes. Health care costs money. Governments of both Canada and the United States are vitally interested in the health care systems since they need to make the delivery of health care affordable. The U.S. government realizes that the uninsured are costing more money than they would if insurance was provided. The Canadian government realizes that unlimited health care insurance is becoming unwieldy and expensive. Their motivation, while mainly economical, may result in better service for women. They are looking for new, economical ways of delivering health services. Many of these innovative ways to deliver health information are put forth by women, particularly the staff of women's centers, public health nurses, and nurse practitioners. There is a strong feeling in both countries that health care is important, health information is important, and women in particular need better information so that they can get better care. Good information results in better care, which results in lower health care costs—a strong motive for supporting women's need to get information.

As is usual when I start on a research project, I found I was not the only one who was disturbed by women's difficulties. In my travels I met gallant, creative, and caring women who had already spent many years trying to improve the health care system for women. It was encouraging to see the progress some had made, and it was inspiring to see how well women could look after each other when they had the room to do so.

I had thought that most women were "looked after" by medical professionals. I had, after all, entered this project from a nursing background that prejudiced me in favor of the medical model. It was not long after hearing women's stories that I developed a fierce anger toward the medical community—so much abuse, so much neglect, so much indifference. At times after hearing a particularly difficult story I struggled to keep my feelings contained. I am very grateful to the staff at the Port Coquitlam Women's Center near my home who listened to me, allowed me to vent my anger and frustration, and served as my balance and safety valve throughout this project. After the emotional reaction came a greater understanding of the problems women face in getting health information and an appreciation of some women, women's organizations, hospitals, and medical centers who help women get the information they need.

This book is an exploration of women's need for information, their history in acquiring health information, the barriers that prevent them from finding out what they need to know, and their hopes and visions for a different system.

There is a tremendous movement among women to harness the technology, research, and medical miracles available in the world for the benefit of women and to place such health care into a broader system of healing that would encompass much more than just medicine.

I invite you to write me and tell me of your experience, your ideas, your community's efforts to deal with this problem. There has never been a better climate for change.

1

Women in the World of Health and Healing

The Caregivers

Women have been caregivers for centuries. We have been the custodians of health for the family; the first aid, nutrition, and nursing experts; the healers, the midwives, and the herbalists. Much of what they have always done, we still do. We look for health care for ourselves and our families. We look for information, treatments, and advice trying to protect and nurture in the traditional ways of women. While we are the hub of the health care systems—the most important consumer—today's health care seems to whirl around us encompassing and affecting us without our direction or control. We need to connect with the sources of information: the health care providers.

Most health care providers work in fields of illness and treatment, not in health promotion and disease prevention. Women are not comfortable in a male-dominated, disease-model health care environment. We have tried to manage this inhospitable world with a network of knowledgeable friends, family remedies, and alternative treatments. We read books, magazines, and

5

newsletters looking for safer, more women-directed ways to get health care.

The women I talked to—54 young, old, employed, unemployed, rich, and poor women—told me that they wanted to be the ones in charge of their health. They wanted to see the relationship of their problems to their life and to see what options were available to control or eliminate the problems. They wanted to be the ones who made the decisions. Most would accept first aid in emergency situations when they were so badly injured they could not make decisions; but barring that rare situation, they wanted to be the ones with all the information needed to decide what was best for them. In order to do that, they need to get accurate, current health information.

The Need

Women, because we conceive and bear babies, are vulnerable to problems, ailments, and painful experiences that never come the way of men. We have unique health problems because of our biology as well as unique problems that are a result of social, economic, and political culture pressures that differ from those of men.

We are talking here about the problems of menstruation, childbirth, birth control, abortion, and menopause as well as the frustrating problem of not being able to find the information we need, not finding the remedies, surgical procedures, and drugs. These are the problems of the socialization of women that makes it difficult for us to demand answers to questions about our health problems and the political and social culture that denies funding to research that is gender specific to women. In 1991, breast cancer research in Canada received $950,000—in spite of the fact that breast cancer was the number one killer of women ages 34 to 55. In 1992 that amount was increased to $20 million—still a small effort. In the United States, Congress allowed $400 million in 1992, up $250 million from the year before, but it is still very little.[1] It is frustrating for women to realize that governments tolerate death from breast cancer as the price its female population pays for being female.

Women use the health care system more than men; we make more visits to doctors not because we are neurotic, hysterical, or overdependent, but because we are women. The medical system has declared women's normal cycles as "medical problems" so that visits around normal cycles of menstruation, pregnancy, delivery, and menopause become "medical" visits. Women also are more likely to be subjected to violence than men: 22 to 35% of all visits by females to U.S. emergency rooms are for injuries from domestic assaults.[2] We also live with harsh economic realities, such as inadequate housing, unsafe workplaces, and sex segregation at work. As much as 45% of the pay gap between men and women is caused by sex segregation in the work force.[3] More women than men live in poverty[4] and are, one suspects, therefore less able to get adequate nutrition or preventative care—and more old women are disabled.[5]

Of course, we can't talk about women as if they were a bland, homogeneous group that thinks and reacts like a school of fish, turning and moving in unison. Women are diverse. We have different needs, social backgrounds, expectations, and ways of coping. It is impossible to represent all women in this book. But it is possible to give the ideas and concerns of some women whose ideas and concerns are common. By understanding the common problems women have getting information so we can make decisions about our health and the common problems we have staying in charge of our health, we are better able to make changes. There is no definitive word, no final answer to any proposal on this subject, only efforts at greater understanding, efforts to recognize what is wrong with our present American and Canadian systems and to create a healthier healing environment for women. Women are ready for it. We are growing more distrustful of the "helping professions." We need to look at the healing environment around us and see how we can make that system more useful to us.

Using the System

Some women avoid the medical system as much as possible and use alternative medicine; some use the medical system as an occasional necessity to be endured; others use it as a resource, an occasional source of treatment; and many have no healing environment *but* the medical system. Most women must use the medical system at some time in their lives, but all women use a health care system of some kind. What they use and where they look for health information is part of the way they cope with the world. They interact with health, illness, and the health care system in ways that are unique.

For many women the cultural and social pressure they live with is reflected in their bodies. An anorexic women tells us with her body that she feels unimportant, almost invisible. A single mother struggling to work at housecleaning tells us with her sore back that she is carrying too heavy a load. A teenager finds that the harassment from her math teacher gives her a pain in the neck. It is amazing how often our bodies give us information in puns. We do respond physically to our social environment.

We think about our bodies and talk about them with our families, our friends, and at the doctor's office in ways that are acceptable to those social groups. We learn to consult about our bodies only with those whom our culture deems appropriate. One of our greatest barriers to accessing good health information is the cultural and social restrictions that confine our efforts to narrow resources and inadequate help. Such cultural restrictions give control of our bodies to people outside ourselves—particularly to doctors.

Our North American society has determined that the physical aspect of illness is the most important one and that the doctor owns it. Many women have experienced being talked about as if their ears and their brains were out of the room. If they weren't so ladylike they'd yell, "Talk to me. It's my body!" But they don't because women are conditioned to passively accept the voice of authority. Our culture tells us that when our bodies are ill, they do not belong to us; that a "wiser," "more correct" voice is the voice of the health care professional; that the "reasonable" thing to do is to allow the medical industry to decide what our bodies need and what our illness means.

The social and cultural aspects of illness are denied in most North American societies where the community does not involve itself in any illness that has not been validated as a community concern by doctors. Some diseases are recognized as social: AIDS, rabies, and tuberculosis. Most other illnesses are considered the private domain of the doctor. As the owner of the disease the doctor can decide what should be done about it. This attitude has been so well accepted in our culture that anyone who tries to retain control of his or her treatment is most often considered presumptuous and ignorant. "Overanxious" is the kindest term; "bitchy" is the more common.

Bernie Siegel, the cancer guru and a medical doctor, has given women permission to fight such an attitude. He declares that women who do fight their doctors have a greater chance of surviving cancer than women who do not.[6] We have long suspected that we would be better off if we were in control of our lives.

Serving Women

Women are not always helped by the male-dominated patriarchal medical system. Women are less likely to be investigated for coronary heart disease even when presenting the same symptoms as men and are less likely to have treatment for lung cancer.[7] We are less likely to get kidney transplants.[8] We were far more likely than men to have lobotomies—that totally debilitating and cruel "treatment" for mental illness.[9] This comes as no surprise to most women. I met many who had personal experiences with doctors who treated their health problems as unimportant, ignored their questions, resented their quest for information, ignored conflicting medical opinion, and resented any opinion that wasn't in line with theirs. If you want to test this, sit with a group of women around a restaurant table and mention doctors. After a few remarks about how wonderful "my doctor is," the stories emerge and the anger grows as every woman adds her negative experiences. Most of the women I interviewed respected the doctor's knowledge and his or her ability to work well in an emergency but were angry that the doctors they knew couldn't see past the presenting symptoms and couldn't recommend any treatment not in the drug cupboard.

Because our society has designated the doctor as the gatekeeper of knowledge and the dispenser of treatment, women are not accustomed to taking charge of our own health care or making demands on the medical system for cures. In a bid to find autonomy, better answers, and more choice, however, some women are looking at alternative medicine: Chinese, First Nations, and folk medicine, and more information in videos, books, and pamphlets. Some are even considering the magical prognostications of mystics, star-readers, and clairvoyants. Women are increasingly aware that the present symptom-oriented, drug-centered medical model is not serving them well.

The following three women were all, in their own way, passionate about women's ability to get health information.

Connie, 56, short, thin, and constantly moving, was furious at the way she had been treated. She told me about her diagnosis of breast cancer and her experience with her doctor:

> The doctor told me I had to have my breast off. He told me I had cancer and that I had to have my breast off. It wasn't until I phoned my daughter who is a nurse and checked into the library and the Cancer Association that I realized I had other options.
>
> I'll never forgive him for the shock he gave me. He treated me like a commodity, lined up for him to mutilate so he could make money.

She had come through a bad marriage and a divorce and then had dealt with the shock of her diagnosis and the stress of cancer treatment. She became a strong, aggressive woman determined that other women should not have to suffer as she did.

I interviewed independent, elderly Mrs. Sanders in her comfortable, spotlessly clean high-rise apartment and heard reminiscences of her life as a young woman in wartime and as a housekeeper of the rich. She survived World War II in Germany. "I was bombed out twice and rebuilt everything twice. If I could do that, I could do anything." She had firm opinions about how to get information. She subscribed to two very credible health information newsletters and read books and newspapers. She knew how to deal with doctors: she avoided them.

> I haven't let a doctor do all that intimate stuff since my son was born—and he's 48. Who needs doctors? Once in a while for a cold, other than that? No. Stay away from them. They make you sick.

While I could not accept her position for myself, it worked for her. How could I argue with a 71-year-old woman who was vigorous, energetic, and healthy?

Pat, 37, the mother of two boys, a teacher, and happily married, is forthright and logical. She has a style of getting information that is as unusual as it is admirable. She figures out what she wants to know, then figures out who has the information, then asks:

> My doctor is my source of information. When I want to know anything, I either go and see him or phone. He gets me the answers I want. That's what he's for.

Most women are frustrated by the social attitudes and social conditioning that make self-sufficient, hell-raising, fire-spitting achievers sit meekly for hours in a doctor's office, bewildered by conflicting advice, confusing medical tests, and frightening cures. Women want to see order, control, and choice come back into their hands.

2

Women in Medicine

A Historic View

The Healing Path

Women have always been at the hub of medical care. In the Middle Ages they barely survived as healers, but they persist as innovators and practitioners. Western medicine has changed in its travels from primitive societies—out of Egypt to Greece and Rome and then through our European culture to North America—but women always have been important and influential figures. They have been the scientists, healers, surgeons, gynecologists, psychiatrists, nutritionists, and pharmacologists working, learning, and practicing medicine.

The Ancient Days

In the ancient days communities had their own healers. The practice of assigning one person in the community the role of healer dates back perhaps 20,000 years. Many of those healers were women because the ancients believed that women held the key to life. Riane Eisler wrote an account of women in the history of the world in which she tells us that ancient societies thought female deities controlled life, and so women, aligned with the

Goddess, were considered to be powerful healers.[1] When a community agreed that supernatural power was part of the healing power of a few women, medicine women and shamans had authority.

Shamans have been important mystics in communities since ancient days. They were more than just spiritual leaders in the community; they were healers responsible for the health of the individual and, more importantly, the health of the community. They used ecstasy and altered states of consciousness to communicate with the spirit world so they could advise the corporeal one. They also practiced imagery—an early and effective form of psychiatry, manipulating the patient's belief system and the meaning of his or her illness in the community. They did not try to destroy the disease so much as augment the power of the sick person.

Practical Healers

Ancient healers expected to produce results. It was not enough to have spiritual power; a healer needed practical tools as well. In the grave of the Queen of Ur of Egypt (3500 BC) there were surgical instruments and prescriptions for pain relief. She expected to make a difference in the lives of her patients. It is clear that, along with spiritual practices, healers were expected to be skillful and knowing. Many queens of ancient Egypt, such as Mentahetep (2300 BC), were known for their medical knowledge. Queen Hatshepsut (1500 BC) was exceptionally learned. She supported three medical schools in her kingdom and stressed the importance of sanitation and hygiene.[2] Moses and his wife Zipporah studied at the medical school in Heliopolis, which catalogued extensive information on drugs from India. Seven hundred drugs as well as rules for diet and medicinal baths came from India to augment Egyptian medical information. Male and female doctors in Egypt of this time knew how to perform surgical operations and even inoculate against smallpox.[3] The doctors of these times, men and women, were not just midwives and herbalists but surgeons and students of medicine. They believed in science, but they also believed in the mental and spiritual powers of the patient. They watched and learned. The queens of Egypt from Mentahetep to Cleopatra (1st century BC) were students of medicine.[4] They knew, even in Cleopatra's time, thousands of remedies such as the use of poppy juice and mandrake for controlling pain. Egypt had a women's college where gynecology and obstetrics were specialties. From good scholarship came good doctors, and the work of Aspasia (2nd century BC) became the reference work for physicians up to the eleventh century.[5]

Archaeological evidence teaches us that for thousands of years women of Egypt served humanity by using diagnosis, intelligent treatments, herbs, and surgery as well as the incantations and magic of their times. We know about the queens and the important doctors of the times, but we have lost the names of the local doctors—women who got up at night to attend births (as they do today) and who tried to prevent disease and alleviate suffering. There must have been thousands of skilled women working in the towns and cities of Egypt: practitioners, innovators, and teachers of medicine. In this climate of learning and freedom to practice, women were important and useful practitioners of medicine, not only in Egypt. Around 600 BC, Queen Macha of Ireland founded a hospital that was used for 600 years.[6]

Holistic Healing

The Greeks in ancient days expected their shamans or healers to be learned people, but they also expected them to understand the importance of the whole person. Mental attitude and spiritual peace were important. Asclepius, a mythical folk hero and supposed teacher of Aristotle, Hippocrates, and Galen, advocated a holistic healing center where the spiritual and emotional aspects of a person's life were given a high place in the healing process. Some physicians today refer to Asclepius' philosophy of holistic healing as a model of patient care.

Accumulating Knowledge

Queen Artemisia of Caria (circa 350 BC) was, like the queens of Egypt, a medical student and a botanist. She was particularly interested in the use of herbs in medicine and investigated and named many herbs. The herb that takes her name, artemisia, was used to prevent abortion or, with elaterium, used to cause abortion.[7] When I visited France in 1993, I saw artemisia growing in the herb garden where Jean-Jacques Rousseau had lived in the eighteenth century. If artemisia has been cultivated for that many centuries, women probably knew how to use it. Perhaps it was one of the secrets women passed on to other women down through the centuries.

The women of Greece were accustomed to competent female doctors. Women doctors lectured as professors of medicine and practiced as physicians. Herophilus (4th century BC) taught large classes of men and women medical students in Alexandria. Women learned surgical techniques, elements of physiology, pathology, pharmacology, herbal medicine, the significance of symptoms, treatments, and obstetrical wisdom. Women doctors were particularly skilled at the care of women in labor and in diagnosing and treating eye diseases. It was normal and certainly practical to educate and sustain women as doctors in the Greek society.

Aristotle

One of the great influences on medicine came out of Greece with the writings of Aristotle. In *De Anima*, particularly Book II, he carefully and logically defined the science of biology and applied it to human activity. His efforts to categorize and explain human senses gave subsequent physicians a base of reference for understanding the nature of how our senses work. Although he thought that people should study the physical body, he believed that they should primarily study the soul since the soul was related to the body in a sustaining way. Aristotle believed that spiritual life was the driving force of the body, and the body was only one part of the whole human. Still, he observed physical phenomena and believed in systematic learning. He and his wife, Pythias, spent their honeymoon on the Island of Mytilene where they collected specimens, catalogued them, and later wrote an encyclopedia with special reference to histology and physiology. Pythias' work in medicine was overshadowed by Aristotle's writings. There is a lesson there somewhere.

While Aristotle wrote down his observations, many of the busy doctors of the day who practiced well and diligently did not leave behind written evidence of their knowledge. It is likely that better medicine than Aristotle's was practiced but lost in time. Many tombstones have been discovered that were erected to women physicians who were beloved by their communities and praised for their skillful work. As in many societies today, the women were too busy working to write.

In Greece the medicine around the first century AD was still very good. Women doctors "... attended classes at the best Greek schools; they studied surgery as well as general medicine and they were obliged to have practical experience in obstetrics before taking cases of their own."[8]

When Corinth was taken by Rome in 146 BC, Greek medical knowledge spread with educated slaves to the rest of Europe. Medicine had a sound and scientific start in the hands of women.

Before the influx of Greek doctors there was little scientific or systematic study of medicine in Europe. Many Romans appealed to the gods and goddess to intervene in their illness. However, "... there were many Romans in those early days who, when in pain, trusted more in their mothers and grandmothers than in the gods."[9]

Remedies and practical medicine were part of an accomplished matron's talents. After the first century, many Greek women doctors practiced in Rome, and gradually medicine improved.

Women as Doctors

Women worked as skilled doctors for centuries. They traveled the homes with their remedies, commonly containing eight or nine ingredients,[10] to diagnose and prescribe for the ill. They were competent surgeons of their day and often collected high fees. I can see these women bustling through the centuries, bag in hand, working, learning, and evolving practical medicine that served the people of the times. A woman worked in her community throughout her life, often adding the responsibilities of a wife and mother to her work. Women doctors served both men and women, but women patients were seen only by women doctors. Obstetrics and gynecology were the specialty of women doctors who taught and practiced particular skills such as version (turning the child in the womb).

Early Christian Era

The early Christian era in Europe produced healers who continued in the medicine of the Greeks. Doctors studied the Greek methods of diagnosis and treatment and relied on remedies and careful treatments from the past. The new Christian religion sparked interest in all areas of human life, so it is not surprising that questions of a new medicine and a new morality occupied the mind of philosophers such as Augustine (351–430). He and his mother Monica trained in medicine and studied biology. They once held a long argument by letter over "when is a fetus a child." They finally decided that a child was alive from the second month in its intrauterine life and that it was a legal being from the fourth month. The family compromise of Augustine and Monica's settled this particular problem, influencing questions of abortion and maternal and paternal responsibilities for the Catholic Church for centuries.

Practical Medicine

Philosophers might debate points of medical ethics, but the people of the time were more concerned about practical care. Women gave that care both as nurses at home and as doctors in the community; they were custodians of health in their families and educated physicians who attended classes at schools of medicine, studying surgery as well as medicine and interning to get experience before they started their own practices. They worked through the sacking of Rome in 410 by Alaric and the carnage that followed Attila the Hun in the fifth century, tending the sick, delivering women in labor, repairing saber cuts, establishing hospitals, and studying medicine. Medical science suffered competition after the fifth century when Bishop Gregory of Tours insisted that the relics of saints worked cures. Spiritually inspired shamanism was replaced by a politically motivated religion that established a system of church-dominated cures. People paid the Church for a cure. Then, in an effort to corner the market on cures, the Church closed the medical school at Athens in 529.

In 581, the theological question debated by the Fathers of the Church was whether women were reasoning humans or just animals without a soul. Church theologians met to discuss and debate this weighty question. The answer was of serious concern to the organizers of the Church, since those who have no soul are treated much differently from those who do. In the years that followed, the Church decided that women did *not* have a soul and therefore did not have any position of authority in society (Council of Nantes, Canon III, 660 AD). Women still worked as doctors because people needed them. The Church said only God had the answer to disease, but many people still saw medicine as a better alternative. Women doctors needed education, and, in spite of the Church's definition of woman, abbeys became centers of medical learning. In the seventh century, for instance, the Abbey of Chelles near Paris was renowned for its medical knowledge. The English abbess, Mildred of Kent, was educated there as were many famous women practitioners of the time.

The Work of Women

The crusades of the twelfth and thirteenth centuries created great needs for medical treatment, as many of the crusaders arrived in the Holy Land ill or injured from battle. War seems to stimulate medical development. We saw that World War II and the Vietnam War demanded creative ways of dealing with injury and disease; the same was true in the Middle Ages. Bertha of Constantinople in 1126 built a hospital of over 10,000 beds, the Pantocrator. The hospital had five divisions with a medical woman doctor in charge of workers: midwives, nurses, surgeons, and barbers. Some of the doctors came from foreign lands. Edina Rittle of Essex County, England, who studied and worked at this hospital and at one time was in charge of it, took knowledge back to her home country,[11] most likely to St. Bartholomew's Hospital in London. In this way medical information spread to the edges of the European world.

Heloise (1101–1162) was probably the most learned woman doctor of France in the twelfth century. Students of literature remember Heloise for her passionate love for Abilard and the tragedy of their union when her uncle ordered his castration. The letters between Abilard and Heloise are poignant, beautiful, and exquisitely literate. Few realize that Heloise was a skilled and competent doctor. In spite of Abilard's influence in closing the universities to women, Heloise managed to practice medicine from her own abbey. Separated from Abilard, in charge of her own abbey, she encouraged the education of her nuns, including their medical education. Women doctors with women's medicines and remedies were a necessary and strong part of the French community.

Great personalities such as Hildegard of Bingen (1078–1179) created pockets of medical learning. She had a formidable intellect and a prolific pen with which she carried on correspondence with all the important people of Europe. In addition to her influential political activities (she advised the Pope), Hildegard studied and practiced medicine. She wrote *Simple Medicine* and *Causes and Cures* and pointed the way toward understanding the circulation of the blood, and the nature of the transfer of impulses along nerves. Some of her visions occurred when she was suffering from the effects of premenstrual hormones. Possibly she had edema (excess fluid) on her brain. Not surprisingly, she thought that the moon influenced behavior. She had some remarkable ideas: she predicted the Reformation, and she was one of the early believers in the sun as the center of the universe and the moon as the controller of tides. While Hildegard would have been an exceptional woman in any era, she was not the only medically minded woman of influence. Nuns, noblewomen, and queens were botanists, physicians, midwives, and surgeons who wrote and collected medical texts.

The Church objected to women as healers at the same time as the community needed them. The constant warfare, plagues, and epidemics of the Middle Ages gave medical men and women many work opportunities. They were important and necessary. The remedies and treatments of the past, plants and herbs, the poultices and emetics, the bone-setting procedures, and the concept of hygiene and nursing care from Egypt and Greece were carefully documented and passed on through the ages.

Suppressing Women Doctors in the Middle Ages

Again, the Church seemed to see women's medicine as a threat to ecclesiastical powers. Pope Sixtus IV (1471–1484) pronounced an edict against the practice of medicine or surgery "by

Jews or Gentile men and women who were not graduates of a university." The laws of most countries refused women admittance to universities, although Italy, in spite of the Pope and perhaps because of diverse and competitive political factions, continued to open its universities to women. Spain also educated women as doctors at universities by issuing a special dispensation or educating them privately at home. Again, no doubt, the rich and influential managed to protect themselves from the power of the Church. But the Pope's edict cast a spell of disapproval over the women who practiced medicine, and that disapproval soon turned to persecution. The need for the women doctors was obvious—women still wanted to consult women doctors. The Pope's edict only made it easier to prosecute and convict women for the crime of healing.

The Church persecuted women healers of the Middle Ages and beyond—from approximately the fifteenth century to the eighteenth—eventually killing 5 million[12] of them by calling them witches, heretics, and evil beings. While it has been accepted as historical fact that the witches were killed and also accepted that a "witch" had been defined as such by the Church officials, the extent of the slaughter of women was buried in history texts until recent writers and filmmakers began to investigate. *The Burning Times*, a film about the witch hunt, gives extensive information, and Judy Chicago in *The Dinner Party*, Barbara Walker in *The Woman's Encyclopedia of Myths and Secrets*, Riane Eisler in *The Chalice and the Blade*, and many others give more. The "witches" of those days were the most advanced scientists and herbalists of that day, so the Church, with its witch-hunting and murdering rampage over three centuries, obliterated much of their specialized knowledge, twisting the "science" of medicine and crippling its development.

Replacing Women Doctors with Men

In place of knowledgeable women, the Church and state licensed male healers, many of whom had little training and certainly little knowledge of herbs, remedies, obstetrical techniques, and psychological approaches that the women healers had developed. Doctors were often political appointees—for instance, a bishop might grant a medical license after questioning an applicant on his religious beliefs without assessing his medical knowledge. When those who had medical knowledge were denied the right to practice and those who were ignorant were allowed to practice, it did not take long before ignorance replaced knowledge in medicine. We have seen in North American over the last 200 years how quickly the aboriginal people lost their knowledge of herbs and drugs when such knowledge was considered wicked and actively discouraged.

Because men were privileged, their works were often accepted if religiously correct even when those works were impractical or medically incompetent. Jean Astruc (1685–1766) wrote a book on obstetrics while admitting that he had never even seen a woman deliver a baby. The careful work of the Egyptians, Greeks, and Italians in obstetrics and gynecology had been reduced in many areas of the world to ignorant and dangerous interference in childbirth. The Church at this time even demanded that the attendant at childbirth work blindfolded if the child was illegitimate.

Midwives and women medical practitioners held onto some of their knowledge from the past, but they were barred from scientific education. While the women may have been skillful in delivering babies and preventing maternal deaths, they had little chance to get a university education. The university doctors had the advantage of new knowledge as well as the advantages of prestige and opportunity to practice without fear of death from the Inquisition. Not only were women denied entrance to most universities, but they also had no control of the university-educated doctors and did not regulate doctors' practice and methods. Men now controlled the medicine women received. This was a great change in the history of the Western world.

The Printing Press

The printing press, developed in the mid-fifteenth century, allowed for all kinds of knowledge to spread, including medical knowledge. It allowed medical textbooks, particularly the practical and informative work of Trotula of Salerno, to be reproduced quickly. The books from the printing presses had fewer mistakes than the old hand-copied manuscripts, and they were soon available throughout Europe, though cautiously and often surreptitiously. Because death as a witch was a threat that hung over knowledgeable women for three centuries, medical knowledge usually spread to women in a clandestine, underground movement.

Women of wealth and influence, however, could sponsor the development of medicine and practice it more freely. Lucrezia Borgia (1480–1590), the daughter of Pope Alexander VI, had a book of gynecology dedicated to her.[13] She was interested in medicine and through her political and financial power encouraged medical investigations. Oliva Saburo Barrera of Spain (b. 1562) wrote a book describing the effects of pain, fear, and other mental states on the body. This was not widely circulated because the Inquisitors, the death squad of the Catholic Church, objected.

Queen Sophia of Mechlenburg, mother of Christian IV of Norway and Denmark, taught birth control and maternal health and compelled midwives to study. Her efforts were so effective that Scandinavia developed excellent maternal–child health standards.

The New World

The threat of death as a witch discouraged the development of skilled women doctors in the New World; they killed "witches" there. In spite of such oppression, some women managed to gain knowledge and skills and serve their communities, but not openly and not easily. Science was regarded with suspicion; religion had a monopoly on cures. The standards of education and skill had deteriorated both in Europe and the Colonies until by the seventeenth century such standards were lower than they had been in the twelfth century at the time of Trotula.

The Seventeenth Century

By the seventeenth century, doctors' knowledge was a combination of meager medical facts, folklore, and common sense. Many doctors, because they had a strong economic interest in medical care, tended to promote that which made money and ignore that which did not, regardless of the benefit or lack of benefit to the patient. The difference between a doctor and a quack may well have been only social status.

There were, however, advances in science. William Harvey explained the circulation of the blood, reasserting Servetus' claim that the blood did not mix in the heart. He wrote *Exercitatio Anatomica de Motu Cordis et Sanguinis in Animalibus*.[14] In the progressive English society of 1628, he was not burned at the stake as Servetus was in 1553, but accepted as scientist. Other ideas of this century included the invention of the microscope by Leeuwenhoek of Delft; the use of obstetrical forceps; the systematic description of disease outlined by Thomas Syndenham; and the increasing body of knowledge developing at the universities. However, the purpose of the universities still was to train ministers to serve the Church. A university medical education was a patchy affair with some fields of advanced scientific knowledge surrounded by bogs of great ignorance. Even though few women in the seventeenth century were able to obtain a medical education, in this climate women without a university education were often as medically knowledgeable and skillful as men with one. Women were still the best obstetricians because they listened to their patients and developed practical skills.

The Eighteenth Century

The eighteenth century saw a widening gap between the knowledge of the university-educated doctor and the lay doctor. There was more knowledge to be learned: the use of the stethoscope, the understanding of the lungs as the site of gas exchange, and the discoveries in chemistry in the work of Mme. Genevieve Charlotte d'Arconville (1720–1805).[15] Surgery remained primitive with some work done by John Hunter (1728–1793), who used cadavers to teach surgical technique and stressed the necessity of being skillful.[16] In America, men had entered the obstetrical field for the first time and introduced the concept of childbirth as a medical event. Medicine was a nonstandard hodgepodge of the skillful and the ignorant with controlling attitudes of paternalism for the medical community—where authority was often assumed even when there was little knowledge. The preacher John Wesley, the founder of the Methodist movement, wrote a very unscientific book of medicine.

The Nineteenth Century

By the nineteenth century many more discoveries in anatomy, chemistry, biology, and physiology expanded the body of medical knowledge. Male obstetricians began to control the lives of women by stressing more surgery and more intervention in childbirth. Medical knowledge became more technical, while acquiring that knowledge remained difficult for women. They could obtain a medical degree only in Italy, although women in England could study privately and did. Medicine in these days was a man's profession. Women were still fighting for the chance to look after one another.

The New Women Doctors

Elizabeth Blackwell was a Scottish obstetrician and general practitioner (1712–1779). Another Elizabeth Blackwell, apparently no relation to the first, was an American doctor who was the first woman allowed to study at St. Bartholomew's Hospital in London in 1850. Although she had graduated from medical school in the United States, it wasn't until 1859 that she was allowed on the Medical Register in England. She was the only woman doctor registered until Elizabeth Garret joined her in 1866.[17] The universities of Britain refused to accept women as medical students until the late nineteenth century when, in 1882, Edith Shove was the first woman to graduate in medicine. The British Medical Association would not accept women doctors as members until 1910, and the Royal College of Physicians refused women membership as fellows until 1925![18] Women in America faced similar prejudices when a doctors' registry was established in 1847. No women belonged to the American Medical Association at this time. There were, however, no educational regulations for doctors to practice as doctors—anyone who could gain community trust could be a doctor and did not have to be registered with the AMA—so women practiced as doctors without belonging to the AMA. There were as many as 7000 women doctors in the United States by 1900. At about this time women doctors suffered organized objections by those male doctors who, with little regard for history, claimed that medicine was too difficult for women and, more accurately, that women took patients and income away from them. The Harvard Medical School accepted Harriet Hunt in 1850 as a student, but the objections of the male students forced her out. They did not allow women as students again until June 5, 1944.[19]

The Male Model

With the opening of the universities, women were able to get the education they needed to work as doctors once more. They particularly needed to work as doctors for women patients. However, the male-dominated university education programs had for so long excluded women's needs, concerns, and life cycle problems that women doctors were required to train themselves to accommodate a "scientific" and male-defined point of view and to practice medicine in this manner. Many women doctors simply ignored this pressure and developed their medical practice in a manner that suited them and their patients. They viewed woman's hormonal cycles as normal, women as reasonable, and women's questions as legitimate. But many other women doctors modeled themselves after the prevalent male ideal and defined the male body as normal, only male concerns as legitimate, and males emotions as standard. Women's views of health and illness as a physical and social problem were, if not lost, at least ignored.

We may blame Descartes (1591–1650), in part, for this narrow view. He initiated the scientific process by suggesting that all knowledge could be catalogued in patterns. This process of systematic learning, of placing facts into patterns, allowed humans to use their brains to store and relate a great deal of knowledge. Over the centuries medicine developed into a collection of knowledge governed by patterns of scientific groupings that for the most part seem to explain illness and disease. But as the ability to evaluate tests and diagnose symptoms was developed, the meaning of the illness, the social context, and the circumstances that worked on the individual to produce the illness was lost.

Attitude toward Patients

People became objects of science. They became "things" to be examined, prescribed for, and cured. This doctor–object attitude was a logical outcome of the past centuries' emphasis on the study of isolated systems and the exclusion of all aspects of the illness or disease that did not relate to the knowledge of the doctor. Women doctors of the past had been well grounded in the pains and problems of their patients. When they were forced out of the field of medicine by the Church, the science of medicine developed without this balancing influence of women.

Doctors throughout the last 300 years have trained themselves to learn with their eyes, to study that which they can see. This excludes what they can learn by listening and feeling. Whole areas of patients' lives are ignored or left unexamined because the patient's view of the illness and the patient's feelings about it and the meaning the patient gives to the illness and the meaning the community gives to it are not part of the diagnosis. The patient becomes an object without meaning.

It is this position that leads to some of the limitations of science. Doctors can only diagnose within the limits of their knowledge. They make little use of the patient's or the community's knowledge. Doctors today take a very technological and detailed understanding of physiology, anatomy, biology, and chemistry and put with it a very elementary knowledge of psychology and an even more elementary knowledge of social science. They fit the patient into this knowledge system, but it is an uncomfortable fit. They seldom fit this knowledge around the patient.

The Meaning of Illness

Women, with their historic emphasis on the meaning of relationships, look for meaning in illness and are not satisfied with the doctor–object dialogue that has replaced the ancient healing relationship. They are still not in the position of their ancestors of tenth-century Rome who could rely on women practitioners educated in the latest scientific methods and who had women's hospitals and medical schools that specialized in women's ailments and life cycle difficulties. Modern women are forced to evaluate the advice of male physicians who have in the past recommended lobotomies for women schizophrenics, clitoridectomies for "unruly wives," forced feeding and punishment of anorexic women, and, from the mouth of a modern 1993 surgeon, hysterectomies on *all* women past menopause. While many male physicians can be compassionate, effective, and knowledgeable, in general, women prefer their own sex. Not only do women see women as less threatening and more supportive than male physicians, they see women as more flexible and more likely to understand and prescribe for emotional, mental, and spiritual needs.

Control of Healing

Today women are reaching out for simple remedies that give them more control over healing. They are not prepared to turn their back on miracles—the antibiotics that eliminate pneumonia, the surgery that makes walking possible or hearts work longer—but they want to have more understanding of their bodies, direction over their treatment, and control over therapy. They are not content to give control and responsibility of their bodies to medical personnel nor are they willing to be a scientific object.

Kate, 30-year-old mother and community activist, said "Male doctors can try, but their reality is not my reality."

Women want to reinstate women doctors to the position of healer and trusted advocate that they held in ancient days. Women have a long history of attendance by competent, educated women caregivers. They want that comfort today.

3

Different Problems at Different Times

The women of North America can't be viewed like a school of fish, all identical, all moving to the same stimulus and responding in the same way. They differ one from another, live in a variety of circumstances, react to pain and pleasure, and try to control their world in their own way as much as they can. Women in this eclectic society face individual and unique challenges, but they also face common problems. At different ages and stages of life women have common needs.

The Teen Years

Feeling Inadequate

It may be hard to remember the vulnerability of our teen years. We repress memories of pain, forgetting how humiliated we felt so often in those years: how "klutzy," how unlovable. We forget the feelings of naivete, inadequacy, and incompetence, the years of wondering how we were going to survive in the fast and competent world of adults. That world of adults was not a welcoming place. It didn't seem to want us or even tolerate us. Even now, teens are rejected, relegated to a "teen" role that doesn't have adult responsibilities or adult rewards. Teens are told to "look good," "study hard," and "stay out of trouble until you grow up." There doesn't seem to be a necessary, positive role for them in the adult world. Society pressures young women not to be productive and useful but to "look good" and "be perfect" and young men to "look like a hunk" and "be strong." The media encourages teens to be perfect students with perfect talents and perfect bodies. Illness is an imperfection that happens to other people. There is an innate implication in advertisements that if you are smart enough, you will not get sick. This world of perfect people that the teen sees is not an easy climate in which to find out about health problems. It's not easy to admit having a health problems and it's hard to find information. "Even when you're gutsy and determined," one young woman told me, "it's still hard to find out what you should know. People won't talk to you."

Finding Information

For a young woman, the healing environment is a strange world full of authority figures and people who can be cruel. It is not easily recognized as helpful. A teen knows that doctors have health information, but she often knows of few other resources. She is afraid to look for help because she is afraid of being blamed, ridiculed, or abused.

"I'm not going to see the school counselor," one 16-year-old young woman told me. "Everyone would see me in the office and they'd think I was crazy. Besides, she'd tell my mom."

It is hard for her to find someone she can trust who also has good information. She is surrounded by half-truths, speculation, advertisers' "facts," and misinformation in the media of television, radio, and magazines. Other teen advisors can give incorrect information. School health programs may be sources of information about drugs, alcohol, suicide prevention, and gender differences, but they are rarely sources of information about mental health, troublesome physical symptoms, birth control and abortion, or alternative healing practices. In cases where school counselors might be helpful, they may be so overworked and overscheduled that they are only available to the students by appointment. This makes it hard for a teen to approach a teacher or a counselor informally. Even if it were easy to get information, schools still may not be the most appropriate source of health information. When I interviewed women about how they got their health information and how they judge the information they did get, 95% said they would not rely on the information they got from teachers. These women placed greater faith in information from nurses. It makes sense, then, to think that teens will get more correct and more believable information from nurses.

Teens can sometimes find nurses at their schools or health units and certainly at the offices of Planned Parenthood. Many teens are aware that Planned Parenthood clinics are a non-threatening source of information available to them in many communities. Young women can get counseling there about reproductive problems or concerns. Young couples can also get counseling so that decisions about birth control are mutual and the birth control is likely to be used. Many teens also appreciate the low-key, casual atmosphere among the volunteers of the Planned Parenthood clinics and the predominantly female medical staff. Janine, a 26-year-old medical practitioner, said, "The nurse's desk is in the center of the room and she's friendly. You don't feel like there's this barrier between you and the nurse."

Although Janine is used to working in the clinical world, she prefers the accepting and comfortable atmosphere of the Planned Parenthood clinic when she is looking for her own care.

Women's health centers usually offer the same casual atmosphere. One center in Winnipeg, Manitoba, ran movies on video for the clients while they were waiting. Teens crowded the meeting room, jammed together on the couches, sprawled on the floor, talking and watching videos, relaxed and sure of their welcome. This was in dramatic contrast to most medical clinics, where rigid formality and clinical coolness is the norm.

Fearing Abuse

Teens have a realistic fear of health providers. They are particularly vulnerable because they have had little experience with medical examinations and are not sure what is usual. They often don't realize that a doctor may sexually molest them until they are molested.

I met Gwenth at a restaurant near her apartment. We talked for 2 hours while she told me of her experiences in the medical industry. She was one of the many women who remembered sexual abuse or harassment by a doctor. She said:

> I came in for a swab from my infected throat and he had me completely undress. He touched my breast and it hit me that this was weird. I mean, touching my breast when my throat's the problem? I grabbed my clothes and backed out and dressed in the hall. He was really weird.

Teens usually don't know where to go for information except the doctor's office, and they seldom report incompetence or abuse. Sexual abuse in the community is a problem for at least one third of the female population. The secrecy, threats, and violence around the huge problem of sexual abuse make it hard for young women to look for help about this problem. It takes courage to make that doctor's appointment. If they meet abuse in the doctor's office, they have even more reason to avoid medical help.

Abuse in Different Forms

Anna, 32, told me that when she was 20 she was pregnant and did not want the baby or a relationship with the father. She went to a local doctor and asked for an abortion. He gave her "counseling" and told her to return the next week. She did that and he repeated the "counseling" and again requested her to return. She told him each time that she wanted an abortion. Finally she was approaching 3 months gestation and getting desperate. She looked up "Women" in the telephone book and found a women's resource center. She told a worker there her story and got help that day. "I was so naive," she said. "It took me two months to figure out that the doctor was just using me to play out his own brand of needs. He probably had personal objections to abortion, or got off on helpless females." It is hard to know how often this happens since vulnerable, frightened, anxious young women are unlikely to report it.

Health Units and Nursing Centers

Many health units operate youth clinics, particularly for birth control and abortion information, where teen women get information, counseling, and practical help. In some remote areas of Canada, the Red Cross Outpost Station serves as the center for advice for the teen population—some are superb and some are not. In one-nurse stations, health education is limited by the knowledge and attitudes of that one nurse. If she is competent, she gives information, pamphlets, books, and phone numbers to the teen. If she is not, she gives cursory and sometimes incorrect advice.

Few Resources

Many teens live with conditions such as eating disorders that the medical model often fails to help. Controlling weight and shape is one way young women deal with emotion and cope with the pressures on them to perform and to be perfect. The medical model has offered little to young women except life-saving treatment in severe cases. Woman-to-woman support groups, experienced nutritionists, and psychologists have a better grasp on treatment but are not always available. Medical personnel, nurses included, are only slowly coming to understand how to help. In many areas of the country teens have little real help or useful information, and they are are often blamed for their conditions. "If she'd just eat, she wouldn't have the problem." Medical personnel look for a fix-it answer in a drug cupboard and ignore the social context of this problem. It seems that by blaming the teen, many medical practitioners feel they have pointed to a solution.

The medical industry has done little to help suicidal teens. This is another condition with a strong social context. Suicide is the second cause of death for teens, yet there are few community or medical resources set up to help with this problem. Phone-in crisis centers operate in large centers and most small ones. Even remote and rural areas can access the nearest crisis center by phone. In practice, however, teens often can't get through the busy lines or they don't realize they can access them. Some schools offer courses in suicide prevention and peer counseling, and some counselors offer suicide prevention information through the school libraries. Doctors are much more aware of the seriousness of teen concerns than they were even 10 years ago, but there are still many who ignore signs of suicide. In my interviews with teens for the book *Teenagers Talk About Suicide* I found that teens usually didn't know where they could get information and help. Few teens consider mental health workers who may be educated in suicide prevention as part of their healing environment. Mental health counselors seem to be part of the adult world—a world that needs a referral and money.

Lack of Money and Privacy

When teens look for help from others besides a doctor, they often are afraid they can't afford it. In some cases teens do not have the money for the services. In others, teens' insurance plans are billed for medical services and a copy of the bill is sent to the parents. Since they often want to keep their health concerns a secret, this discourages teens from getting help. Most teen women are reluctant to consult the family doctor because they think he or she will report to their parents. In some states and provinces, teens can't be treated without the consent of their parents, and so doctors aren't able to promise confidentiality.

Lack of Knowledge

Typically, teens are uncomfortable with their bodies and are unsure of what is normal. They have gaps in their knowledge and lack life experience and thus find it hard to judge the seriousness of their symptoms or to evaluate the information they do get.

Teens justifiably are wary about approaching adults for health information. Some counseling organizations, particularly pregnancy counseling groups, are aggressive and manipulative with teens.

One 17-year-old young woman told me:

> I wanted an abortion so I phoned one of those ads in the paper that says they'll help you. They showed me this gruesome film on abortion and told me how horrible I was. They didn't show me any gruesome films of childbirth or tell me how dangerous it was. I was 14. They were vultures.

Adults often assume young women know more than they do or that their knowledge of health information is more uniform than it is. Being a teenager means having patchy and incomplete knowledge, yet we seem to expect teens to make good health decisions without good information and with little confidence. As a society we do very little to give a young woman a sense that her body is a wonderful functioning miracle that can heal itself of many problems—a miracle that deserves respect and admiration.

Young Adult Women

The First Pregnancy

If young women have avoided the medical system during their teen years, they often meet it with their first pregnancy. Suddenly they have a great need for information about their health, their child's health, nutrition, preventative medicine, medication, and treatment. It is often at this time that women realize they know very little about their bodies. Because they are searching on behalf of their child, most women find the courage to ask questions and make demands. Women at this stage of their lives can be aggressive about finding information. They read articles, follow up recommendations of friends, and interview health care workers. They look at the many sources of information now available to them—doctors, midwives, prenatal classes at a public health unit or a private clinic, hospitals or home birth consultants—and read a great many books and pamphlets and watch educational videos. They have a sense of urgency about their search for information. This baby will arrive in 8 months, and they have only that much time to become experts.

The Self-Help Psyche

Through the challenging self-help years of the 1960s and 1970s, women created a culture around childbirth that demanded more choices and more cooperation from the medical profession and health care consultants. Prenatal classes conducted by lay personnel and nurses in private practice challenged the feet-in-stirrups delivery position, the routine episiotomies, and the doctor-directed deliveries. As a consequence, childbirth is one of the few areas of a women's experience with the medical and health care system where she is expected to try to stay in charge of her health.

"What do you mean *you're* going to delivery this baby?" one woman said in the hospital case room. "It's *my* delivery! *I'm* doing the pushing here."

It still takes a great deal of energy and assertiveness on the woman's part to stay in charge, but she has some social approval for her efforts. Because some births are medical emergencies, the medical professional has designated all births as potential emergencies and all births medical problems. Women are fighting this concept, trying to take back control of childbirth. They want to see childbirth as a family event and medical intervention only an important resource for a few.

Learning about Health and Illness

A young mother still uses her doctor a great deal for descriptions of normal child behavior and the crisis of child rearing: communicable diseases, immunizations, fevers, colds, and accidents and the problems of bed-wetting, thumb sucking, temper tantrums, moral dilemmas, discipline, and learning disabilities.

Her questions about her own health and the health of her children seem to arise with the problems, yet there is little attempt to educate her in advance of problems so that she knows what to expect from her body and from her children's bodies. She buys books and phones her friends and her relations, but there are few programs parallel to prenatal programs to give mothers an education that would make them more competent with their own health problems and those of their children. Women with young children crave education. Pat, the energetic mother of two little boys, said:

> Of course, I want to know. If my little boy gets ear infection after ear infection, I want to know why. Don't just give me antibiotics. Tell me what I can do to prevent it. I'll ask the doctor; I'll ask the health nurse; I'll look it up in the library; I'd phone the Pope if I thought it would help.

Increasing Education

At this stage in their lives, women are not encouraged to be strong and independent. They are not encouraged to believe that their bodies are, for the most part, useful and efficient. There is no program within the medical system that encourages young women to develop into self-reliant, responsible directors of their own health. Women's health education is not an important part of the medical delivery system. There is, in fact, encouragement for them to become dependent on doctors and drugs, to ask their doctors for all the answers to their questions, and to trust the doctors to care for their health on an incident-by-incident basis. The answers to their questions are limited to the knowledge of the doctor they consult. If they had a wide number of people to consult, they would learn more.

Knowledge and Ability to Cope

When prenatal women started to consult health nurses, midwives, private nutritionists, and fitness experts as well as doctors, they increased the amount of knowledge the average woman had before she delivered. The same could be done after childbirth. Women could learn from a wider number of consultants about the various childhood crises, the basic changes in their own bodies, useful concepts of visualization and imagery in health, sound nutrition facts, community resource sources, and how to judge medical advice. This would broaden their base of knowledge, stimulate change in the medical model, and give women a greater sense of control over their health and the health of their children.

One young woman I interviewed, an intelligent product of high school and 1 year of post-secondary education, said she had so little understanding of normal childhood events that she felt as though the first 3 years of her child's life were a constant response to crisis, never knowing what to anticipate, never knowing what to do, always feeling like an incompetent mother, and embarrassed to be yet again at the doctor's office. Some women feel there is a "conspiracy" in the health care field to make them feel incompetent.

> At first I thought I was an idiot and then I realized that the doctors wanted me to feel that way. The woman who answers my doctor's phone makes me feel like I'm neurotic, like any fool should know what to do with a kid's fever, like I'm a nuisance. I put up with her because I need the answers.

This woman's natural concern and her attempts to help her child are twisted by the medical system to appear abnormal. Again, a young woman is blamed for not having medical knowledge while at the same time she sees no social avenues for her to find that knowledge other than the "ask the doctor" route.

Defining Normal and Abnormal

Psychiatrists within the American Psychiatric Association have defined, in the *Diagnostic and Statistical Manual of Mental Disorders*, two diseases peculiar to women that are not diseases at all. They have designated the conditions *premenstrual syndrome,* thus describing a normal hormonal process as abnormal, and *masochistic syndrome,* wherein a patient "rejects help, gifts or favors so as not to be a burden on others" and "responds to success or positive events by feeling undeserving." This is a description of a woman socialized into typical female behaviors in our culture, yet it is defined here as an abnormal psychiatric syndrome. Normal behavior is defined as sick. Both syndromes have been given a billing number and now can be described as diseases that need medical treatment. It is like defining a woman as basically sick and in need of medical supervision because she is a woman. It is an amazing way to define women as faulty human beings.

The Mid-Years

By the time a woman is in her 40s she has gained some knowledge of the medical system and a great deal of knowledge about the frustration of dealing with it. By now, she usually has alternate sources of information, a network of friends, a resource center, a library, a doctor she can work with, and some understanding of her own body. If she has not tried alternative health, naturopaths, vitamin therapy, fitness, meditation, or faith healing, she usually knows they exist.

The Prospect of Aging

In North America she lives in a society that makes being young a virtue and being old a vice. In her middle age a woman faces the prospect of aging with less equanimity than in some other cultures. She is enticed and coerced by advertisers to remain forever young, as if getting old was socially repulsive. Medical practice endorses licensed cosmetic surgeons who promise the appearance of youth to an aging body—pulling the wrinkles away from eyes, lifting the sagging breasts, excising the abdominal rolls, tightening the neck. The dangers of these operations are ignored. Health is not the goal of cosmetic surgeons; beauty is.

Forever Young

Middle-aged women are besieged by the media to deviate from healthy ambition, from the productive world, and from energizing activity to the search for beauty. This pressure to be ornamental starts young and remains part of the culture of women in our society. It is intensified in a woman's middle years, when she begins to lose the beauty of youth. Some women who have cosmetic surgery may be happy with their larger breasts or smaller noses, but it is unlikely that surgery creates happiness as the original unhappiness often had an emotional or social basis. Women who have breast reductions do not usually fall into this category because they have breast reductions most often for reasons of physical comfort, and they rarely return for other cosmetic surgery. Physical changes with surgery usually make little difference to a woman's feelings of being unacceptable or unlovable. Women who have cosmetic surgery usually go back to the surgeon for more snipping, cutting, and pasting, looking for illusive perfection. They take health risks in order to "be perfect."

A woman in her mid-30s came to visit me. She had heard that I was researching this book and she wanted me to know what her search for perfect breasts with silicone implants had done to her. She told me about her increasing pain, her search for help, her rejection by the many doctors who told her she was imagining things. She showed them the bulges of silicone that began to emerge under the skin of her abdomen. Her pain was so severe she had a double mastectomy that removed the implants, her breasts, and the tissue around them. This did relieve the pain.

Her reason for the implants in the first place was to make her breasts more attractive. She pulled up her shirt and showed me her chest. Big scars from the mastectomy disfigured both sides. Smaller scars slashed randomly like whip marks around the larger ones, giving evidence of small excisions for the removal of silicone lumps. She pointed to an area of paler skin. "There's another one ready to come out," she said. "Silicone has traveled all over my body now. My brain as well." She was blonde, blue-eyed, and attractive. The skin on her chest was as grey as a cadaver and badly disfigured. "I wish I had a noble reason for all this pain," she told me, "but I just wanted to look great."

The "perfect body" is an impossible goal that requires a woman to buy many beauty products and some surgical procedures. This pressure to be thin, attractive, and young fuels a big economy contributing millions to the beauty industry. It does not necessarily contribute anything to the happiness of women.

The Older Woman

Older women in our culture, the over-65-year-olds, face a world of prejudice against age and often a world of poverty and disability. Those who have enough income for food and shelter are expected to remove themselves from the mainstream of society and live outside productive, creative, and useful environments. While increased activities for seniors are advertised in our "Sunset Centers," few activities are geared to productive, able women. Most are time-filling activities of busyness that assume the women involved have led a life of semiliterate incompetence. While some older women organize around causes and work to create changes (the Grey Panthers, the Raging Grannies), little is expected of most. Older women are invited to live frivolous lives pursuing trivia—endless crocheting or television watching—and they are invited to play. The lives of the "retired" bear great similarities to those of adolescents, where play, comfort, and amusement are the focus of living and society requires nothing useful from them.

At the health centers and medical centers older woman are expected to have time to fit into the schedule of the practitioner, the productive member of society. The women are expected to accept their treatment with gratitude, to be quiet and complacent. The rare woman who bangs her cane and says, "No!" is considered "quaint" or "a character," not representative of her age.

Needs

The needs of older women are often ignored. Research done on healthy young males is applied to women and results in errors in medication both in kind and in dosage. Older women usually lack political organizations to make changes. Since they are considered socially unimportant and even expendable, recent media discussions on euthanasia must be terrifying to them.

Poverty

It is easier for society to ignore the poor than it is to ignore the rich. Most older women live in poverty. Sixty percent of women ages 65 and over live at or below the poverty line.[1] Women in this age group are often homeless and helpless. They are in no position to rail against the world and demand service.

There are exceptions that give us hope. One women called me to say, "I'm 77, dear. Do you want my opinion?" When I assured her that I did, she had trouble fitting me into her schedule because she volunteered all day, every day. We settled on an evening interview. She lives in her own home with her cats and is comfortable and self-sufficient. She is currently very concerned about the prejudice against the mentally handicapped in her community and is trying to organize help for them. She is energetic, useful, a necessary part of her community, and a great role model!

Future Attitudes

Perhaps as the baby boomers reach old age sheer numbers will force attention to their problems. Perhaps as more women who are accustomed to managing their own lives, their own finances, and their own future reach old age, they will make more demands on a health care system and insist on a healing environment that serves them. If teens, young women, and matrons change the way they get health information, change the way they view the healing environment, and insist on staying in charge of their own health, they could develop into a community of informed, educated, inquisitive, knowledgeable old women.

4

Walls around Us

Health

Health is more than the absence of aches or illness, more than freedom from disease. We speak of being "healthy" when we mean energetic, happy, and full of vitality. Janine, a 26-year-old doctor, offered me her definition. She said: "It's everything working well: my brain, my heart, my love, my competence, my work, my optimism. Everything."

Healing

Healing is more than the physical repair of bones and tissues. Healing is a process that involves physical change, spiritual energy, emotional acceptance, and mental direction. For hundreds of years society has tried to name and explain parts of the body, examining their composition and physiology so we could better understand how we function. As we became more sophisticated and detailed in our knowledge we began to believe that the body was *only* the parts we could name and describe. We reduced our idea of a person to a collection of scientific facts ignoring the complex and intermeshed mental, emotional, and spiritual activity occurring in that body. We lost the concept of a whole person.

In our new view of healing, we see a whole person, one who is more than just a physical machine and one that interacts with the world around us. We know science is important. We want laser scans, antibiotics, microscopic surgery, and miracle drugs, but we know there is more to healing than a pill or a chemotherapy treatment.

Healing is a process that occurs in the mind, spirit, and emotions as well as in the body. It depends not only on diagnosis and treatment but also on cooperation of our physical, spiritual, emotional, and mental lives. This seems a very simple idea, full of common sense—almost obvious—but our medical industry does not accept this definition of healing as a principle of care. When we understand that healing is a broad concept, we understand that no one can direct or control it but us: not our mothers, our doctors, or our therapists. We are responsible for our own healing.

Directed Healing

Dr. Candace Pert of Rutgers University, New Jersey, spoke to Bill Moyers on Public Affairs Television about the amazing ability of our body to organize itself. She said that emotions may be information molecules of peptides interrelating with the immune system.[1] If this is so, and peptides roaming around our bodies carry emotions to our immune system, then how we feel may direct our body's ability to heal. More and more scientists are suggesting that a person may be more in charge of their healing process than our old textbooks ever considered. This is not news to faith healers, shamans, and folk healers, but it is uncomfortable news to most of those who had the scientific method taught to them with their multiplication tables and who see illness and health as outside personal control.

Changing Ideas about Healing

There are many popular magazines, such as *Glamour* and *Elle*, that carry health sections. In such magazines we read the latest information on breast implants, liposuction, AIDS, uterine cancer, and cardiac disease. The content of these articles may be influenced by the advertisers—a magazine that runs cigarette ads may not run articles on lung cancer—but in spite of that kind of restriction we do get snippets of knowledge that often alert us to new ideas. The casual reader is coming to understand that science is constantly reinventing itself. Ideas that were guiding principles in the past are no longer reliable as new information forces new rules. Science can rarely give us infallible answers, only the best answer for this time. We would like to have solid, dependable responses to our questions, infallible rules that guaranteed health, such as "beta carotene prevents heart disease," but we often can get only probabilities, reasonable guesses, or "most-likely" scenarios. Individuals still react individually to stress, deprivation, and disease.

In our search for more specific information about our bodies and our health, we may run into barriers that have little to do with the amount of knowledge around us or the kinds of knowledge we need. One of the greatest barriers to finding health information about ourselves can be our own attitudes.

Attitudes

Many women have been socially conditioned to see active, aggressive pursuit of personal knowledge as masculine. Women are supposed to wait quietly until told what they need to know. They have been taught that asking questions implies lack of confidence in their doctor; that it is not in good taste to demand answers. These women often see the doctor as their only source of information.

Five years ago when she was 48, Joan, a quiet, petite retired music teacher, had a serious heart attack and subsequent emergency bypass surgery. She had visited the doctor two weeks before her attack. The doctor neither listened to her heart nor ordered tests.

> JOAN: This was a new doctor and I never told her that I had high choles-
> terol in the past. It's her job to ask me, isn't it? I thought she would
> check whatever needed checking.

> ME: But didn't you know why the doctor in the past had been worried
> about your high cholesterol and why you had been on a special diet
> for years? Didn't you realize that you were at risk for heart disease?

> JOAN: No, I didn't ask. I'm a passive person. I thought the doctor would
> look after me.

Our authoritarian schools and churches encourage women to place their confidence in a benevolent father figure who will make good health decisions for them. This leads some women to believe that there is one source of health information, a wise and kind doctor, who will have all the information they need. The woman only has to find that person, follow his advice, and all will be magically well. This attitude is pervasive in spite of the feminist movement, the advances in education and increased opportunities for women, and the self-education that is prevalent in our culture. Women often are bitter about what their doctor has not done for them but just as often are convinced that there is one "good" doctor somewhere who can "look after" them. This attitude prevails even when women know that no one is as concerned about their health as they are and that one health care worker seldom offers all the knowledge a woman needs. Women need more than one source of information.

Cultural Conditioning

Low self-esteem is legitimized in our culture as the social norm for women. Gloria Steinem, in her book *Revolutions Within*, quotes studies by the American Association of University Women that showed that 67% of 9-year-old girls feel "happy with the way I am." By high school that percentage drops to 29%.[2] College women fare even worse. Twenty-one percent of college students who had been valedictorians at high school graduation entered college feeling "far above average." After 2 years that rate dropped to 4%. By the time these students graduated, 25 percent of the men had an estimate of themselves as "far above average"— but *none* of the women did.[3]

They had been socialized to devalue themselves. Researchers Carol Gilligan of Harvard and Lyn Mikel Brown of Colby College tell us that adolescent girls lose their ability to know themselves and learn to please others.[4] Gilligan and Brown point out in their study that the change occurs usually between the ages of 8 and 13. Most of us have empirical evidence of our own to back up this finding. We know that 8-year-olds are more aggressive, opinionated, exuberant, and definite than 11-year-olds. We need to ask why 13-year-olds want to please others so much that they will negate their own opinions or needs to do so. This is not news to most of us. Our experiences have taught us that women are not valued. Living as a woman in Western society puts us through a process that essentially devalues young girls. This process does not create a demanding, curious, responsible health consumer.

On the contrary, our culture creates women who do not demand and do not question and who feel they do not deserve the best advice. Little girls are taught to accept authority and to think of others first. They are taught to care for others but not for themselves as if they do not deserve fair treatment. Some women only learn to demand answers to their health questions when their child needs help. It is socially acceptable to be aggressive on behalf of a child. Brita, a petite 34-year-old mother, said:

> Once I had my baby, I could ask questions about him. Before that, I didn't think I should. Like, it was okay to push a little when I was asking about Mike, but not when I was asking about me. I can't believe I was that timid.

Other women manage to survive in our society with an entirely different attitude. Pat, 37, is confident, knows her resources, cheerfully demands satisfaction from the medical professions, and stays in charge of her health. She recently had a gall bladder operation and had a surgeon who used the latest techniques. Postoperatively, when the intern ordered her catheterized, she was anything but passive."Listen, Charlie," she said, "I know my body better than you do. When it wants to pee, it'll pee. Leave me alone and let me get comfortable. When I'm ready, I'll pee."

Pat is rare—wonderful, talented, admirable—but rare because most women do not have her confidence or her ability to get cooperation. Most feel incompetent and unable to deal with their health problems. They don't have a family of knowledgeable aunts and grandmothers to give them advice and to help them develop a philosophy of health and an understanding of what health and healing mean. Many see health as luck and healing as a procedure given to them by someone else. Most don't look inside themselves to discover what is wrong with their health, nor do they look inside themselves for ways to heal. Usually dependent on someone else, particularly a doctor, to diagnose their illnesses and prescribe their treatment, they don't feel like a partner in discovering the problems or in discovering a healing process but are subservient participants in the health care system. They are often resentful, angry, worried, and anxious because they haven't been able to give the doctor a complete picture of their illness and because they haven't been given the options they think they need. Rarely do they confront the caregiver or object to treatment. They put a high value on being liked by their caregiver and less value on getting good treatment.

What happened to the confident, courageous little girls that Gloria Steinem talked about who entered first grade with such hope? Many became hesitant, self-effacing, intimidated consumers of medical products. Their experience made them that way.

"Ask the Doctor"

It is common to hear comments such as "What did the doctor say you should do?" "The doctor won't let me on my feet for two days." "*They* won't let me go back to work." "I don't know why I have headaches. I haven't been to the doctor yet." Such comments reveal the extent to which women give the responsibility for their health to others.

Women often agree to suggested treatment, even to treatment they don't understand or procedures that are harmful or unnecessarily, painful because they think "the doctor knows best." They don't believe the doctor knows best because he has a good reputation in this area of illness, because they checked his professional credentials, or because his advice makes sense. They believe he knows best because he is a doctor and doctors are supposed to know best. Women still give doctors power over their bodies even when they have been harmed in the past or when they are afraid.

Connie, 56 years old, quick moving, talkative, and full of compassion for others, is a cancer survivor. She looked at life after divorce and after cancer as a new beginning. She felt she had "wrestled alligators and won," and nothing would ever be so hard again. She had some strong views on how women see themselves:

> We don't think we have any rights to start with. If you come out of a dysfunctional family system, as I did, you don't have the self-esteem to ask for what you need because you don't think you deserve it.

Like Brita, Connie at first had a hard time seeing herself as a valuable person who was capable and who deserved answers. Many women have little faith in their own ability to understand their bodies. They are not taught to understand what their bodies are telling them, to interpret the metaphors of meaning that bodies often convey, to deal with pain and unhappiness, or to trust the healing powers within.

Anne is 36, dark-haired, tiny, vivacious, and intense. She had lived through a difficult time with strep throat, skin ailments, depression, and a divorce to become a self-sufficient, stable single mother of two small boys:

> I learned that what happens to us has to be processed. Somehow it has to be processed physically, and we get sick. We use our bodies to let truth come

out and sometimes that is really uncomfortable. We need to see meaning in our illness and work at dealing with the pain that is underneath the symptoms.

Anne is looking for much more information about health and illness than symptom relief. Many women, while not as articulate or philosophical as Anne, realize that they are looking for a broader view of health and a more complete knowledge of their own health problems than they usually find in the doctor's office.

Confidence

If a woman believes that she deserves good information and that she can find it if she asks enough questions, she will persevere until she gets it. With good information she can make good decisions. If a woman believes that she must accept the opinion of one advisor—that she is neurotic, self-centered, foolish, and hysterical when she wants answers to her questions—if she believes that she only need do as she is told to get well, then she is doomed to inadequate, ineffective care.

Rita was a wife and mother of two little children who did not go for care until her cancer was inoperable. She was a big woman, and she said she was tired of being told that all her health problems would go away if she just lost weight. She was humiliated and hurt by constantly being told her size was not acceptable and she was frustrated by having all her physical problems attributed to her weight. She preferred to accept her health problems rather than put herself through the humiliation of a doctor's visit. She died of her cancer, not her fat.

Many women know that an increase in self-confidence can increase their ability to get information. They look around and see that self-confident women are treated with more respect than self-effacing women and that they usually get more answers to their questions. Confident women continue to search for the information they want in spite of rejection or indifference on the part of the caregivers. Many women understand that in order to find information in our health care systems they have to believe they have the right to know. They need to understand that there are different sources of information and that they can reach many of them. They need to view themselves as worthwhile so that the effort they make to find information is a reasonable activity. They need to see themselves as valuable, important, and worthy of attention.

Linda, a feminist and community worker, said:

> Big project. Most of us have been so intimidated by the medical establishment we can't think around them. They use jargon in a way that excludes us, but it's done in such a way that we're embarrassed to ask what they mean. I manage better now that I'm older. I'm bolder. It's wonderful to be 44 and not give a shit.

The Rare Ones

Some women do see themselves as worthwhile. My friend Judith, a 42-year-old woman who was being treated with radiation for fast-growing breast cancer, was told at the beginning of the last week of radiation that her dosage would be increased and the angle of delivery changed so that instead of the rays hitting her from the side and avoiding lung tissue, they would hit her directly. The technicians assumed she would cooperate and started to move the equipment. "Wait a moment," she said. "I haven't agreed to this." They waited. She continued. "Today, you will radiate me as you have done in the past. And then we will talk."

The caregivers were annoyed and refused to talk to her that day. The next day they tried to insist that she have the radiation as they wanted it. She insisted on a consultation. She asked what risks were involved in the different treatment. They reluctantly gave them to her. Then she asked for other options. She found an option that satisfied her, was not as damaging as the one they first suggested, and seemed to be acceptable to them as treatment. While she got the treatment she wanted, she had to struggle with her caregivers to get it. No one made it easy for her. She had to demand choice.

Judith is an exceptionally strong and determined woman. Most people lying on an X-ray table would give the responsibility for deciding the dosage and treatment to the caregiver. Judith insisted on retaining control. "After all," she told me, "who's going to trust a medical profession that makes money taking off breasts? It's an industry and you'd be a fool to forget that." She tells me that cynicism is an important part of her independence. She trusts herself and her decisions.

For many women, the process of raising their self-esteem starts with a network of encouraging friends and may include courses at the women's center, community center, college, or church school. It may include group or private therapy or a course of individual reading and study. Once a woman realizes that the reason she can't ask questions and can't seek information from the health care system is that she feels unworthy of that information, she can work on her own attitudes and make changes.

Even the Confident . . .

However, some of the most confident women I know are intimidated by a doctor's office, and very strong women are terrified of hospitals. We all need to consider why. It may be the lack of control they feel in these situations. For some, lack of information equals lack of control, but even articulate, aggressive women with good research skills may have problems finding their way around the medical system.

I interviewed Cathie, a 36-year-old clinical psychology student, in her high-rise apartment. She told me that she usually managed to get the information she needed but occasionally she was frustrated:

> I don't need to be patronized. I'm relatively intelligent and I'm eager to learn. I told the doctor my symptoms but she didn't give me any idea what

she was thinking. I wanted to know if my guess was incorrect, which would help me to self-diagnose better in the future. I do need information—I like to know what is happening with my body. I also think it makes me a better patient, less dependent perhaps on the medical profession. But it also helps me understand what it is I can do toward actively preventing more injury. She can be the doctor, that's okay with me. Doctors know more than me in this area. I'm happy to ask them, that's why I went to her. But I came out of there no further ahead. I got such an enormous run-around I couldn't believe it. I'd never go back.

Medical doctors misdiagnose, mistreat, and do harm. They also discover, explain, and help. Doctors may be good sources of information—even wonderful sources—but they do not know your body the way you do, nor do they know your problems the way you do. Their opinions are not a substitute for your common sense; their directions are not a substitute for your decisions. Their role, except in emergency situations, is to advise so that you can make good decisions about yourself. They should be a good source of information but, in most cases, only one of many sources of information. Women must remain responsible for their own health, exploring different sources, asking questions, and getting advice until they can make decisions that help them to become healthy and remain healthy.

5

Walls around Information

The Information Network

A woman in our world of health and healing should be like a spider sitting in the center of a web, receiving information from a network of interconnected systems covering all her world. In our society women are not at the center of a web of information. They are on the edge collecting bits of knowledge, trying to weave meaning without enough material. They scurry through the various systems—medical, public health, library, friends, relatives, support groups, and private organizations—looking for the information. The information is so fragmented that, although a woman may have perfected how she gets one kind of information, she has to discover a new system to find out about another. She may know whom to call about measles but may have no idea how to get advice on a hysterectomy. Almost every new disease or problem requires a new source-finding process. For every problem, she has to construct a new web.

While some women are able to build a network of information, most find that their sources shift and change: the person they relied on from the medical field leaves or retires; the women's resource center that used to carry current information has their budget cut and can no longer get up-to-date information; their neighbor, a nurse at the hospital, moves away. Few women have family members who can give them generations-old herbal remedies and practical advice.

Gilda, now 43, lives in a tidy, suburban townhouse with her adult daughter. We sat at her kitchen table while she told me how hard it had been for her to find information when she was a young mother.

> It seemed I gave birth to my daughter and then went into a deep depression and I didn't know what was wrong with me. I just felt absolutely hopeless and helpless. I was crying all the time and I put on this big front, you know, but I was a withering, soppy person inside. I don't know how, but I just kept on going. I didn't tell anyone. There was no one to tell.

Like many women, she didn't know where to turn to get help or information. She had no idea what postpartum depression was—that deep pit of despair and helplessness that can be triggered by childbirth—until she was long past it. Now, she has compassion for the young woman she had been, and she believes that no one should be so unhappy, so confused, and so alone, cut off from empathy and information. She wants a better system for the young mothers of today.

Isolation

Most North American women do not live in communes or small villages where women can meet everyday at the town well and talk. Some women do retain the extended families of their old country and manage within the North American society to have ethnic subcultures—in the East Indian communities of a big city, on the native American reservations, at the family gatherings of Italian Americans, or even daily gatherings in someone's kitchen where women share information. Most women live in one-family homes or apartments. The less a woman has contact with other women at work or in school, the less likely she is to find alternatives to her information sources. Often, there is excellent health information available through societies such as the Cancer Society and the Diabetes Association, or through women's resource centers, doctors' offices, community health units, books, and videos, but some women, isolated in their own homes, do not know where to start—women like Brita. She told me that after having her first child she felt lost:

> I phoned my step-mother and she told me about the yellow pages. Can you believe it? I didn't even know enough to look through the yellow pages in the phone book.

Researching

Many women are not used to researching their own information. Information sources look like a mess of unconnected lines with no starting point. These women aren't comfortable traveling through the telephone book, phoning one agency after another until they find what they need. They might make one or two calls—but they will not make five. Others don't know where to look and they are afraid they won't understand the information if they do find it. Some have greater research skills and know how to use the library and how to persist when a contact is lost or when sources are unwilling. There are computer whizzes who are comfortable on the computer information superhighway and know how to pull information from journals and articles all over the world. Some who may have excellent research skills have training in the medical model and distrust any alternative healing. They limit their research to doctor-controlled sources and dismiss a source of help and healing that could be useful to them.

This attitude is changing as our understanding of healing grows and broadens. Television talk shows, magazines articles, and newspaper stories speak of "energy sources," "harmony of spirit," and "positive imaging." What the First Nations people have called for centuries the "Healing Circle" is now being called the "biosociopsychomedical model," a comprehensive view of healing. It really means that doctors and nurses are trying to see the patient as a whole, that is, "holistically," and are beginning to approve healing methods that have been outside the medical model. Medical consumers are eager to see a broad view, and slowly the narrow bands of medical knowledge are stretching. Soothing touch has been used by many nurses for years but now has an official name. The Nurse-Healers Professional Association has defined "therapeutic touch" as: ". . . a consciously directed process of energy exchange during which the practitioner uses the hands as a focus to facilitate healing "[1]

The CEO of Mercy Healthcare Sacramento, Sister Bridget McCarthy, uses stories and imagery to create an atmosphere of healing in her hospital. Health care consumers trade doctors' advice, read popular magazines, and watch television and find that some doctors are more "holistic" than others, that there are alternative healers and healing methods that might help them, and that there are drug-free solutions to some problems. Yet alternative medicine looks promising and scary at the same time, and many women want a trusted guide to help them evaluate the information they find. They are looking for a gateway through the walls around information. They need an entrance, a way in.

Prejudice

Often that entrance is blocked by subtle, but harmful, prejudice against poverty, illiteracy, gender, diagnosis, age, and size that still exists in our health care systems. There is no one totally free from some kind of prejudice. It's human nature to respond to past experiences positively or negatively, but it does help to realize that some of the difficulties women face when they search for information come not from their diagnoses or personalities but from the prejudices of the health care workers and the society from which we all come. Some conditions are more likely than others to prevent access to information.

Poverty

If the health care system were a holistic one and women could find broad information within it, poverty could still keep them ignorant. Poverty is a barrier to finding health information even in our world of public libraries and our democratic commitment to public information. Without money, women can't buy books or videos on health information or pay for health education courses. They may not be able to pay for the tests they need to get an accurate diagnosis or the treatment they need to prevent complications. Their jobs may require that they work too hard and for too many hours to have time or energy to pursue knowledge.

My neighbor stood under my office window one sunny afternoon, threw out her hands and said, "I haven't read a book in two months! And I work in a library! Life is moving too fast."

Some women may not have the time it takes to make the five phones calls to the library to get information or the strength to track a telephone trail of referrals to get an answer. Poor women often feel intimidated in the doctor's office and in hospitals. "I always dress up when I go to the doctor's," Brita said. "I think he'll treat me better if he thinks I can afford him."

In countries such as the United States where not all patients have medical coverage, the kind of care patients receive is most often directly related to their ability to pay. I spoke to Laura, a 42-year-old white woman who sold health insurance in Alabama. She said:

> Patients don't get the same kind of care from free clinics as they do if they have an insurance plan and can pay the doctor. Free clinics don't do as many tests or investigate as far; treatments aren't as complete and sometimes not even close to adequate. There isn't any respect there, you know. Patients don't see the same doctor twice in a row and the doctors are usually young and using the clinic as a way to survive until they can start their own practices. In my state, most of the poor people are black so the problems of poverty look like problems of race. It's really basically the inability to pay for medical insurance that is at the root of poor care. Black doctors have white patients. We have no problem with any one of any color with money. We just don't look after our poor people very well.

When I first started selling insurance here I was told not to sell to black people because they wouldn't keep up their premiums. I soon saw that many black people didn't have full-time work, so they didn't have the means to pay for the health insurance. It's pretty clear that my company was anxious to sell insurance to people who could pay for it and not anxious at all to sell it to people who had trouble paying. Naturally. That's the system. It was a problem of cost efficiency, not race. Eighty percent of the population of Alabama is black; 80% of the management, the university professors, or the doctors are not black. The reason black people don't have steady jobs and enough money to pay for health insurance sure could be a problem of discrimination.

I tried once to sell a policy to a black family who needed it but the company rejected them—not on the grounds that they were black, of course not, but on the grounds that they didn't have enough money to keep up the premiums. And so it goes.

In Canada where ability to pay is not supposed to be a factor, there is still prejudice against poverty. The poor receive less instruction and have fewer options than the rich, and even with "universal" health care the insurance will not pay for "elective" medical care (that is, the medical care that the medical industry does not think is necessary).

Jessica, an architect and mother of a 4-year-old, told me that midwives were not covered by insurance in the Northwest Territories of Canada where she lives:

Cost is a real prohibitive factor for most people here. I had to get a midwife to come from the south and stay for a 2-week period and hope that I had my baby in that time. I had to pay the midwife compensation for the births she wouldn't be able to take on while she was up north with me and then I had to pay her air fare. All together it was about $2,500.

Poor women in Jessica's district, the vast area of the north, don't have the option of home births with a midwife, and poor women without Jessica's education would not be as informed about their health choices. They don't have access to long-distance telephone lines, FAX machines, or credit cards, nor do they have her ability to use the language to persuade the local medical personnel to back up midwives in an emergency. Jessica's ability to research and read information helped her greatly. Poor women are more likely to be illiterate than rich women or to be literate in a different language, so health care information is often written in a language they can't read. Poor women without literacy skills have few choices, as they must rely on word-of-mouth information either from friends or from the health care workers.

Literacy

The literacy rate in the United States is difficult to assess because different researchers use different standards to measure it. Forest P. Chisman and Associates, in their report on *Leadership for Literacy: The Agenda for the 1990s*, state that 20 to 30 million adults in America have not mastered basic literacy skills,[2] roughly 8 to 12% of the population. In Canada, 12% of the population cannot read and write a simple message.[3] Of those 88% who *can* read a simple message, some would not be able to read well enough to understand a health pamphlet.

Since many women are unable to receive health information through reading, television is an important source of education. This information is good, bad, and mediocre. The women I interviewed rated television documentaries on health as more believable than the information they received from nurses or doctors. Whether the health facts given on television are true or false, many women rely on them. Perhaps when interactive television is common—the kind that allows the viewer to ask questions and receive answers—the information from television may be more reliable. It may be, though, that our prejudices will simply carry on into the new technology.

Gender

One of a woman's greatest barriers to consulting doctors is gender itself. Women often feel that, because they are women, they have to prove themselves as reasonable humans before they can get the information they want. And they fear the abuse that comes from this prejudice. The fear of sexual abuse haunts all women when they are alone in their houses or when they walk down an empty street, so it is no wonder that it is part of their fear of doctors' offices. Many women have been sexually abused and fear that if they allow themselves to be alone in a room with a man, a man who has social power and who requires that they take their clothes off, they will be sexually abused again. The incidence of abuse by male physicians is high enough to justify this fear. In British Columbia in 1992, 208 women phoned in to the physicians' hot line to complain about sexual abuse. The response was so great that the physicians' association installed a permanent complaint line. This is really not a way of dealing with the abuse, but it does recognize the problem. Studies in the United States show that 10% of doctors are guilty of some form of sexual misconduct toward their patients.[4] As long as male doctors are the main source of health information, women are prevented from getting that information by their reasonable fears of abuse.

Janey, a 33-year-old mother of one told me about her experience:

> I was 17, unexpectedly pregnant, and I went to the doctor who was going to do my abortion. Because my condition had to do with parts of my body that were part of my sexual being, I knew the doctor would pay attention to them. I didn't know whether what he was doing was usual or not usual. But I was very young and I was totally unsupported and feeling terribly awful about the predicament I had gotten myself into. I was very, very vulnerable. Whether this man was out of his jurisdiction or not I felt I deserved it.
>
> I felt I deserved to be sort of punished for getting pregnant. I mean, I didn't do anything careless. I was living with my husband, a teacher. A doctor had told him that he was sterile and since he'd never made anyone pregnant we didn't use birth control. He was saying that based on what a doctor had told him. Again, you know, the information of the doctor was taken as gospel.
>
> But this particular doctor I went to see had me take my clothes off in front of him; and he watched me. There was no female attendant present and I felt terribly uncomfortable about that. He fondled my breasts and said suggestive things that I felt were ... well, I didn't know. Your body language tells you. My stomach was crunching up and so on. It's like something's not

right here. But because I didn't know and because of my vulnerability, I didn't report him. The heightened vulnerability creates, I think, more victims because of the terrible power imbalance.

When something happens to us in isolation I think we believe that we're the only person in the world that this is happening to. We don't have any other experiences to compare it with.

When I was 17 I had no idea that the doctor was acting outside his realm. It was only when I was an older woman and when I had other healthy experiences with healthy doctors who did not overstep their boundaries that I realized the first doctor had been wrong.

When I go to a doctor I open myself up to this person. He's a potential helper, my healer, my confidante. I'm worried. I'm sick and I'm depending on this person to hear me, to listen to me, and to help me. When that person recognizes all those things about me and then goes in for the kill, I think that is inhumane.

Suzanne, a Dene woman, native of the Northwest Territories, is 37 years old and a cook at a geological camp; she sat on the porch of the Women's Center in the late daylight of a northern evening and told me about her experience with an emergency Cesarean section:

The doctor cut down each side and across the front, took the baby, and sewed me up, down, and across and back up . . . like an envelope.

"You know they can cut low, a 'bikini line,'" I said, "or cut a straight line?"

Yeah, I know." We sat in silence for a few moments. She looked at me out of the corner of her eyes. "He was just having a joke, eh?"

A sick joke. She carried the scar of his disrespectful "joke" for the rest of her life. I held her gaze for a long moment and then the tears filled my eyes and spilled down my cheeks. It was too much for me this time. She should never have had to carry such a brand. The doctor, a white man, in this community of aboriginal people thought of her as a second-class citizen and treated her that way. She knew it and anyone who saw her scar knew it.

Sometimes, the abuse takes the form of a casual disrespect of patients. Fay, a 30-year-old social worker, told me about one of her experiences:

> Not too long ago I was having an ultrasound done on my breast at the hospital and people walked in the room without even knocking. There was a curtain right there but no one pulled it. This worker just walked in the room and went on doing what he came in to do. I pulled the technician's hand away and pulled the sheet up over me and I said, "Excuse me, would you mind locking the door or something? Is this Grand Central Station?"
>
> I know that other people may not be as mouthy as me. What a horrible experience for them, and no wonder they walk away feeling violated.

It is very easy to hear stories like this. Any group of women will offer them. Such treatment is common.

Diagnosis

Because health care practitioners come from a society that has prejudices, they carry prejudices into their health practices. Women with certain conditions have a difficult time getting information because they often are considered incapable of understanding the information or not deserving of it. Women who have been treated for mental illness find it difficult to present themselves at the doctor's office as anything other than a mentally ill patient, even when they are no longer ill. They may be a successful wife and mother, a competent teacher, a valuable social asset to a community, but they see themselves in a defined and unchanging role in the health care system, a mentally ill patient. The diagnosis creates prejudice. A woman experiencing a schizophrenic episode for which she is hospitalized may find her children under the care of the state 2 weeks later when she is discharged. The state may serve notice on her and remove her children while she is incapacitated. Had she been a diabetic and hospitalized for an insulin reaction, she would be far less likely to lose her children. Women with mental illnesses are more likely to have their financial powers taken over by the state and their job opportunities narrowed. Because the consequences are so drastic, women are afraid to look for information about their condition or to expose their diagnosis to the ruthlessness of the health care and social systems of their state or province. Mental illness is still seen by many as a lack of will power. Such social prejudice also exists in the diagnosis of AIDS (although there seems to be greater understanding of this disease than many others), tuberculosis, or venereal disease, or any disease that is seen to be infectious and, for some, has overtones of immorality.

Women who have been treated for symptoms of stress are often considered mentally ill. Most women agreed during the interviews that revealing that they had consulted a psychiatrist would threaten their job prospects. One woman told her insurance company that she had taken tranquilizers for 1 month during her exams in university. Now, 2 years after graduation, she could not get professional disability insurance because the insurers considered her mentally ill. Our society encourages women to go to the doctor and psychiatrist early to prevent severe reactions to stress, then labels them and socially penalizes them for doing so.

Age

Older women find health care professionals prejudiced against them. There is a stereotypical vision of elderly women as mentally incompetent, socially powerless, and undeserving of information. Elderly women are often prescribed many drugs. In my years as a community health nurse I can remember the drug profiles of some elderly women. One doctor prescribed 17 different drugs to an old woman. When that doctor was away on holiday, his replacement substituted 3 drugs that she *did* need. When the regular doctor returned, he put the woman back on the original 17 drugs, forcing her to deal with all the interactions between the drugs and the side effects they produced. She trusted her doctor and thought he would give her a long life, so she took all the drugs. Recently, a practicing hospital nurse told me that many elderly women are admitted onto her ward suffering from the side effects of overmedication.

Drug abuse is often prescribed. This may be the result of the beliefs of medical personnel that health is defined as the ability to work.[5] The elderly, who don't work, are therefore defined by doctors as unhealthy. An unhealthy person then requires treatment or drugs. Doctors also have a general tendency to define all suffering in terms of health, ignoring social and environmental responses to poverty and loneliness; thus, elderly women are handed drugs as a solution to all their problems.

Size

Prejudice against big women is common in our society, so it is not surprising that this prejudice is alive and well in the medical industry. Large women receive little information about their health problems that isn't related to their size. Mary, a matronly size, an advocate for the poor in her northern community, and a busy mother, complained:

> I'd like to go to the doctor with a cold just once and be treated for a cold without being told to go on a diet. Diets don't work anyway. You'd think they'd know that. They do know that, so they're only putting me down.

Forty-seven percent of British women are size 16 or larger.[6] Instead of being considered normal, big women, larger than the media-designated "ideal weight," become targets for a diet industry aided by the advice of doctors. Stable overweight is healthier than yo-yo dieting, yet few doctors advise women to maintain stable overweight. There is little money to be made by telling women to enjoy their bodies as they are. A huge diet, fitness, and medical industry tells women that their bodies are not good enough and that they need pills, potions, diets, exercise therapy, and plastic surgery in order to become "ideal." Often the ideal is a beauty myth, not a health goal. Many large women avoid health care professionals because they find it difficult to get useful advice.

The Need for Health Information

The health care systems in our Western society do not assume that a woman *needs* health information. Information does not flow out through the walls around the medical industry. Giving information with a diagnosis is not automatic; we don't necessarily get education with our prescriptions. We do assume that school girls need information about puberty, birth control, sex education, nutrition, suicide prevention, and drug and substance abuse, and our schools very often provide this information. We usually do not assume that the same detailed knowledge is needed about most health problems.

As a society we have come to understand that good information is necessary to a pregnant woman, that understanding the stages of pregnancy, labor, and delivery is important to good perinatal care. We don't want to return to the days when a woman went through her pregnancy in ignorance and through labor in fear and prayer, comforted only by the knowledge that most women survived. Now, everyone expects doctors and health care professionals to explain and teach pregnant women the information they need. It is perhaps not coincidental that women have been given more choices in labor and delivery now that their male partners have been allowed in the delivery rooms during birth.

While we now believe that pregnant women must have good information, we don't have this expectation for women dealing with menopause. Are they supposed to pretend that nothing is happening to their bodies? They are rarely given good information about their age and stage of life, perhaps because the research and recommendations are not reliable. There are few doctors or health clinics that prepare and deliver health care information on menopause or any other life stage with the same thoroughness with which they deliver perinatal information. Why not? Perhaps because doctors don't receive enough education in this subject or perhaps because there isn't enough information. One of the reasons women don't ask doctors for information on menopause is that they don't trust their advice. They do look for information at women's health centers, which are often established and organized to give information about reproductive cycles.

Maddy, a 51-year-old homemaker, said: "Doctors don't know anything about menopause. Men don't know what women are experiencing. They make us feel old."

Typically, women receive symptom relief at a doctor's office, not education for all kinds of concerns. A 34-year-old woman suffered from severe back pain. The doctor gave her medication for pain and advised rest. The chiropractor she consulted gave her mechanical adjustment to relieve pain; a video to teach her how to walk, sit, and lift; pamphlets and books on back care; and several follow-up visits to be sure that the woman understood how to strengthen her back muscles and avoid injury in the future. With the doctor the woman felt like a patient who was acted upon. With the chiropractor she felt like a cooperative member of a therapeutic team. Health information is available at sources other than doctors' offices and women are beginning to shop for it.

We have many sources of health information—radio and TV shows, pamphlets, books, school talks—but most of these information systems are not presented, as pregnancy information is, at the optimum teaching moment: the time of diagnosis. There is often no program of education, no effort by the health practitioner to initiate or continue the patient's health education. Most doctors will answer questions initiated by the patient and they may often know what most patients ask when first diagnosed, but they seldom go beyond a few short remarks. Few patients know where to look for further information.

The "Insiders"

Some women know *exactly* where to find medical information. These are the nurses, physiotherapists, laboratory technicians—the insiders. One who seems to feel able to get necessary knowledge is a nurse, Gina. She works at a big urban hospital and has many friends who are nurses. She is also acquainted with doctors and knows which ones have good knowledge and which are not competent. She is able, without appointments or charges, to ask advice of doctors casually during her workday. She can stop an internist on the stairs, have coffee with a cardiologist, or check drug dosages with her friend the pharmacist. When her husband suffered a heart attack, she got the information he needed very quickly and was able to evaluate and assess that information with her nursing friends:

> I get what I need either through experience or I know somebody who works in that department and they just grab the first expert that comes through the door. I had somebody who worked at the hospital in the recovery room and I asked which anaesthetist should I have? I get information that way. I know somebody else who is a supervisor and I get her opinion on different specialists. I am lucky, really. I am lucky to have this network.

Gina never considered investigating complementary or alternative health care. She never thought of checking with a naturopath or any other kind of healer, since she was isolated from any contact with practitioners that were not part of the Western medical model:

> I don't know much about alternative medicine. I believe in acupuncture. I don't know why I believe in it, perhaps what I've read or seen on TV. But I haven't thought about it for myself. The only thing I've done is go to a chiropractor. Lots of doctors don't believe in chiropractors. Well, I was getting to the point where I was so frustrated with my frozen shoulder that I did try a chiropractor—but it did nothing for me. Now I don't think I went in there with a negative attitude, but maybe I did. [She thought her resistance might have impeded a cure.] I know they work for some people. I know quite a few people who go to them regularly. You know, they get stiff and they go for their session and they feel great. My philosophy is that if it works for you, that's good—no matter what it is. I mean other than if it is illegal. But if a naturopathic works for you, if acupuncture works for you, if pressure points work for you, take that route. Whatever really works for you should be fine.

Alternative or complementary medicine was not part of her education or her practice. She feels capable of finding out what she needs to know within the community of health care workers that is her everyday environment.

Gina works within the walls of the medical industry. Most women, however, feel barred from the privileged world of knowledge that Gina finds so accessible. Most women must consult a doctor or health care professional for their information. Often, they don't know what questions to ask or even whom to ask. The world of knowledge becomes a mystical, protected, specialized world that women can only approach from the outside, looking for a way in, anxious to get a few pieces of information, forced to take advice on trust, and unable to get enough information to make wise decisions.

6

Why Doctors Don't Give Health Information

The Social Position of Doctors

Doctors in our North American society are well-organized, well-funded, and socially powerful. They often decide who is sick or well, who is competent or not competent, who can return to work and who cannot, who can get insurance and who cannot, even who is guilty of criminal intent and who is not. Life insurers depend on a doctor to decide who gets insurance. Immigrants depend on a doctor to decide if they can be admitted into the country. Society has given doctors power far beyond their first calling as healers. We have created modern shamans, patriarchal and dictatorial, who are supported and sustained by an industry that maintains their position. Doctors have become the central focus of this powerful medical industry. Their social control of the population is encouraged and entrenched by the economic activity they produce.[1]

One young doctor told me:

> I think society is geared to give the doctor a special social status whatever his or her real social status may be. Maybe to create professionalism, to create in the patient a sense of faith in the doctor. The trouble is, it also creates a "holier than thou" attitude in the doctor. It's hard to deal with.

Doctors' pay is not dependent on how much the patient knows. A doctor gets paid for his or her services whether or not the patient receives useful information or even useful treatment. Rewards don't depend on the patient's satisfaction but on a medical association's definition of appropriate care. We have developed a system where doctor-controlled medical associations decide what care, treatment, and behavior are appropriate and then reward and occasionally chastise their members for adhering or not adhering to those standards. It's a bit like asking the Ford Motor Company to set the safety standards for cars.

Janine, a 26-year-old doctor, explained:

> Doctors don't understand you because most of them aren't smart enough and don't spend enough time with you. I think our system is crazy because we go to doctors for all our information. It's expensive and not really effective. They all have the same type of training. Doctors contend that naturopaths and homeopaths are dangerous. What they forget is that they themselves are also dangerous.

Becoming a Doctor

We pick the brightest of our young people, encourage them, financially support them, and then yoke them to years of struggle in universities where they wrestle with difficult studies: anatomy, basic biology, chemistry, and physiology. They interrelate that knowledge to create a useful background to the study of diseases. They learn about drugs and treatments that may help the body overcome disease. By graduation they have absorbed an amazing amount of information stored systematically in patterns in their minds. We then have what we hope is a reliable, skillful practitioner.

Many of the facts they have learned change as scientists discover new information, new technologies, and new methods. Doctors must continue to learn as they practice. They must understand the latest surgical techniques, newest drugs, and latest information on illnesses. They read medical journals and attend continuing education classes in order to keep their medical knowledge as current as it can be. All of this produces doctors who move into their position in the medical industry as skilled technicians. It produces doctors who have excellent information on disease processes and treatment protocols and who believe they are responsible for curing patients. It does not necessarily produce doctors who work in tandem with patients or who are committed to preventing disease or educating patients to help themselves.

As patients, we think that doctors have the answers to our questions; that if we could only ask the right questions, we would learn what we need to know to help ourselves. We expect doctors to be one-stop, all knowledgeable health care sources. We, the consumers of medical practice, are socially conditioned to expect cures from doctors. We hope when treating us the doctors will be empathetic, intuitive, wise, and kind, even though doctors' training stresses the analytical and thorough, not the wise and kind.

The Problem Solvers

In order to be good at his job, the doctor has trained himself to look at problems, analyze them, and break them into smaller problems. He has taught himself to find solutions to specific problems, to consider possibilities and work with the greatest probabilities. And he has learned to work with technicians, nurses, specialists, and insurance agents to deliver his share of health care. He has not trained himself to look at the world from the patient's point of view or to work with the patient's hopes, fears, and emotions. We need to tailor patients' expectations to fit doctors' capabilities. We do not, after all, go to a plumber for advice on electricity.

Pat, a 37-year-old teacher and mother, was a refreshing optimist compared with most of the women I interviewed. She was breezy, intelligent, and competent. She told me of her expectations of doctors:

> Any new doctor I've ever been to sits down with me and talks about the technical aspect of my health. That TV garbage about the doctor sitting there

and having a nice discussion with me about my life and telling me I can take all the time I want to ask whatever I want is not the way life is. I know that medicine is a business, and I realize that I'm dealing with people who are busy and I realize that I'm dealing with people who don't have that "extra time" to sit down and do the human aspect of things. I do expect information, and, because I expect information, I am prepared to do what it takes to get it. I don't expect the doctor to sit down and give me information, I expect to ask for it. My health care is 90% my responsibility, and I treat it the way I would treat a job. If there are things I need to know, I write them down. If there is information I need, I write it down. And I will sit there with my pad and paper and jot things down or I'll add extra questions as he is talking to me.

When you have pain—not the kind like a tooth that eventually you have to get fixed, but pain that is wrecking your life—you know something must be done about it, so you have to take control of the situation. In order to get your health back, you have to take control. I don't like not being able to function. I don't like not being in control. So I go for information. I won't be rushed either because I just keep asking.

While Pat says she gets the information she needs from the doctor, she is aware that she has to be very aggressive to get it.

Solution Givers

Doctors see the world as a bundle of objective problems that need solutions. They are not trained to look at diseases and conditions as meaningful ways that women deal with the pressures of their lives, to see a woman's physical pain in the context of her life, or to see how it is expressing that life. Doctors may give a drug that relieves the pain of a headache without exploring the abusive relationship that contributed to the headache. Julia, 44, mother of three and a homemaker, took Valium for years because she was often "upset," weepy, and anxious. The doctor knew that her husband punched her and slapped her every few weeks, but, other than sympathy, offered no alternatives to her life beyond the comfort of his drug cupboard. Yet patients should not expect doctors to go beyond symptom relief, because the world of social context, emotions, and spiritual needs are outside the doctors' competence. Our expectations of doctors are far too high.

Because their training is solution-oriented and they believe that most problems can be solved within the disciplines they study, doctors often believe that if they do not understand something it is insignificant and even, if they haven't studied it, it doesn't exist. In spite of doctors' perspectives, social and emotional pressures remain an integral part of our lives and influence how we feel, how we get sick, and how we heal.

Julie took her aching back to her doctor who recommended muscle relaxants. Julie did not want to take pills so she went to a chiropractor who dealt with the pain by adjustment and massage. When Julie returned to her doctor and told him that the pain was gone and why it was gone, the doctor was not interested in the chiropractor's work. He chastised Julie for not taking the pills. Anything outside of his treatment and control was not acceptable to him—even when it worked.

Many women have similar experiences. After an initial negative reaction by a doctor, women who had enough assertiveness to look for help outside the medical model rarely reported back to their doctors. By their dismissive reactions, doctors trained these women not to tell them how they dealt with their illnesses when the methods they used were outside of the doctor's knowledge. In this way, experiences of healing and pain relief go on outside the jurisdiction and knowledge of Western medicine in a kind of clandestine manner and stay separated from it. I was amazed, when I started looking, at how many women sought healing experiences outside the medical industry. It was as if there was a two-tiered system of healing—the medical model and the alternative model—used by the same people.

Educating Doctors

Kate was the only woman I interviewed who felt an obligation to educate her doctor. She had a hysterectomy at age

29 to deal with huge uterine fibroids. She had studied all the literature she could find, interviewed five surgeons, and decided on a taciturn doctor with few communication skills who did neat and uncomplicated surgery. Kate advised him that he would do fewer operations if he knew more about holistic medicine and that it was his moral obligation to do fewer surgeries:

> I made appointments with him to discuss the things I'd learned. I'd make up education kits and send them to him and then I'd make an appointment and go in to discuss the information. I told him about primrose oil and low-estrogen diets. I thought of switching doctors but I thought, "No, I've had him so long I'm going to educate him," and I have. He told his colleagues about primrose oil. He's still a close-mouthed jerk, but he's now a jerk with information.

Doctors are taught to be decisive, confident, and organized. They also are paid well for their work. This combination produces men and women who see themselves as powerful and elite. Like rock stars who believe their own publicity, many doctors believe that they are indeed more worthy than others in society and therefore entitled to special status. This attitude of hubris, an arrogant belief in one's own superiority, contributes to the difficulties patients have in asking questions of doctors and the difficulties doctors have in relating to patients. It also makes it unlikely that alternative and Western medicine will dance together in health care.

It is hard for young medical students to resist the seduction of the "god complex" in the drama of life-saving procedures, in the deference of hospital personnel, and in the obvious importance of doctors in a legal system that requires a doctor's signature on most aspects of health care. After spending several years in this heady atmosphere of hierarchal and patriarchal authority, doctors would have to be strong characters indeed to resist the conviction that they were entitled to a special position of power in society. Some of them do resist it, but most accept their special status.

Dominant Doctors

Once out of medical school and practicing in a hospital or community, doctors join organizations that are designed to maintain their position of privilege: colleges of physicians and surgeons and the medical associations. There is something logical and almost inevitable about the domination of doctors over the medical system. There seems to be a law of self-propagation that insists that those in power stay in power. Doctors' signatures are required on procedures that nurses are competent to do. Nurses can't give medications without a doctor's order. Yet, it is amazing how that law is circumvented when it is useful to doctors to ignore it. When I worked as a community health nurse we had "standing orders," that is, a doctor 500 miles away gave us permission to give immunizations whenever we saw fit. Nurses in rural areas also give medication and emergency drugs under "standing orders," which allows the law that gives doctors sole power over prescribing drugs to remain in power while at the same time allowing nurses to give medication. The law is not safeguarding the patient here. Nurses are capable of deciding what and how much medication to give and are legally liable for their decisions; the law protects the doctors' privileged relationship with the drug industry. Midwives who are more capable and safer than doctors in many childbirth situations[2-9] are not legal in some areas and only under a doctor's supervision in others. Nurses who make diagnoses, prescribe treatments, and deliver babies in rural areas such as northern Canada, Kentucky, and New Mexico, somehow need doctors to supervise them when they move to areas of greater population and greater affluence. The dominance of doctors in our health care system has little to do with the needs of patients and everything to do with the needs of doctors.

Constraints of Practice

Once in practice, doctors move into the medical system as a health care delivery person in a fee-for-time basis. Unless he is on a salary, as few are, this means that the more patients he sees, the more money he makes. A doctor usually designs his practice so that he allots time to receive facts, make a diagnosis, and give the solution. Doctors seldom allow time to hear the complete story or view the physical complaints or illnesses from the patient's point of view. And as Kate pointed out, there seems to be little difference between the male and female graduates of medical school:

> Women gynecologists are taught in the same system as men. If you're seeing a female doctor, it doesn't mean she'll be any better than a male.

Female doctors seem to absorb the paternal model in medical school and fit into the authoritarian system.

Social Meaning

Doctors of either gender rarely try to access the social meaning of the illness: why the patient has the illness, how it is serving her, or what change this illness might effect in her life. Such assessments take time and are not considered the priority of the doctors. They are vitally important to the patient, but as yet are rarely included in a medical diagnosis. Patients do want symptom relief, but they also want information about the cause of this problem, their choices of treatment, and the ways to prevent reoccurrence. Their illness is affecting *all* their life, not just their physical comfort. Doctors, because of their training and continuing education, are interested in primarily providing drug or treatment solutions.

Learning on the Job

Patients do teach doctors—not usually as directly as Kate does—but a doctor does learn through contact with patients that all is not as clear as the medical textbooks suggest. He sees healing that is influenced by sadness, by optimism, by family support, by love, and by fear. He learns that there are undefinable forces of healing, such as confidence and faith, that affect the body in ways that seem uncontrollable. He learns that his own personality and attitudes help or hinder healing.

In spite of their training and socialization and the continual reinforcement of their power, many doctors, those with a compassionate nature who have managed to retain that compassion, deliver patient treatment in a caring and flexible way. Some try to understand the holistic nature of their patients and recommend therapists who can assist them on their way to a healthy life. A few work with herbalists, psychologists, and support groups to offer patients a more rounded view of health.

Fitting into the System

But generally, patients are required to fit into a medical system that serves doctors. When a medical system is designed and run to serve doctors, it is not important to the system whether the patients are informed. The system is judged on the number of doctors and doctors' clinics and hospitals there are in the community, not on how healthy or unhealthy the people are. In a system revolving around doctors, the rest of the population is trained to respond to the needs of those doctors.

Compliance

Some women feel that their education, their whole social conditioning as women, sets them up to be ideal users of the medical system, helpless and easily manipulated. Jeanne, 29 years old and tiny, talked to me in her counseling office. She had a great deal of experience with doctors and hospitals because she had been born with hips that did not fit together properly:

Two things ended up happening to me. Doctors were kind of like God. They would tell me what to do and tell me what was going to happen to my body. I asked no questions because I thought the doctor knew best. The other part of my life was religion. I was taught to pray about my problems. If I trusted in God, everything was supposed to get better. It was kind of like I was supposed to work hand-in-hand with two patriarchal systems.

I decided at a certain point in my life that I wasn't buying that crap any more. I'd had enough of doctors walking all over me, just walking into the room and pulling back the sheet and doing whatever they wanted to my body and paying no attention to who I was as a person. Giving me no dignity, no respect of any kind. So I started talking back and fighting them.

I was about 20 or so when I realized I could ask questions and I sort of got a grip on the fact that this is my body.

One of the really abusive things—it still makes me shudder when I think about it—was when I was a teenager and I was in the hospital. It was a big training hospital and the specialist that I had would walk in with anywhere from 20 to 50 student doctors and they'd all gather around me and discuss me in medical terms. That was just one of the most abusive things that could have happened. Sometimes I got a "Hello," and sometimes I got a smile. Like what do you do when you've got all these people around you staring at you, and they're talking about a part of you and not communicating with you at all? It was really awful actually.

I asked Jeanne if she got the information she needed from the doctors. She said:

Doctors are notorious for answering a question while they're walking out the door. That way they make damn sure you don't get another question in on their time. It's a really slick trick. Before you know it, they're gone.

Women complain about the doctor's lack of listening skills, his inability to understand what their illness means to them, and their fear that he is missing something important in their care. While some women want greater empathy and more information from their doctors, they often do not look for a replacement.
Jessica told me:

It's a social thing sometimes. Some women have really strong ties with their doctors. It's interesting how that plays a social role. Like I don't want to hurt my doctor's feelings by going to someone else. In a small town that social thing is really important.

Kate talked about the expectations on her to be a passive recipient of surgery:

> There's social pressure just to be quiet and obey the doctor. Most people don't understand that. The pressure on me was not in the hospital, it was through friends and acquaintances. They told me, "Don't be ridiculous!" "It's only a uterus." "What's the big deal?" It's *my* uterus and it's an amputation, you know? I'm grieving.

Teresa, a 41-year-old entrepreneur from Calgary, told me:

> Unless women have a strong reason to pursue information most of them will keep going to the doctor they had and not question his advice and hope that their problems will go away. A lot of people think they have a good friend in their doctor and will not change him because they've had him forever, even since childhood. Even though those doctors may be near retirement, they won't look for someone more modern. I also have friends who, when they don't know what is wrong with them, push the problem away and don't try to find out about it. I think that is kind of scary.

These women are giving the responsibility of their health to the doctor as if they were slaves of an all-wise master. They may find it easier to allow others to make their health decisions, but they then have all the problems of slaves: ignorance, fear, abuse, lack of control, and the subjugation of their needs to those of the master.

Choice

In a small community, the doctor's power may be exaggerated. A woman fears that if she offends her doctor, she may be vulnerable to that doctor in the future. A woman from the north asked me:

> So what do you do? There is only one doctor in the town. He's not very good but he's all we have. In an emergency he could save your life. So we go to him. The medical plan won't pay for us to travel to someplace else. We go to him. That's all there is to it.

There are things she can do. She can take an advocate with her when she visits him. She can report any transgressions to the medical association. But people in small communities are afraid that their doctor will move away—many small communities have no doctor at all—so they are willing to accept second-class care rather than have no care. Traditionally, doctors in small rural communities work very hard for a short time and leave. The people of those communities know that a good doctor will leave soon, but so will a bad one; so they are quiet, and wait.

Advocates

Doctors often respond positively to advocates. Women can often get more information from their doctors if they take an advocate with them. Many women use their husbands and partners as advocates during labor and delivery. Some women use the workers at the women's centers. Others use their public health nurse or their social worker. Sometimes, they use a friend.

Jessica described her experience as an advocate:

> I went along with my friend, wearing a variety of hats: one was as a friend, one was as a supporter, and also as a recorder to record everything that was said. I also went as a prompter and an advocate because I'm a little removed from the problems and can come up with questions or suggestions that she might want to ask—which we wrote down in advance. So when we were there in the doctor's office he answered the questions and I madly wrote the answers down. It is interesting. He'd tell her something and there would be this screwed up look on her face and she'd say, "Yes, doctor. Yes, doctor." I knew from her face that she didn't have a clue what this guy was saying, so then I turned to her and said, "Did you understand this or did you have some more questions about that?" She said, "Well, actually, no. I didn't understand."
> So I would paraphrase back to her what I thought she was thinking and I was usually right dead on. It surprises me that doctors haven't got a better ability to read people. But then I knew her. She's my friend so I knew when she wasn't getting it. Time is precious. She has to get all her questions answered now. She doesn't want lingering unanswered questions like, "Is this cancer?" She'd suffer. That's the worst place to be, in purgatory like

that. Tell me I'm going to die, tell me everything's fine, but don't leave me hanging with, "What if? What if?"

Being an advocate is very much like working as a translator. An advocate interprets, rephrases, and records. In addition, an advocate demands, defends, explains, and acts as a witness. More and more women are taking their friend or partner with them to the doctors' offices and relying on them to defend and protect them.

Women who do not take an advocate with them to the doctor's office very often debrief their doctor's visit with a friend so that they can be sure they understood what the doctor said and so they know how to use his or her advice.

Only Source

Sometimes women cooperate with their doctors because they do not know where else to get information. Jeanne, with her years of experience with the health care system for treatment of her hip problem, still did not know any options for health information other than the doctor:

There isn't anywhere to go. If I'm not getting the information I need from the medical people, I'll go to some books, but otherwise I can't even think of any place to get information.

Jeanne is a professional woman working as a counselor in a government agency for drug and alcohol addiction. She has more ability than most to find information. She had the research skills that allowed her to get her university degree, but she has been conditioned to find her health information from doctors and, in talking to me, was surprised that she had never looked for other options. That was astounding to both of us.

When a woman does not get the information she needs from her doctor, she often does without the information. Fay, a social worker, told me:

I question the doctors, but I think other women wouldn't necessarily question. Like my mother had a hysterectomy when I was in grade seven and I remember going to the hospital to see her. I talked to her about that later as an adult and asked her why she had the hysterectomy. She doesn't know. She had a hysterectomy and she doesn't know why. Lots of people don't question. They just don't question what their doctors tell them. And my Dad. He was on high blood pressure medication. I looked at this stuff (all kinds of medications) and I said, "Let's find out why you have high blood pressure." So I sent him back to the doctor with a list of questions. "Don't leave until you get the answers." He wouldn't have asked if I hadn't done that. I think younger women are more committed to owning their own bodies and finding out what's wrong, to being an active member of the whole system of health care.

Some younger women seem more committed to asking questions, but there are still some who are intimidated and fearful of doctors.

Some women are grateful for competent, empathetic care from their doctors. They don't expect it and are pleased when they find it. One woman told me that her doctor had discovered uterine cancer and referred her to a specialist.

"Is it important that I see the specialist soon?" she asked.

"Yes, very soon."

"Then I want to see him today."

That was arranged. She went for surgery the following week.

"That surgeon," she said, "had healing in his hands. I felt it. He gave me healing. Is that crazy?"

Not as crazy as one might have thought years ago. More and more we are realizing that one's attitude to health and healing plays an important part in that healing; this woman's recognition of her doctor's ability to heal may have done a great deal to keep her cancer-free for 3 years.

The Doctor's Role

Doctors often initially see themselves as healers but come to act as drug dispensers. Many doctors fight to retain their role as healers in society against a strong pressure to be instant diagnosticians with magical cures in time-pressured practices that require they make enough money to support staffs and pay overhead.

One doctor told me:

> I know this patient needs an hour of my time twice a week. I understand this. She has no one else to go to and I can regulate her medication and help her get a grip on her life. But I can only be paid for 15 minutes and I have a wife and two kids and overhead. So I see her twice a week for an hour, and four other patients like her, and my wife goes out to work.

This doctor responds to his patient's need. Many doctors will respond to the insurance company and will give only the amount of time they will be paid for.

Many doctors schedule patients tightly to fit efficiently into the doctor's time. They book two patients for the same time slot so that the doctor does not have to wait. June, a 45-year-old secretary, told me: "I'm working and my time is important. Why should I have to wait in his office? My dentist isn't late; why the hell should my physician be late? It's an insult."

Most women understand the nature of emergencies, even of a sudden need of a patient for more time that day. What they expect is an apology for having been kept waiting. When they do not get it they quite reasonably assume that the doctor does not value their time, is not at all concerned with how long they had to wait, and expects them to wait on his convenience. Patients feel used and angry. Yet they seldom complain to the doctor about this. Perhaps doctors don't know that patients are angry over waiting, or perhaps they believe that patients expect to wait.

Doctor's Etiquette

Sometimes women are caught in the professional games of doctors. Fay was hospitalized with sudden abdominal pain. She had an appointment already set with a female doctor who was a specialist in gynecology and decided that, since she was in the hospital anyway, she would not take the doctor "on call," she would see that specialist. The specialist was annoyed that Fay would not see her colleague.

> My first meeting with her was quite yucky because she was offended that I didn't think her colleagues were good enough to talk to and I insisted on seeing her. That whole "doctors together" thing. I was really taken aback by that. I thought, "Oh jeez, we're off to a good start here. How are we going to cooperate in my health care when she's already angry with me because of this?"
>
> But eventually she and I found common ground and worked in my best interests. She ended up doing the surgery and did what she promised to do—that is, she was conservative and saved my ovary.

The Oppressor–Victim View

The idealistic, compassionate, hardworking, intelligent medical student comes to be viewed as an oppressor once he becomes a doctor. The specialized knowledge of the doctors seems to remove them from the world of the patients. Doctors seem to have little to do with the world of the female patients and have a wide gulf of disparity to bridge before making a personal connection with them. Doctors, while perhaps recognizing that patients are uncomfortable with them and reluctant to speak easily with them, may not realize how this lack of communication inhibits good medical practice. A good "bedside manner" is considered a bonus, a frill, by many doctors. The ability of the patient to understand, cooperate with healing, and make changes in her life is not evaluated as a healing force in medical schools. The doctor's knowledge and skill are evaluated, but not his ability to make that knowledge and skill useful to his patients. If a doctor genuinely feels judgmental about people, if he sees some patients as more worthy of his time than others, if he see women as less worthy than men and "nonworking" women as even less worthy, his prejudices and judgmental views will prevent him from acting as an effective health consultant. All the knowledge and skill in the world are not going to benefit women unless the doctor can receive information from them, reflect on it with his own knowledge, and give back information in such a way that it can be translated into changes in the patient. Knowledge and skill must be communicated. It is at that point, the point at which the patient communicates her need to the doctor and the doctor understands and responds with practical advice, that our health care system is weak.

Prescriptive Technicians

Doctors are part of a medical industry delivering health care, one of the many integrated parts of a health care system that includes druggists, technicians, nurses, and specialists. They are *prescriptive* technicians[10] in the same way mechanics are technicians in the automobile industry. On the other hand, patients see doctors as *holistic* practitioners, artists who control the process of healing with their own skills and knowledge. It is this difference of perception that frustrates women and leaves them dissatisfied and angry.

The Imbalance of Power

It is also difficult to create a partnership in health with doctors who are trained in power and control and patients who are trained in passivity. It is doubtful if doctors will share that power unless it becomes inevitable. Patients are unlikely to demand power over their own health decisions if they are socially conditioned to see such demands as inappropriate. Women have to deal with their own attitudes; doctors have to deal with theirs. We need to make social changes in order to bring about an atmosphere that allows doctors to share information. For, at present, the medical profession sits comfortably in a prescriptive medical industry and ignores the patients' need for a holistic service. The medical profession needs to ensure that the ability to give information and to educate patients is a necessary skill of doctors.

7

Alternative Practitioners

Complementary or Fringe Figures

When I worked as a community health nurse, I initially thought that everyone trusted and used Western medicine, that scientific brand of medicine practiced in North America, Europe, and most of the developed countries. It had standards of diagnosis, treatment, and a code of ethics that were governed by medical associations all over the world. I thought this was the only medicine; I was naive. Fresh out of university, imbued with the zeal of magical medical solutions, I saw few choices for my patients. It took me only months to understand that medicine was a much bigger field than my textbooks admitted. Patients told me of their experiences, beliefs, and effective solutions to medical problems. I learned from them to see value in remedies developed outside Western medicine—in Grannie's poultice and Uncle Archie's cough syrup. I learned to ask them what they thought would help and to assume that they looked for more solutions than the doctor's prescription. Alternative medicine flourished.

The Office of Alternative Medicine

Congress established an Office of Alternative Medicine[1] in 1991 at the National Institutes of Health in Washington, DC, to study theories and practices of medicine outside the Western medical model. Its purpose is to encourage primary care and the prevention of disease through therapies that are alternate to established medical practice. This office encourages scientific methods in the study of alternative medical care: the careful measuring of controlled experiments and cautious conclusions. This may be official recognition of the way Americans actually look for health advice—at chiropractors' offices, at herbalists' clinics, at the shaman's—or it may be the first step in regulating and controlling alternative medicine. A government office investigating alternative medicine makes some people worry about government regulations, control, and suppression. Alternative practitioners are not sure if they are going to be helped or hindered.

Understanding Illness

Western medicine is changing so quickly that it has difficulty setting guidelines to regulate itself, establishing its boundaries, and defining its influence. Knowledge and technology have grown so rapidly that our philosophy, morality, and laws can't keep pace. We have the ability to implant a fetus in a surrogate mother before we understand the moral and legal implications of doing so. We still have little understanding of why people need illness, what their illness is expressing for them, or even what causes many illnesses. Our understanding of needs, meaning, and causes seems primitive beside the developments in technology, biochemistry, and physiology. The developments in chemistry are moving so fast that we may be able to define cell reactions and "fit" those reactions to antidotes before we understand why they happen. There may come a time when all Western medical knowledge will be a matter of describing DNA codes. Treatment will be the ability to relate coded problems of immune deviations, cancer, and emphysema, for example, to corresponding coded drugs. Illnesses may have chemical engineering solutions, the ultimate in prescriptive technology. Imagine how dehumanizing it would be to walk into a special laboratory and be weighed, measured, and described as a system of coded molecules. It may, however, be effective.

Healing Power

Engineering solutions do not seem as attractive as solutions that lie within our own bodies. Jeanne Achterberg describes in *Imagery in Healing: Shamanism* and *Modern Medicine* the place of imaginary pictures in healing. She comments on the ability of mental images to communicate with tissues and organs and suggests that there are specific nerve pathways for such transmissions.[2] Imagine visions traveling through our bodies, creating changes as they pass through organs—something like a hologram or a TV image. Other authors go even further and suggest that there is an intelligent coordinating system that tries to maintain balance within the body and that this system coordinates the healing process.[3] What would that be—a chemical community? a biological battleground? a soul? Would such a coordinating intelligence be a balancing agent or a defensive army?

Our Western scientific medical community has isolated disease as an invader, an aggressive enemy that has to be fought. Medicine fights disease as if the body were simply a passive ground for the battle. We, in our Western society, have made the mistake of throwing out workable healing methods from the past, such as touching, visualizing, soothing, and balancing food and herbs, and replacing all old methods with disease–treatment–pathology models of scientifically "proven" treatments. Books describing the recent history of medicine reflect the bias of the writers in dismissing ancient ways as "superstitious" and "pagan" without investigating how well such treatments work and without investigating the social effects of those treatments. We have accepted a clinical description of illness as a complete description.

Not all civilizations have given the responsibility of recovery from illness and disease to doctors. Some communities have a two-track system. They consult the Western doctor for advice but also consult their community shaman or wise woman to evaluate that advice and to give them spiritual direction.

The Spirit

First Nations people, Native Americans, are often strong believers in the harmony of spirit that is necessary before healing can take place. They pay attention to their spiritual, mental, and emotional health when dealing with a physical problem and are particularly aware of the need for balance in people with addictions. While Western medicine offers sobriety programs, detoxification programs, and methadone maintenance, First Nations healers advise looking for the cause of emotional distress that is driving the person to the addictions in the first place. They look at the patient's need for spiritual peace. For them, dealing with emotions is the first step in dealing with addictions. They don't try to divorce emotions from disease as Western medicine does; they embrace emotion as an important component of illness and healing.

Western medicine is only beginning to understand the importance of spiritual peace and emotional balance in healing. It's acceptable now to talk about a "healing environment." I recently attended a conference in Oregon where the concept of emotional and spiritual balance with physical cures was offered as an innovative idea. It is, of course, an ancient one and one that flourished in the world of women. Even with a renewed interest in the concept of healing, some of the power and meaning of healing medicine seem to have disappeared over the centuries. Women look for a broad concept of healing in a Western medical industry that can't accommodate it.

Our Western medical process of diagnosis and treatment is increasing the prescriptive technology of doctors and creating distance from the holistic approach women seek. The gap between

Western medicine's definition of disease and cure and how women see their own illnesses is widening. More and more doctors see women as collections of symptoms, vital signs, and test results. More and more women see themselves as embodiments of social and spiritual meaning. In their efforts to get support for their holistic views and individual attempts to control their own health, women look outside Western medicine.

Anne, 36, had lived through a difficult divorce that left her with two kids, a house, and a skin disease. "I felt like all my defenses, including my skin, were breaking down." She talked to a doctor who gave her cream for her skin, but she was still sick and unhappy. She tried naturopathic remedies and was satisfied.

> What I would like to see is doctors and naturopaths working hand-in-hand with no walls between them. If you went to a medical doctor and he honestly didn't know how to help you, he could refer you to a naturopath, a "kooky" therapy guy, or whatever and let you make your choice. When I went the alternative route, I was on my own. Medical doctors pretend they are the only healers.

What Is Alternative Medicine?

When we remember that medicine is an industry that serves the economic needs of the practitioners, it is no surprise to see doctors in positions of power defining what the industry may and may not do. Doctors approve or disapprove of procedures and remedies "for the greater good" of humanity. They defined tonsillectomies for most children under the age of 6 as safe for years in the 1940s and 1950s, but chiropractic treatment as unsafe. Surely more children died from unnecessary tonsillectomies than died from unnecessary chiropractic treatments. "Safe" is that which is under the control of doctors; "unsafe" is anything that is not. This amazing power still has not prevented people from slipping outside Western medicine to find remedies that work for them, nor has it prevented effective help and treatment from developing in fringe or alternative areas of medicine.

Alternative medicine includes such respected practitioners as Qi Gong masters, the Chinese specialists in energy balance, and such disreputable ones as backdoor herbalists who read labels on the bottles and create a new therapy. Women face various alternative medicines with little confidence in their ability to sort the fantastic from the useful. Generally, women depend on testimonials from other women—"I tried it; it works"—and truly don't know how to evaluate any kind of medicine: Western, alternative, or even folk medicine. They often feel reassured that the treatments prescribed by alternative medical practitioners are not as harmful as the dangerous drugs prescribed by Western medical doctors. This is not always correct. For instance, an alternative practitioner who recommends fasting and a series of vitamins can cause harm. A practitioner who prescribes ineffective treatment for a serious illness can delay effective Western medicine until it is too late to use it. But those situations can and do occur within Western medical practices as well. Because many women have little understanding of medicine, they look for advisors who can help them increase their knowledge. They find, in alternative medicine, practitioners and consultants who act as educators and treat them as part of a health team.

The Old Remedies

Family remedies generally are no longer passed down from generation to generation as they were in ancient days; few women have medical knowledge given to them by their mothers. There is no tradition in our North American culture of women's medical lore and no trusted "women's medicine." Of the women I interviewed only 38% trusted their mother's health advice.[4] The comments ranged from: "She's a dear woman but she knows zilch about health. She thinks you shouldn't wash your hair when you're menstruating, for heaven's sake;" to "She reads a lot; she's a nurse. If she doesn't know, she can find out. I'll ask her anything." But most had other, more reliable sources of information than their mothers or family members. Family remedies are generally seen to be unreliable and unscientific.

When the missionaries destroyed the aboriginal religions and replaced them with Christianity, they destroyed the social structure that included the folk medicine that had helped people stay healthy for centuries. In the same way, Western medicine walked into traditional social life and disregarded, dismissed, and destroyed the folk remedies that had served families for years. Mothers replaced their grandmother's advice with new concepts of Western medicine—some of it good and some of it bad. Instead of weaving new ideas into the patterns of the old, Western medicine replaced the old remedies with new ones, breaking one generation's link with another's and effectively removing the herbal and folk remedies of the past. Two remedies survived in my family—one a poultice that got rid of infection and one a method of cleaning wounds. That is all.

Those old remedies were usually part of the knowledge of women. Women grew herbs and collected bark and leaves. They diagnosed and treated ailments using their store of remedies. This power to treat the sick and relieve pain and discomfort moved from the hands of women to the hands of the doctors and into the medical–drug industry. Doctors lobbied for controlling legislation until it became illegal for anyone but those in the medical industry to dispense drugs; women were then dependent on a medical industry.

An aboriginal woman told me that her community had a history of sharing their herbs and remedies with anyone who wanted them, but now they were afraid that profiteers would take their herbs, license them, and then sell them to others, including the native people who had discovered them.

A Place for Alternative Practices

In spite of the medical technology, biochemistry, and microbiology that surround medical advice, women look for simple answers to their medical problems. They are often less interested in complex drugs than in commonsense remedies. One woman from Manitoba drank cranberry juice for a bladder infection. Anyone who has ever had a bladder infection can appreciate the commitment to alternative medicine this woman must have since most of us would reach for an antibiotic and a drug to control bladder spasms; cranberry juice and the body's immune system are not fast enough for us. But many women find simple remedies such as exercising, eating a balanced diet, and drinking herbal tea an alternative to the doctor's care. Most women will seek a doctor's advice for serious ailments like broken bones, hemorrhages, heart attacks, and strokes but will continue to look for answers outside this advice to health problems of a less immediate nature, such as painful menstrual cramps, skin rashes, yeast infections, and fatigue. Alternative medicine gives them a nonthreatening, understandable treatment and appears to be within their control. They want to be in charge and, in alternative medicine, they can be. Often, women are looking for the cause of their symptoms, not just temporary relief from them, and they want a more inclusive, balanced view of their illness than they find in Western medicine.

Nurses

Some practitioners of Western medicine try to be inclusive of emotions and the social needs of the patients and try to put the patient in the center of care. They taught this notion when I was an undergraduate student, and they still teach it. This is not the same as patient-controlled care, but it is at least a philosophy that recognizes that patients are individuals. Nurses graduate from universities with a science education in biology, physiology, chemistry, microbiology, psychology, and sociology, as well as courses in communications and ethics. While there are still some nursing schools in North America that concentrate on teaching manual skills, most nursing schools teach knowledge in the core courses of science, sociology, and communications. There are nurses in every community who are skilled in Western medicine and combine that with empathy and the ability to listen and communicate. While nurses are not taught to give patients control of their care, the education they receive at university and the education they receive from patients make them the most likely Western medical practitioners to respond to the needs of women. Some nurses, such as aboriginal nurses who serve aboriginal communities, combine Western medicine with ancient folk medicine because that is the kind of medicine that is accepted in their communities and that is the kind of medicine that is useful in their patients' lives.

Eva, a Kquaiquewal native nurse who works with her own people on Vancouver Island, said:

> I feel okay recommending traditional medicine because I have yet to see side effects with our herbs, unlike Western medications. Anyway, my mother used to use herbs and remedies all the time and I learned about them before I learned about drugs.[5]

She also explained her view of the difference between aboriginal medicine and Western medicine:

> Today [in Western medicine] if you have a headache, you treat the headache. We [aboriginal people] treat the whole person, what is underneath.
>
> About 30 years ago my mother was diagnosed with cancer. To this day, it has not gotten worse because she continually drinks Indian medicine. Another time, they [doctors] told us she was going to be crippled with arthritis of her spine. Again, she has defeated the white man's medicine. She is 96 and is able to walk because of her traditional lifestyle. She was diagnosed with diabetes when she was 85 and was on Western medicine for 3 months. She got her blood sugar down and has never gotten it up again because she did away with all those cookies and cakes and pies which we never had long ago. She went back to eating traditional foods. So there is hope for us in a healthy lifestyle.[6]

Nurses seem to be the most flexible medical practitioners and responsive to patients' needs. Some nurses have private practices in counseling, advocacy, and information services. Nurse practitioners work as midwives in all the states in the United States and a few areas of Canada.[7] Two provinces in

Canada, Ontario and British Columbia, have passed legislation to make midwifery possible soon. Clinical nurse specialists see patients, diagnose, treat, and advise. Slowly, nurses are beginning to be consulted as private practitioners by patients in the community. Most nurses are women; most women prefer to consult women about their health. Perhaps in time women, through the work of nurses, will regain the skills they once had as healers, and perhaps they will become health teachers. While nurses may not be, strictly speaking, alternative practitioners, they can deliver health care in ways that are alternative to the present system.

Fragmented Care

Our Western culture offers few trusted advisors who can diagnose and treat and who are given the power to do so. Psychiatrists come from the same training schools as medical doctors and tend to see the patient from a similar viewpoint. Psychologists usually come from a liberal arts program and should have a broad view of the causes of illness, but they are not skilled in physical exams and do not prescribe remedies. To the patient, Western medicine seems to be a very fragmented, impersonal, and scattered service, where parts of them are sent for examination but the whole person ignored.

Lay Counselors

In an effort to find advice that is full of common sense, practical, community-based, and affordable, many women consult lay counselors. Lay counselors have an unreliable set of skills. Some are very good; some are very bad. They are concerned with the emotional lives of their clients and can give a different approach to illness and therapy. Some have little understanding of medicine and are not skilled at knowing when to refer patients for additional help. Others become very knowledgeable and are excellent sources of information. The Women's Health Clinic in Winnipeg, Manitoba, Canada, provides health information to callers through a lay researcher who is most effective at giving information on problems of women's reproductive system although she will help a caller find the information she needs on almost any other question. She is a friendly, interested voice on the telephone and a valuable resource. Our health system may be missing a cost-effective service by not encouraging this position of lay advocate and researcher.

Naturopaths

Naturopaths are an alternative for many women, usually those who have been brought up to value naturopaths as "doctors." Naturopaths and homeopaths may be accredited by professional organizations such as the American Institute of Homeopathy, the National College of Naturopathic Medicine, or the American Association of Naturopathic Physicians. Naturopaths usually have 8 years of schooling: 4 undergraduate years and 4 years in a school for naturopaths. Long thought of as outside normal medicine, naturopaths are being considered more and more as useful parts of the healing world. Naturopaths still diagnose and try to give solutions as medical doctors do, but they pay attention to the emotional and social life of the patient, what the illness means to the patient, how it appears to her, what the patient expects from the illness, and what the patient's belief system is. Naturopathic medicine uses a natural system of healing, including homeopathy, a system of treatment that uses remedies containing herbal ingredients. Naturopaths often include a prescription for lifestyle changes, such as "Cut out coffee and alcohol; increase exercise," and seem to try to give the patient the responsibility for her own health. The patient is in charge of the care and works with the naturopath for her own improvement. They are paid under some medical plans, but often the remedies they prescribe are not.

One woman who was subject to asthma attacks found that the snake venom she had been prescribed by the naturopath effectively controlled her asthma. She had not had an asthma attack since she started taking the remedy. "And I haven't had any urge to rear back my head and strike anyone with my teeth."

I initially rejected this remedy as being fantastic until I remembered that one of the drugs that anesthesiologists use just prior to surgery was originally used by South American Indians as poison on the end of their weapons. One may be just as fantastic as the other. Still, there seems to be an aura of magic about some of the naturopaths' remedies—but then magic may be one way of describing what one does not understand.

I tried to get a naturopath to tell me what was in the remedies he prescribed. Biologically, how did they work? Essentially, he didn't know. The remedies work on the principle that an infinitesimal dosage of something creates an ability in the body to deal with that kind of substance. More than that, no one knows.

Naturopaths do not seem to work with general practitioners, although there are naturopathic physicians. Generally, women do not tell their doctors that they are seeing a naturopath, as if naturopaths were in the same class as tarot card readers or psychics—outside medical "science" and therefore vaguely clandestine.

Chiropractors

Chiropractors, on the other hand, have gained a place in recognized medical treatment in many communities. Chiropractic education in the United States and Canada usually takes an additional 4 years after 2 years of preparatory classes in university. In most colleges chiropractors receive an education similar to that of medical students in hours spent in study, with some differences in subject matter. Like medical doctors, they are licensed by a professional board that maintains standards and has the power to remove a license if the practitioner does not meet the standards.

Chiropractors use manipulation, spinal alignments, and adjustments to promote unrestricted nerve function and relieve pain so that the body may heal itself. Their services are often paid for by health insurance plans that recognize the cost-effectiveness of chiropractors.

I tried a chiropractor when I was researching this book. It was a new experience for me. He did help me deal with hip pain, for a fee of $5 and my government insurance plan. He also seemed to be very clear on what he could *not* treat.

Because they do not prescribe drugs, chiropractors have been allowed to develop treatment and healing methods without the influence of the drug companies and are therefore an alternative to some forms of medicine. Some medical doctors refer patients to chiropractors—some never do. As a nurse within the medical system, I frequently heard about the work of chiropractors from my patients but never from within the medical community. If any of them used a chiropractor, they never admitted it. We were dismally ignorant of any kind of treatment that was not part of our textbook education. Patients took responsibility for themselves in working with chiropractors and did not use their doctors as referral agents or advocates. In spite of the scientific, professional basis to chiropractic medicine and in spite of the public's widespread use of chiropractic medicine, it has, for the most part, remained as a tolerated alternative to Western allopathic medicine: not a part of it, but more like a successful second cousin who is ignored by the family.

Massage Therapists

Massage therapists work on muscles to relax them and prevent the injuries that result when stiff muscles are overused. They also try to induce an emotional peace in response to the soothing physical attention. A professional friend who runs her life in 15-minute appointments schedules an hour every week with her massage therapist just to create some peaceful time in her life. This massage experience was one of the most relaxing ones of my research. Some women use massage to relax muscles so bones can move freely, to promote healing of an injury or to prevent repetitive motion injury. Alternative medicine like Ayurveda from India uses massage as a regular activity in a healthy lifestyle. The degree of effectiveness of massage seems to relate to the skill of the masseuse and to the beliefs of the client. There is no question that some masseuses have "healing hands" or "therapeutic touch," terms that are new and innovative in the Western medical world and ancient in the world of shamans and aboriginal peoples.

There are some therapists who are skilled in cranial–sacral work, which is not massage, although it feels like massage. The woman who worked on me had a science education—Bachelor of Science, Master of Science, and Masters of Arts degrees—and she was licensed as a physiotherapist. In spite of her Western medical education, she used an "energy system" of treatment that was not accepted by the medical industry. I didn't understand how it worked; it seemed unscientific, but she effectively reduced the pain and improved the mobility of my injured hip. It is this "I went in there on a cane and I came out walking freely" kind of personal recommendation that creates interest, respect, and acceptance by the people in the community. Alternative medicine establishes its own credibility. The physiotherapist I consulted also used Qi Gong Chinese medicine and acupuncture.

Acupuncturists

Acupuncturists have been practicing in the world for thousands of years, but only recently has our Western society considered acupuncture seriously in medical care. Both Canada and the United States have certificate programs that allow trained people to practice acupuncture. Some Western medical doctors learn acupuncture in order to offer it as pain control to their patients. Perhaps with the increasing dialogue between North America and China, some Chinese medicine will gain respect in the Western model. Western medicine has an astounding arrogance when it gives a stamp of approval to an acupuncture procedure that has been accepted and used for thousands of years. Chinese practitioners happily borrow what they need from Western medicine. Perhaps Western medical practitioners need to borrow from the Chinese.

Other Chinese Medicines

Chinese medical theory stresses keeping the body in balance, keeping the yin and yang in harmony. With balance the body can resist disease. The treatment for disease then is to restore the balance. Qi Gong practitioners "see" auras and colors of disharmony and harmony and, with their healing hands, mold the energy of the patient's body into balance. They also diagnose by seeing the disharmony in the body.

Chinese doctors and herbalists believe in the body's ability to withstand disease when in balance. They believe, for instance, that cancer is always present in the body but that a weakened immune system allows cancer a chance to grow. Chinese herbalists and doctors are in high demand in the Chinese communities if the practitioner I met was any example. Clients called him on the phone continually and walked into his office looking for advice.

Potpourri

The business section of the phone book reveals many different types of healers: reflexologists, kinesiologists, faith healers, pain and stress management counselors, herbalists, nutritionists, nurses in private practice, and psychologists. Most people find help in alternative sources not by skimming the phone book for a likely name but by getting a recommendation from someone they know. Word of mouth seems to be the most trusted recommendation. I visited a healer, recommended by a friend, who offered to put my energy in balance. I sat on a chair while she moved her hands about 3 inches from my body, starting at my feet and working up slowly to my head. She was respectful, intent, and obviously sincere. She "took away" muddled or bad energy to allow my body to maintain a balance. I found the experience interesting, mystical, and in some ways self-affirming. I saw its value in convincing the client that her body was strong and capable of health. It seemed similar to my experience with Qi Gong medicine. Both left me feeling calm and capable. However, the Qi Gong experience actually caused physical changes in my body that I could feel. Perhaps, because of that, it seemed more believable.

Women go to healers such as the one who promised to take away my "bad energy" and the iridologist who diagnosed my ailments by studying the patterns in my eyes. I had to work hard to find useful information here. Women go to alternative practitioners because they want to get all the information they can about themselves, to be in control of their health, to avoid drugs, or because they can't find information in Western medical sources. And perhaps some go because they are fascinated by a different approach to medicine. Certainly some of alternative medicine, like the Qi Gong experience, seems exotic.

Nonprofit Societies

Some sources of information are on the fringe of the medical industry, not because they are unproven, mystical theories, but because they don't make money. Nonprofit societies such as the American or Canadian Cancer Society, the Diabetes Association, and the Kidney Foundation are not part of the industry because they are nonprofit and because they exist to serve the client. These organizations usually have excellent information and often good referral information. They know what treatments are being offered and how effective they are. They may employ counselors to help with the practical problems encountered by those with the disease; counselors are often people who have the disease, so their advice seems to come from the patient's own community. They are usually aware of nonproven and dangerous treatments, can give advice about many folk or alternative treatments, and often have a 1-800 phone number. They usually work in conjunction with Western medicine and often with local health units.

Health Units

Local health units are usually good sources of information. Again, they are usually nonprofit organizations but are part of the medical system, with nurses, nutritionists, technicians, and doctors as staff, although they seem to have a certain independence from the control of local doctors. Local health nurses often act as advocates for people in their district. Committed nurses may even fight for their patients. The nurses are usually well educated and informed and seem to be used as advocates more in rural communities than in urban communities. Sometimes they are seen as social workers and advocates for the poor, sometimes only as maternal–child health experts or screening technicians for school children. They work in most areas of the country and are good sources of information on disease entities, treatment programs, and new concepts in health. Health units usually employ nutritionists who can answer questions from the public, and many can counsel as well. Health units may have mental health units attached to them where counseling is available. Generally, their services are free to the consumer.

Family Service Centers

In some communities, nonprofit Family Service Centers offer counseling, advice, and information. Churches, synagogues, and temples have counselors, some better than others. Women's centers may employ counselors. Some of these counselors are informed and excellent sources of information, particularly about women's reproductive health, rape, or the problems of battered women. Community centers may offer support groups where women can get advice and acceptance. Any gathering of women will produce some information, and within the group may be women with lines of information into other sources.

Computer Information

More and more women are computer-literate and able to research the vast data systems of North America. New computer programs offer medical encyclopedic knowledge. Some programs allow users to type in their symptoms and then receive diagnosis and treatment options. This instant answer system is too simple to be reliable. It can add to women's knowledge of their problems, but it leaves out too much. For instance, spotting between periods can be a sign of cancer; it can also be perfectly normal. Between the risk of a dangerous disease and no risk at all lies more knowledge. Also, the advice given by a computer will only be as accurate as the knowledge of the person loading the program. Errors are likely to be repeated until they are taken for truths. Still, it is intriguing to think that health information could be available on computer to anyone who wanted it. Perhaps, when such programs are more widely used and more widely available, all that women ever wanted to know about health care will be on the computer, and we will consult with doctors and practitioners only to help sort out the information we already have.

Some women with a computer and a modem connect to the Internet system and can send out questions to a bulletin board, hooking up with thousands of people who may give them advice. This may be most helpful as an emotional support system and a place to get leads on information. While great information may come from this kind of connection with people, great misinformation may come as well. One of the advantages of this kind of information is the anonymity of it. Women don't have to disclose who they are or where they live in order to get information.

Confidential Files

Some women look for alternative medicine, not because they do not trust doctors, but because they do not trust the confidentiality of the medical system. Care from a Western doctor is usually entered into a billing procedure that can betray information about the patient. A woman I know was very reluctant to go to her doctor for medication for high blood pressure, because when she was billed for her visit her diagnosis would be available on a data bank. She was particularly anxious that it not be known by her life insurance company. The fear of having personal medical information stored on a computer for the use of insurance companies makes some women, particularly women in business who need to borrow money or buy insurance, wary of consulting doctors. These women are interested in black market medicine, where they can get the drugs and treatments they need without leaving a paper trail.

Choice

A woman in a community looking for health information can waste a lot of time trying to find her way through agencies and individual practitioners. She wants more than just the medical advice. Most women want to know what options are available to them, not just in their community but all over the country. If endometriosis is being treated more effectively by the conservative surgical treatment of Dr. Redwine in Bend, Oregon, while their local surgeon is still doing hysterectomies, they may want to go to Bend, Oregon, or they may want to persuade their Women's Institute to send a local surgeon to Bend, Oregon, to learn the technique. A woman may find an herbalist in her town who is getting good results in relieving the pain of endometriosis and will want to try her remedies. There may be several ways for a woman to make her choice of treatment, but she needs the information that will allow her to make that choice.

Most women are willing to ask a doctor for advice. They have been conditioned to do so and usually feel that it is wise to do so. But few women believe that the doctor has all the information or even the correct information—only 38% of the women I interviewed trusted their doctor's advice.[8] Women want other sources of information from which they can get what they see as more respectful, more comprehensive, and more meaningful advice.

8

The Nature of Quacks

What Is a Quack?

If a medical quack was a loud circus hawker harassing a crowd to buy his "Lydia E. Pinkham's Vegetable Compound," he would be easy to recognize and easy to avoid. Quacks who seemed obvious when they sold "Hostetter's Celebrated Stomach Bitters" or "Kickapoo Indian Sagwa" have changed shape and appearance. Today, it is hard to distinguish quacks among the advocates of bee pollen, garlic, transcendental meditation, and immune enhancement therapy. Today's quack is likely to operate with smooth words, grave attention, and a brand of logic that seems acceptable. Between the stereotypical quack of the 1900s and the smooth, distinguished, academic owner of today's latest "cancer cure" lie hundreds of variations.

Women aren't necessarily more vulnerable to quacks than men, but since they seek health services more often, they are more likely to meet them. Rich people aren't more vulnerable either, but quacks are more interested in those with money than those without. They advertise in magazines and newspapers so that in our free society we can choose any therapy we want and can question the usefulness of some of the remedies we're offered. Look through the following advertisements with questions in your mind. Could this practitioner do harm? Is this *only* a method of parting me from my money? I took these ads, word for word, from a magazine available in my area:

> Health Clairvoyant: By projecting her consciousness to internally view the inner functioning of the body, assess the body's physical health, and stimulate cellular intelligence and healing, a partnership is formed.

> I am here to co-create light space in you and to help you tap into the source inside yourself of strength, love, and health . . .

> Florbalance: May help improve GI symptoms, food sensitivities, yeast infections, etc. . .

> Aromatherapy for Women: With a full body, face and scalp massage using botanical essences, I specialize in stress reduction, cellulite, premenstrual, menopause, headaches, muscular pains, asthma, and face toning.

> Fasting: The ultimate wellness vacation.

All the above share a common trait; they cost money. It is also common to see advertisers take an idea—the mind and emotions influence healing—and stretch it into a credo that says *only* the mind and the emotions influence healing. The concepts of self-control, emotional and mental influence, harmony, balance, and stress reduction are increasing areas of interest to Western and alternative medical practitioners, and a free-for-all circus of opportunity for quacks.

Initially, we may think of quacks as flourishing in the mystical and magical world of Mexican *curanderos* or witch doctors, in the world of the shamans of the Salish tribes, in the hills of Appalachia and the mountains of Quebec. But quacks are more likely to be in the cities where they can make money. Quacks can live on the fringes of sophistication as well on the fringes of folk medicine. Folk medicine can be a strong protection against quacks, since folk medicine often serves its community with a solid, social presence that helps the people of a community. A quack is a solitary entrepreneur whose commitment to a community lasts as long as the community's commitment to his or her wallet.

Because the eccentric, the well-intentioned, and the quacks are all protected by laws against slander, it's easier to look back on quacks who have been through the court system and been proven quacks than to name current candidates.

Freddie Brant, a Louisiana-born opportunist with a stolen diploma, practiced as a doctor in Groveton, Texas. When discovered, he was not prosecuted because the townspeople said he was the best doctor they had ever had.[1]

More dangerous are those quacks who assume authority, present themselves as knowledgeable, and prescribe and treat in a money-making power game. Unlike Freddie Brant who liked being a doctor, liked helping people, and safely referred conditions he did not understand, many imposters are motivated only by greed. They won't work with medical doctors or refer their patients to others. They cause harm.

Victor Kollman

In the 1980s, Victor Kollman was recommending *Blue-Green Manna*, a green algae, for the treatment of many problems from allergies and Alzheimer's disease to leprosy. A Federal Drug Administration analysis of 5 ounces of *Blue-Green Manna* found it contained mainly impurities such as flies, maggots, mites, and feathers.[2] If the patients managed to deal with the flies, maggots, mites, and feathers and the algae itself did them no harm, they may have delayed getting effective treatment for their presenting diseases. Often, the direct harm that results from unorthodox treatment is insignificant beside the harm that delay causes. Kollman presented himself as a doctor. When pressed, he said he had a PhD, but had no record of graduation from any PhD program.

Fraud

A quack may be someone, like Kollman, who poses as an expert in medicine. He may not have a medical degree or certificate from an accredited school but may present himself as if he did. Federal and state or provincial laws should make such fraud difficult because patients can always ask to see the credentials of their doctors—but most don't ask. One unusual young woman, Janine, stood and read the certificates on her doctor's wall. "I wanted to know from what school he graduated and when." It should be obvious to other medical personnel when an imposter practices medicine, but the sad fact is that medical people work around enough incompetent practitioners who *do* have licenses that they may not recognize one without. I remember a secretary who used to listen in on the telephone extension as her boss, a physician, prescribed medication. She corrected his prescriptions in kind and dosage. He did eventually lose his license. As medicine gets more and more technical, an unskilled imposter may be easier to detect, but many conditions and diseases don't require extensive technology for diagnosis and treatment, and women may still meet dangerous advice.

"Good" Advice

Women are aware that medical knowledge has given us some very bad advice. Over the years women have been prescribed mind-altering drugs without consent or enough information. Medicine has made enough mistakes with women throughout recent history that women are naturally skeptical of the doctors' desire to own all knowledge. It seems healthy to most women to consult other sources besides the patriarchal medical system for information about their health. After all, it was not quacks who caused deformed babies with prescriptions of thalidomide, nor is it quacks who perform unnecessary hysterectomies. John Smith in *Women and Doctors* said that 90% of the hysterectomies are done for reasons other than medical necessity—and it is licensed surgeons who do them.[3] The level of trust in doctors is low enough to make other sources of information attractive. What looks like quackery to many doctors represents a second opinion to many patients.

It's hard to judge health information. Women know that some practices that were considered unmedical and foolish years ago are now medically advisable. Someone who meditated in the 1940s was seen as a little strange; someone who meditates today is seen as mentally healthy. Midwives who were frowned on in the 1950s are advocated in the 1990s. The aboriginal people who used herbs, roots, and bark 30 years ago and who were seen as backward and ignorant are seen as wise today—drug companies are interested in their herbs. What is condemned by the medical profession today may be praised tomorrow, when new knowledge makes the obscure and foolish seem wise. This makes it hard for us to decide what is good for us and what isn't. On the one hand the Western medical community condemns homeopathy as useless and even dangerous.[4] Steven Barrett in *Health Schemes, Scams and Frauds*, tells us to beware of homeopathic remedies: "Homeopathy is based on nineteenth century theories that medical science considers nonsense."[5]

On the other hand, Western medicine uses homeopathic principles when administering allergy shots—a little pollen will create a reaction in the body that may increase resistance to a bigger dose of pollen. Western medicine condemns homeopathy, and yet half of the licensed homeopaths in the United States are MDs.[6] There isn't an easy way to distinguish the helpful practitioner from the harmful.

The medical industry itself is not without its peculiar and harmful quacks who *have* a license. What difference is there between an MD and a quack if their advice is equally dangerous? If one is a quack, why isn't the other? It would seem that an MD may act foolishly, even dangerously, without being labeled a quack. Several doctors in my area do chelation therapy, a process unsupported by the medical association, although apparently not condemned, and not paid for by the health insurance companies. One woman reported to me by phone that she had taken treatment to reduce her high blood pressure:

> There were 15 of us every Tuesday and Thursday and, I suppose, another 15 on Monday and Wednesday. The doctor started the IVs and we sat there until noon. It took him about an hour to start all the IVs each day. We paid him $1,000 each for the month, so I guess he was making $30,000 a month for 3 or four hours work a week. I'm a nurse and I was pretty skeptical. I'm still skeptical but there is no question that some of those people that started with me were much improved. It did reduce my high blood pressure, but I'm not sure that sitting in a chair for 3 hours twice a week for a month didn't have more to do with it than the therapy.

So are these doctors quacks, or just ahead of science? If they were not MDs, would they be quacks?

Outside Medical Knowledge

Some define quackery as that which is outside medical knowledge. As we have seen, medical knowledge is constantly changing: what is true today is not true tomorrow; what is advised today is condemned tomorrow; what seems new and innovative in treatment turns out to be dangerous. Doctors make the best judgments they can based on the knowledge they have at the time. We do place a lot of faith in the education, judgment, and common sense of doctors, but we cannot accept the definition of quackery as that which lies outside medical knowledge because, in addition to the constantly changing nature of medical knowledge, a great deal of worthwhile folk medicine, use of herbs, and alternative medicine lies outside medical knowledge. Unfortunately, some medical practitioners define useful knowledge as only that which they have learned. If they don't know about it, it doesn't exist. And so the problem seesaws between the rigid definition of the medical industry and the common sense of the consumers.

A Broad View of Medicine

It also moves between what is defined as medicine by the doctor and by the patient. Many women consider their reflexologist a practitioner of medicine. Many doctors would consider a reflexologist outside the industry of medicine. It is very hard for someone like myself with my medical education to accept a diagnosis based on the study of the feet or, in the case of the iridologist, on the study of the iris, but many women will give credence to information received in this way because it seems personal, pertinent, and practical. Instead of placing such practitioners outside the medical industry and into the suspect category of quacks, they broaden their understanding of medicine and include them. Since diagnosis and healing do occur in many incidents that seem strange to medical workers, society needs to accept that some people find relief and help outside of the medical industry. Women do get better, overcome disease and chronic conditions, and attain wellness through unorthodox and remarkably "unscientific" practices. Many members of the medical community have little idea of how much or how often patients consult fringe, alternative medicine and quacks or what the individual means by the term "medicine." It's a diverse, rich, and active field.

The Placebo Effect

Quacks use the body's ability to help itself and claim credit for it. For many years, medical science has recognized that patients respond to a placebo in many treatments. That is, patients given a placebo (a non-active pill such as a sugar pill) will get the same positive results 30 to 35% of the time as those given a drug.[7] This remarkable ability of the body to cure itself is utilized by doctors and quacks alike. Good medical practitioners try to work with the body's healing capabilities and not claim they are in charge of them. They understand that "a treated cold disappears in a week and an untreated cold in seven days" and don't claim they control and cure everything. Quacks have no such inhibitions. They will claim cures for almost anything.

The Definition

For the purposes of mutual understanding and communication, let us define a quack as *someone who pretends to have medical knowledge and who promises to cure—but who does harm.* Quacks promise to cure diseases such as cancer but do not, to cure mental illness but do not, and prescribe drugs, remedies, or treatments that mask illness, delay diagnosis, worsen conditions, and cause disease or create pain. They make money from misery and leave the patient poorer in health and finances.

Diseases That Attract Quacks

Diseases that attract quacks are diseases that have no "cure" in medical science. After all, there is no profit in developing a quack cure for treatable diseases like pneumonia when antibiotics are cheap and effective. Quacks work with diseases that are difficult or impossible to cure and with those that often have unexplained periods of remission when patients feel better—diseases like arthritis, cancer, headaches, chronic fatigue, and depression.

Charles Kaadt

Before the discovery of insulin and in the early days of insulin use, diabetes attracted quacks. Charles Kaadt, an Indiana MD, established a new treatment for diabetes in 1922. He advocated no insulin, eating sugar, and taking a bottle of his medicine. His medicine was saltpeter and water. Saltpeter is a diuretic which, among other things, increases the amount of urine the patient excretes. It does not effect the metabolism of sugar which is the basic problem of diabetics. His advice was dangerous and many people died. His clinics brought him patients, profit, and the attention of the Federal Food and Drug Administration (FDA) which finally prosecuted and sent him and his brother, Peter, to prison.[8]

Harry M. Hoxsey

One of the well-known hucksters of useless anticancer remedies was Harry M. Hoxsey, who deluded thousands in the United States from 1922 to 1960 with the backing of convinced Congressmen and in spite of vigorous efforts of the FDA to restrain him.[9] Hoxsey concocted a paste that contained arsenic and applied it to skin cancer. The paste was so corrosive that by itself it caused the death of at least one patient. After the man's death, Hoxsey was charged with practicing medicine without a license and fined $100. Thereafter, he usually concentrated on promotion and advertisement and left his treatments to hired health professionals. After efforts of the FDA over many years, Hoxsey was finally forced to abandon his "treatments" in 1960. He had managed to keep this ineffectual treatment for cancer, a totally useless and sometimes harmful treatment, before the public from 1922 to 1960. He made an amazing career out of nothing, convincing many. Quacks such as Hoxsey don't necessarily target women. They prey on both sexes, taking money where they can find it.

Fear of Western Medicine

One of the reasons anticancer quacks like Hoxsey are successful for so long is that the reasonable cancer treatment—disfiguring surgery and poisonous chemotherapy—is so horrific. Almost anything looks worth a try when faced with the "reasonable" but frightening recommendations of modern medicine.

Fear of the medical system, of not being in charge of their health, drives some people out of the medical model and into the arms of quacks. Instead of taking the information, treatment, and drugs they need from the medical system, they discount it completely.

Women like Reena, 65, who said, "You can't trust a doctor. They don't listen to you."

"They all work for the drug company," Kate said, as we sipped our tea and let the busy life of the restaurant swirl around us. "Do you think they have quotas? Like they have to sell so many drugs in a month?" I assured her I didn't think so, but she was unconvinced.

Unlike alternative medicine, which rather than truly being alternative is often complementary, quackery is incompatible with Western medicine. People like Hoxsey and Kaadt are not at all comfortable with medical science, and, unlike alternative medical practitioners, don't wish to have patients in charge of their treatment. The quacks' "cures" are designed to be administrated without the help (or interference) of the patient. Belief in his or her advice or, preferably, blind faith in that advice is a necessary part of the "cure."

Why Quacks Are Successful

Quacks pay attention to the needs of patients in the way many medical professionals do not. Typically, they listen to the patient's stories, empathize with their needs and aims, and give patients information and reasons for complying with their treatment—attitudes and practices that women want from the medical system. Quacks are good salespeople; they give flattering attention, take time to listen, and sound convincing.

Almost everyone believes that they can spot a phoney, that they have enough common sense to make good judgments; it is only other people who lack common sense. We don't question our own common sense or believe that we would be gullible enough to be duped by a quack. Some of us will accept advice or recommendations, suspending belief for the moment, willing to listen to the advisor as if we believed, and then later either comply or discard the advice. Others will seem to accept the advice while maintaining an active skepticism. Others will accept advice or treatment if going along with the advice will not harm anyone, without necessarily believing the advice—an "I'll give it a try" attitude. But few of us believe that *we* will be foolish enough to actually believe a quack. Yet, every day, thousands are parted from their money with the promise of hope, simple solutions, and cures. What we need to understand is that it is often very hard to spot a quack.

Sometimes it's hard to tell a quack from a knowledgeable doctor. Perfectly respected, competent medical doctors make outrageous statements. I heard a cardiologist say to a patient, "All drugs have side effects," then say, "Digoxin does not have side effects." The patient had every reason to be suspicious of his advice. "Digoxin has few side effects" would have made more sense to the patient. The same cardiologist told the same patient, "Doctors don't make mistakes." The patient was a lawyer who was well aware of the work doctors give lawyers with their mistakes. Yet this cardiologist was very competent in his understanding of the pathology of the heart. His medical advice was generally good. Quacks can sound like good physicians, and good physicians can sound like quacks.

Personal Experiences

With the definition of a quack as one who has no medical knowledge, promises to cure, and does harm, I looked for examples I thought fit into this category. I stepped outside the medical system and booked appointments with many fringe and alternative practitioners. Generally, I found only well-intentioned people who were conscious of their role in the patient's life and did not do harm. But there were a few.

One was a middle-aged man who had a background in lay counseling and psychic readings and who offered seminars in

"The Child Within." He had a great ability to appear caring and concerned and encouraged women (always women) to reach into their minds and find past problems and to expose those problems to the group. He had no idea what to do when one of the women in the group hit emotionally traumatic information that she had carefully protected herself from dealing with for years. He didn't know how to help her with it and solved his difficulties by driving her home while she was going through a psychotic reaction and telling her husband he thought she had "flipped"—after first carefully getting his fee for the seminar. It took a year of psychiatric treatment for the woman to deal with the pain he had caused her.

This is not to say there are not professionals who might cause similar harm, but professionals at least have a license to lose. This man is bound only by the laws governing the conduct of one citizen toward another in the state or province within which he works. He is not subject to any disciplinary hearing by any board of his peers. This betrayal of trust is a moral problem that is almost impossible to adjudicate in the courts. He would defend himself by saying that he did not claim to be a psychiatrist and that he acted in good faith.

It's hard to tell if the purveyors of exotic medicine act in good faith or are just good sales people. From the same magazine I quoted from earlier, I found many advertisements for innovative medicine: colon therapy—"Revitalize the digestive function of your body and at the same time lower the stress on other organ systems by detoxifying the colon"—and "The Healing Touch: deep trance work and past life regressions." There were pages of "therapy choices" that promised relief from pain and control of life and health. While information from such sources can be stimulating and enriching, I could see buckets of money and weeks of time devoted to sampling any number of these exotic therapies. Are all these therapies not just a variation of the medical industry? I had no quarrel with people who told me they were giving me a mystical, spiritual experience that should increase my ability to deal with disease.

"Listen to your body," the iridologist said. "It talks to you."

"Just relax," the massage therapist said, "and let your body heal itself."

I had more trouble with those who, obviously without medical knowledge or even high-school anatomy, offered to diagnose and treat and who saw their therapies as a replacement for medical advice. I found myself almost apologizing to the herbalist for not having high cholesterol. She clearly wanted me to have it so she could cure it, at $30 a month.

The Self-Help Phenomenon

Quacks use the self-help phenomenon. Since the early 1970s the mood of our Western democratic society has been moving toward self-help and self-control of health. Encouraged by governments who saw self-help as a way of keeping health care costs down, we have become more and more interested in finding answers to our health problems ourselves and less interested in believing the medical professionals, except in times of emergency. In 1974, the Canadian federal government published a paper, "A new perspective on the health of Canadians,"[10] which encouraged individuals to take responsibility for their health. Again in 1986 a policy paper appeared, "Achieving health for all: A framework for health promotion,"[11] encouraging Canadians to learn, among other things, to cope with chronic conditions. The self-help movement was well established in the United States. It is obvious that helping ourselves is a current expectation of adult life. Any number of books urge us to take charge of our health (including this one). The emphasis in the 1980s and 1990s on self-help groups has the virtue of empowering individuals to choose the health care that will benefit them, regain control of that care, and question advice. It is cheaper (for governments and other insurers) to have patients choose alternative medicine or self-help rather than choose the expensive medical system. With the increasing age of the population and the greater need for health care, we can expect

to see more government-sponsored self-help and self-care programs because such programs are cheap and result in a more
active, self-reliant older population. Quacks are eager to help us
help ourselves. If they can't have our blind faith, they will be
happy with our temporary attention. If we "mobilize our resources" and help ourselves, the quacks promise us cures. Failures
are our fault.

Disease itself may be seen as our fault. After all, if self-help
is possible, then disease and even broken bones must be within
the control of the person, either consciously or unconsciously. I
met one healer who believed that we had such control over our
lives that we choose when we wanted to die. "What if I die with
200 other people in a plane crash?" I asked her. "Are you saying
that all 200 people wanted to die at the same time?" She didn't
hesitate. "Yes," she said. "They did." I was speechless in front of
such a blatant disregard for logic. That woman *really* believed in
self-control! If life insurance companies take up her attitude, will
we be held responsible for our own deaths, and will they ever pay
benefits? How far does this "responsibility for health" concept go?
Quacks tap into our need to help ourselves with promises that we,
with their help, can cure anything.

The belief that we are responsible for illness is no doubt
attractive to medical insurers. If illness is under the control of the
individual, then the health care system is no longer responsible
for it. While the movement to greater health care independence
seems to be a social one, it is no doubt primarily an economic one.

Increasing Personal Knowledge

Individual empowerment is liberating, but most women
don't want to be totally abandoned by doctors. They want to be
able to use health information that works in their lives and consult
doctors visit by visit over the years, increasing their knowledge of
their body and its strengths and weaknesses. In addition, they
want to be able to consult alternative and fringe practitioners for

new ideas, useful knowledge, and practical advice that helps them deal with their bodies. Since it is hard to tell the difference between harmless eccentricity, new reliable information, and dangerous profiteering, women need to know who is a legitimate practitioner and who is a quack. In the tradition of the self-help movement, they don't want to rely on the American Medical Association and the Food and Drug Administration to "protect" them from quacks. They want to protect themselves.

The following section will help you make decisions about your health advisors. Are they good? Are they safe? Will you get the best advice you can?

How to Protect Yourself from Harmful Medical Advisors

1. What are your advisor's qualifications?

- Academic
- Life experiences
- Special qualities

An academic degree does not create expertise, but it should give the consumer some idea of the advisor's basic knowledge. A medical doctor, nurse, psychiatrist, medical specialist, and in many states and provinces, an X-ray technician, laboratory technician, nursing assistant, ambulance attendant, and industrial first aid attendant are presumed to have a basic grounding in the normal human body's composition and function.

Look at the degrees posted on the wall of the office. Ask from what university your doctor or practitioner graduated. Ask if they have had any further education. While it may seem socially rude to question the doctor's qualifications by reading the diploma on the wall, remember that you are in a business relationship with the doctor, not a social one.

Ask about your practitioner's life experiences. If she has a degree in medicine but has never delivered a baby, you may think twice about allowing her to learn on your delivery. Perhaps you could engage a midwife and allow the doctor to attend the delivery? Judge your medical advisor's advice against what she has done in the past.

Some people have special qualities that are helpful to you. Some practitioners are empathetic; some are good at knowing whom to call for a referral; some are great at making you feel capable of dealing with your problems; some have a "healing touch"; some spill out information like a computer printout. Decide what you value in this practitioner, and get other qualities from other practitioners. For instance, if you value this person's ability to hear you and understand your story but do not believe they have the qualifications necessary to treat you, use this practitioner to help you understand your condition and your problem so that you can present it well to the one who can give you treatment. Take time to ask questions to determine if this advisor is going to be helpful and useful to you.

2. Is this medical advisor safe?

- Pay attention to the clues you see as you enter his or her office.
- Are there signs that the practitioner values you? Are there recent magazines, comfortable chairs, respect from the outer-office staff?
- Do you have a sense of comfort or are you wary?
- Leave if you are uncomfortable.

3. What is this health care worker promising you? Is he promising you a cure for your problem or just a chance to explore the problem?
4. How much time do you plan to give to this health care worker?
5. How much money will you spend on this health care worker?
6. What are your expectations from this visit or series of visits?

7. What good could this visit do you?
8. What harm could this visit do to you?
9. What do you know about this health care worker's previous work?
10. How long has this person been practicing?
11. Do you know anyone who has consulted this person? What were the results of their experience with this person?

It will take you some time to go through the above list, but you will learn a good deal about your advisors if you do so. Eventually, some of this process will be automatic and you will become more and more capable of protecting yourself against those who could harm you.

9

What Women Want from Their Doctors

Women want a wizard, a magical healer, a wise woman, a guru, a friend, and a confidant all rolled into one doctor and available 24 hours a day by telephone. That is our fantasy doctor. We will settle for a competent, caring doctor who listens. What we know and what we can't get away from in our society is that we must consult doctors.

Permission

Doctors are an important resource. Not only are we conditioned by the medical and drug industry to "check with the doctor" for all manner of discomforts and illnesses, we are also often required to see a doctor by government regulations (prerequisites for licenses or some work situations) and by our employers. Some employers demand a doctor's written excuse when workers return after a 2-day absence. Such regulations give doctors tremendous power and social control. The doctor decides whether we are ill or not, whether our injuries are work-related, or whether we are physically and emotionally competent. Even without legal or employer demands, we are socially expected to see a doctor when we are ill. Doctors, in a sense, "own" disease and illness; we do not even *have* a disease or illness unless the doctor declares that we do. We are not expected to diagnose ourselves, even when we can. Women have been trained by society to "ask the doctor" and accept his diagnosis, and so we do. There are few women who will not consult a doctor. Mrs. Sanders is one of them. She served me homemade apple strudel and wonderful coffee in her comfortable high-rise apartment and told me that good food, exercise, and respectable habits created health—doctors didn't. She declared quite firmly that doctors made you sick and she wouldn't go near one; most women, however, are socially, legally, and morally persuaded to ask the advice of a doctor. And since "asking the doctor" is the adult, responsible thing to do in our society, women's needs and concerns about doctors become very important.

To Be Heard

Women want their concerns to be heard individually by doctors and collectively by medical organizations, health insurers, researchers, and funders of research.

Jeanne sat in her office at the drug and alcohol counseling center and told me about the attitudes and approach of the medical profession:

> Maybe it's a lack of respect for races other than white, and lack of respect for women in general. The medical profession is so traditional and patriarchal that way. It sounds dramatic, but I think it's the basic problem—no respect.

If we feel heard and therefore respected, we can trust. Once we establish trust with a doctor, we can then work with him to help ourselves. Without the first two steps, respect and trust, the third step, healing, is difficult.

We want instant access to unlimited information, but we'll settle for information that is helpful and pertinent. We expect our concerns and fears to be acknowledged and respectfully responded to, not trivialized: "Don't worry about that" or "You don't need to know that." That kind of treatment makes us angry.

Jeanne stared at the plants in her office for a moment trying to crystallize her thoughts about this:

> Women shouldn't trust the medical profession. We're taught to trust them and that perpetuates abuse. When I was a kid getting all those surgeries on my hips, my mom used to stay with me. I think she thought I would be safer with her there, but she thought the doctor was God and she never asked questions; just went along with whatever was said. She'd been brainwashed pretty good in that area.

Jeanne thought the first two steps of respect and trust had been ignored in her case. She had been treated like a body on which doctors acted, not a person who was accepting help.

Women want their doctors to understand normal female bodies. We want reliable information from our doctor and a referral to other sources when we need more information. What we often get is a dismissal of our fears by the doctor. Either the doctor thinks a woman's concerns are unimportant—he does not understand them and therefore will not deal with them—or he doesn't have time to listen to the complete problem. Women, while they generally prefer to consult women as doctors, aren't sure women doctors have any better an attitude than men.

Cathie, a clinical psychology student, tried to stay in control of her health care. She asked questions, read books, and consulted doctors.

> Female physicians can be uncaring, brusque and, well . . . patronizing, even insulting. I can be just as frustrated talking to a female physician who isn't listening as a male.

Kate, the woman we met earlier who sends her doctor education packages said:

> It's an equal-opportunity profession. The women get to be like the men.

This frustrates some women, angers some, and creates fears in others because we don't know where to go when doctors can't help us.

Marie, 51 and a nurse, told me:

> You don't get details from the doctor unless you ask for them. They're not usually forthcoming, but it *is* important to understand your own health problems. You'll probably have to push yourself to get information, but if you don't make your own decisions, someone else will make them for you, and they don't always make them in your best interests.

In our Western society we have made the general practitioner's knowledge the focus of our health information system. Because patients read magazines and talk to people about their experiences, we often demand knowledge from a doctor that the doctor doesn't have. Women hear on television and read in health magazines and brochures that they must "check with their doctor," as if all the advice within the medical industry was complete, accurate, and safe and any advice outside the industry was unsafe.

Accurate and Complete Information

Because we place so much emphasis on the MD license and what the holder of the license *ought* to know instead of concentrating on what he or she *does* know, we place huge expectations on the individual doctor to be our one source of health information. Doctors feel harassed by patients to be some kind of medical encyclopedia, and patients feel frustrated because doctors are not fonts of all knowledge.

Fair Expectations

It really isn't fair to doctors. As a society, we abuse our doctors. A young man I know is struggling with his internship. He has had no more than 4 hours of sleep at one time during the past month working in a busy city hospital. He is worried that his 28-year-old body won't be able to stand the stress of the constant demands and the sleep deprivation. This is called "internship," clinical experience. It is part of the grueling education of doctors. What kind of a system do we have that requires such negative experience? What kind of life is he being trained for?

I sat in my study and allowed the memories of doctors I had worked with and known well in the past to emerge. The memories took their place in a circle around my head, and they talked to me: "How can you criticize us when you know how hard we try? Remember me?"

I remembered Mike. He sat across from me just before midnight one night in the quiet of the pediatric ward. I had called him in to see a young boy who was reacting to his medication. The boy was going to be all right, and we stopped at the nurse's desk to chart what had happened. He picked up a medical journal that I had been reading. "I have to stop working like this," he said. "I haven't read a medical journal in 2 years. Do you know what that makes me? Dangerous. That's what that makes me. I have to get out. I know people need me here, but I'll die working like this." He left our town for a quieter practice, one that allowed him to read his medical journals, have some time with his wife, some time to think.

And there was Ron, who made home visits, sometimes miles out of town in the country, to dying patients so that they and their families would not suffer trying to get to his office.

And Andy, who phoned me to apologize for not picking up a problem with his patient, who was also my patient. "I knew she didn't understand English very well. I should have asked her more questions. I feel terrible." I should have asked her more questions as well, and I shared his guilt. Andy and I stayed with her through the operation that she would not have needed if we had both communicated better. He cared, and he tried, and neither he nor I deserved to be condemned because we weren't always right.

And Shiela, who could not persuade her patient to quit smoking. "How can I help him when he abuses his body so badly? His blood pressure is terrible; his heart is bad. Smoking is going to kill him and he won't let me help." Her frustration was causing her physical distress. "You're going to have high blood pressure yourself," I said. "I know, I know," she said. "What do you *do*?" She was committed to helping her patients and frustrated that she could not communicate what she knew so that she could help them.

And Gary, who ignored the nurse's criticism about the way he encouraged a mother to spend all day with her brain-damaged, seemingly unresponsive son, talking to him, touching him, telling him stories. "She's not facing reality," the nurses said. "She needs to do this," he said, "and I think it will help." That was the miracle child who did recover.

I can see the physical and emotional problems that doctors face. They are asked to be God and Mother Teresa, an infallible technical machine and a loving Earth Mother, a mind-reading magician and a powerful ally. They are, by definition in our society, never quite good enough no matter what they do. They feel alienated from their patients, and they are alienated. We, as a society, have created an impossible position for them.

Occasionally, we do feel as though we have a met a doctor who fulfills our fantasies. I attended a lecture on menopause given by a woman doctor who was not only experiencing menopause herself, she is also an expert in endocrinology. About 150 women listened, asked questions, and wanted answers. The doctor gave answers, straight answers.

A woman stood and asked her, "I've been having heavy periods, 12 pads a day for 6 days for 20 years. I've tried all kinds of things but doctors tell me that I have to live with it."

A collective sigh of empathy from 150 women drifted across the auditorium, for they knew what such heavy bleeding meant in her life. Almost everyone had experienced some days of heavy bleeding and could imagine what that would be like day after day and year after year.

The doctor responded by naming a drug that would help and gave the specific dosage.

"That's it?" the woman said. "That will help?"

"It will help a great deal," the doctor said.

"Why does that leave me angry at the doctors I consulted before? Why does that make me feel that no one before you even listened?"

Maybe no one before this doctor *had* really listened to her. Maybe no one had the drug information. Maybe little research has been done on this kind of heavy bleeding because it is not seen as important. The medical industry seems to swing between treating women's normal cycles as medical problems and treating abnormal cycles as the suffering that women must expect. The women at this lecture felt that, at last, an informed, reasonable doctor was taking their concerns seriously and giving practical advice. They were being heard.

Many women say that they are not looking for all the answers to their concerns from their doctor. They want a real doctor, not a fantasy. They want the doctor to say, "I don't know about that," when he doesn't. They don't want a doctor who, if he doesn't know about something, says that it is insignificant or, as some doctors try to tell patients, that it doesn't exist.

But, as rule, most of us find that we must research our health concerns ourselves. We read books from the library and the health units, phone friends and relatives with medical educations, and ask for advice and references. We go to several doctors to compare opinions, read magazine articles, and check on the alternative sources of information in our area, including women's centers, chiropractors, naturopaths, and ethnic medical advisors such as acupuncturists and native healers. We search the newspapers for articles, watch televisions shows, and try to educate ourselves so that we can get enough information to make a good treatment choice. We find the answer to this puzzle, piece by piece, over time. We are the women who have faith in our research skills.

Like Pat, the mother of two little boys, who demands information from the health care system:

> I want to be in control of my health, so it's my job to find out about it. I think you have to do your homework. I ask questions that might be the same ones I just asked and been told the answers to, but I don't care because I have to get it into my head, understand exactly what the answers are. I'm a very information-oriented person. If I read something in a newspaper that I want to know about, if I have a medical question about it, I'll phone somebody because I'm not an expert and I figure experts are out there to give me information.

Many women have little faith in their research skills and are angry because they find research very difficult.

Vivian, 59, lives in a small urban house with a beautifully landscaped backyard. She and her husband manage with careful budgeting to rent the house and look after themselves. She does need housekeeping help since she finds housework physically beyond her. She responded to my ad in the newspaper because she doesn't want other women to stay ignorant about their conditions as long as she did, and she thought I might be able to change the system for people like her. She said:

> A lot of that information is not something I can understand. Most of the doctors and the people I talk to are very well educated; they all have very good jobs. Sometimes the doctor doesn't explain things easily. Sometimes she has to say it two or three times before I can understand it, or I'll ask until I do get it straight. Other times I get it quickly. The trouble is that with my problem [fibromylagia] the GPs don't know any more than you do. I read all the newsletters about it and I have to educate the doctor. She will always read anything I take to her. Anything I copy that I think would be of interest she takes with open arms. Not all doctors do that; some don't care to be educated. You can't trust those kind.

Appropriate Help

The frustration with the one-stop-doctor-information source has led women to consult with other health professionals outside the Western medical model. Women are reaching outside the medical industry to get advice on pregnancy and birth. There is a strong move to demedicalize birth, to renaturalize it. Midwives are becoming a useful and reliable source of health information about pregnancy and delivery.

Pat, with her great confidence in her ability to work with others, said:

> I would have my kids in a minute with a midwife. It's really a shame that we don't because if you look at Australia and you look at the Philippines [and parts of the United States] where the midwife is recognized as a medical profession, it's a different experience. I was watching a documentary about a woman delivering and she had her baby at home and all the circumstances of pregnancy were very positive. It would have been nice to have had my babies at home the way she did. I would just love to walk around my house during my labor and not be in the hospital where all these weird things are going on and people you don't know are all around you. Who the hell wants to be with all those people when you're in labor? You're testy enough that you don't even want to be nice to the people you love, let alone Joe mopping the hallway while you're walking down it thinking, "Get out of my way! I'm going to have a contraction right here!" You want to keep a certain amount of pride and dignity; you don't want to lose it in front of everyone. I would have loved to have gone about my merry way at home; just done my thing at home and had my baby right there. I would have done that in a minute if I'd had a choice. People think I'm nuts because the medical facilities aren't there and both my boys needed them. But you can have emergency services standing by and I'm 7 minutes from a hospital and 3 minutes in an ambulance. And it would have been less costly [to the health insurers] to transport me and the baby to the hospital in an ambulance than it was to keep us all in the hospital the way they did.

Pat had strong emotional reasons for preferring a midwife to help her deliver her own children:

> You know doctors may have delivered a million babies, but you know, at the same time, they're not women; they truly have never had that experience. You know their mind-set. It's the same mind-set that you had before you ever delivered a baby, and that was technically you know what is going to happen. Technically you know how this is supposed to go and how it supposedly will feel. You understand it differently after you've had a baby. Male doctors don't really know.

Women are looking for ways to have babies that are more comfortable, more self-controlled, and less technical than the present "average" hospital experience. Like Pat, they see films about home births and are attracted to the nonintervention, the family protection and support, and the emotional satisfaction of a job well done. Their experience in the hospital is one of obedience to rules, awkward and uncomfortable positions, and frightening equipment and personnel, with the underlying implication that childbirth is too difficult and too life threatening to be left to mothers.

Jessica, who had her child with a midwife in attendance at her home in the Northwest Territories, said:

> We're stuck in this attitude that doctors must control health care. There is an issue of control when the situation is life threatening. But the vast majority of health care consumers use the medical system in situations that are *not* life threatening.

Because medical care is becoming more and more expensive we may see insurance companies pushing nondoctor care. Recent changes in some provinces and states to again allow midwives to practice is encouraging. Nurse midwives are legally licensed to practice in all states. There are nurse midwifery schools in 17 states and certification programs in others. British Columbia and Ontario have passed laws that make midwifery legal. There are nonmedical home births and birthing centers in some areas where only emergency or high-risk mothers are sent for medical care. There are active organizations trying to pull birthing away from the hands of the medical industry into the hands of mothers.

Pat had a lot to say about delivering babies:

> Male doctors don't know how it feels to want to push that baby out. There you are, you're whole being is expelling this thing and they're saying, "Don't push!" which is an *insane* thing to say. "Just hold back. Hold back. Don't push." You know you feel like turning to him and saying, "You know where you can go."
>
> I listened to my case room nurses because, first of all, they were with me the whole time so I'm attached to them and they understand me. And,

secondly, I feel they have more experience than the doctors. Also, I feel that women relate to women in situations of childbirth the way a man never can. Women are tuned into what you're doing. They know the feeling, the overwhelming parts of the experience, when you're going to lose it, when you're going to be in control. I don't think a male doctor can ever be an excellent obstetrician.

Perhaps once pregnancy and childbirth become less of a disease process and more of a normal life process, the same might happen to other patterns and cycles in women's lives. Perhaps menopause will be seen as a natural and normal life cycle instead of a disease process that demands control.

Advice, Not Control

What upsets many women and makes them angry is the supposition that the doctor's advice should be the only information they get and that they should make their decisions about their health only on that advice. Many women realize that they can't afford to do that. There are too many testimonials from women that tell of misplaced trust for a woman *not* to believe that the responsibility for her health rests on her shoulders.

The April 20, 1993, edition of Toronto's *Globe and Mail* carried an article by Jeanette Mathney, a CBC reporter, about her false-negative diagnosis from the doctors who told her not to worry about the lump in her breast. When she found it was malignant she lost faith in the competence of Western medicine. She found herself suddenly learning about homeopathic medicine, visualization, and other less mainstream methods of dealing with cancer while she used what she needed from Western medicine:

I'll continue to research, explore, and experiment—arming myself for battle in my way. Knowledge is power, as they say.

I wish I had known last August what I now know, that young fit women get breast cancer. And that doctors don't always get it right.

I would have been far more persistent. And I might not have been sitting here today, weighing my survival statistics against those of others, as poisonous drugs drip into my veins.

We should not expect doctors to be infallible, yet, even when we know we must have a broad base from which to get information, we still expect much information from them.

Respect

Women want a receptive, respectful attitude from the doctor. Doctors often indicate with their first words to the patient that they do not respect her. The current habit of introducing themselves by their title and calling patients by their first names, such as "Hi, Marion, I'm Dr. Smith" is innately condescending. Women react to this initial contact whether they do or do not confront the doctor about it. Doctors tell me that the public expects to be treated "professionally," and they think that introducing themselves by their title is "professional" and calling a woman by her first name is "friendly." Women don't see it that way. Two women I interviewed did not object to being called by their first name when the doctor retained his title, but most saw it as a power play by the doctor designed to reduce the patient's social status or as indifference to the patient's reaction. Women want their doctor to show respect in the way they are addressed, the way they are heard, and the way their treatment is discussed and recommended.

A Comfortable Doctor's Office

Women look for respect in the doctor's outer office. If patients have to wait for a doctor and the receptionist does not apologize for the wait or in any way indicate that the patient's time is valuable, women usually resent it. Some don't tolerate the experience of waiting.

Bubbly, self-determined Pat said:

> I've never had to wait in a doctor's office . . . and you know what, Marion?
> I think that if I had to wait I'd get up and walk out . . . because what he
> would be telling me is that my time is not important.

Others seethe. Others feel they do not deserve the doctor's time.

Brita, the young mother who had been so timid when she first started taking her children to the doctor, said:

> I felt unimportant there [at the doctor's office]. I felt I was taking up his
> time. I even thanked him for making time to see me at a regular appoint-
> ment! I don't go to him any more.

Office procedures and organization that seem efficient and helpful to the doctors often seem officious, condescending, and rude to patients. Some women have innovative ways of dealing with this. I asked Kate what she did to make herself feel more comfortable in the doctor's office. She said:

> I ask him to take off his white coat. Then I ask him to sit in my chair and I
> sit in his. I do that with social workers too when I'm uncomfortable. I ask
> them if I can sit in their chair or if they can bring their chair out to the front
> of the desk. The environment is important.

She is aware that manipulating the environment creates emotional reactions.

The physical office where a woman consults a doctor often sets the dramatic stage for the attitude behind the closed doors. "Nurses" stand behind high counters, creating a division between the professionals and the patients. Stacks of patient files with color-coded numbers are overwhelming and depersonalized evidence that the patient is one of hundreds. Patients are often led into consulting rooms to wait until the doctor, in an assembly-line and efficient manner, enters with chart in hand to dispense advice and prescriptions. The experience leaves a woman fighting to believe that her concerns are legitimate and important.

The boxlike examining room was not appreciated by anyone. It was condemned by one doctor as an anxiety-producing environment. She told me:

> I don't think patients like it. I don't like it myself. I think our staff out front are friendly and that helps, but I don't know what to do about this room.

She gestured around the examining room.

> I can see it's intimidating but I don't really know anything different.

Linda, an accountant and the mother of a 13-year-old, said:

> There you sit on a high narrow bed without a stitch on, barely covered by a flimsy piece of paper, staring at four blank walls. Comfortable? No.

Magazines in the examining room were evidence for some women that the doctor appreciated the problem of waiting in the room, but others found the experience of waiting there, with or without magazines, anxiety-producing. They felt very vulnerable.

Marie, 51, said:

> I feel like I'm almost in a cell, a tiny cell, almost coffin-like, very tiny. Sitting there with a piece of paper over me.

Women who have been sexually abused and women who have been abused by doctors in the past find this waiting particularly stressful. They want to have someone to talk to. They would prefer to be dressed, and they'd like a more hospitable, comfortable room.

Some women take their husbands or boyfriends with them to the doctor's office when they want to make sure they are going to get the facts they need to understand their health problem and to make sure they are safe.

A Safe Environment

Because one in four women have been abused by men who were in positions of power in their lives and because doctors are seen as powerful people, some women are afraid of doctors. Violence and abuse are linked in many women's minds with all men. Since most of our medical practitioners are men, some women have a difficult time accepting help or trusting them. When they do establish trust in their doctor and are assured of his respect, then they can begin to educate themselves.

Education

Women want a patient library at the doctor's office where they can get pamphlets, videos, and books. Our education should be part of the doctor's responsibility. Doctors are not usually paid for this. In this way insurance companies shape the kind of care doctors give since they usually pay for diagnosis and treatment, not for education. Doctors recognize that patients with conditions such as heart disease and diabetes need education and that sexually active women need information on birth control and sexually transmitted diseases, but patients see a need for education in *all* conditions. Women would like to see efforts to increase patient knowledge as part of the doctor's job.

If doctors are not willing to take the time to give them information, women want a referral to someone who is. Often women are not used to phoning the health unit or the women's center. They have had no method of information gathering to rely on and they feel ignorant. They have had no practice in making five phone calls to get one piece of information and don't realize how tenacious and persevering they must be. They are not prepared for the put-downs, the trivializations, or the criticisms they often receive when they do search for information.

Why shouldn't women get dispassionate, accurate information regarding the normal cycles of their lives? A woman who is entering menopause needs information on estrogen and progesterone replacement therapy, what it will do for her, what it won't, what the side effects of the treatment are, what hormones are specific for what conditions, what conditions are the most likely, what the statistics on osteoporosis are, and what is recommended for prevention. She should not be subjected to the outrageous advice that I heard from an orthopedic surgeon I consulted. Our short conversation about menopause went this way:

> Dr. H.: "All women should have hysterectomies after menopause and go on estrogen replacement therapy."

> Me: "Did you really say that?" I thought I must have misunderstood him, then fleetingly wondered whether he got a cut from the drug companies or the surgeons doing the hysterectomies.

> Dr. H.: "Sure. No woman needs her uterus. It's just useless. Why would you want to keep it?"

At this point I realized that this doctor had very little understanding of women's reproductive system, the role of the uterus in sexual arousal, or a woman's emotions or needs. His advice was barbaric, but he was free to give it to anyone who would listen, and there were many women in his waiting room who might believe him.

Time

A public health nurse in southern Arizona told me about her experience with her doctor:

> I had to see him to get a return-to-work slip after a cold. He came in, asked me what the problem was, wrote a prescription, and started out the door. I said, "Just a minute."

He stopped.

I said, "You came in, avoided eye contact, diagnosed, and wrote a prescription for a drug to which I am allergic—all in 3 minutes. I don't think this is good enough."

He froze. Then he walked back in, sat down, spread his hands out, leaned back, and said, "I'm sorry. Can we start again?"

Perhaps we need to *ask* for better care.

Independence from Drug Companies

Women are suspicious of the drug companies' involvement in a doctor's advice. Most are not as suspicious as Kate:

> Forget the doctors. They work with the drug companies . . . You can't trust the facts that come from the doctors or the health magazines. The doctors write it. They throw in some herbs or some natural stuff, but I don't trust them.
> Drugs companies are selling. Doctors are selling. They want to own health and disease. The economy would fall apart if we took responsibility for our own healing. My God! Women deciding what to do about their own health? Too frightening!

While this may sound severe and unusual, Kate's point of view was repeated in less emphatic terms many times. The recent takeover of the PCS Health Systems Inc. by the drug company Eli Lilly and Co. puts a new twist on the kind of influence health care will take. The marriage of a big drug company to the largest managed health care company in the United States is surely going to create a difference in the way patients view their insurance companies. The purpose of the health maintenance insurance companies with pharmacy maintenance programs is to keep the price of drugs down and to monitor doctors' prescriptions. Is it reasonable to expect a drug company to do this? Since the insurance company pays the doctor, what will be the doctor's relationship to the drug company? As doctors get closer to drug companies, will they get further away from their patients?

I had worked with Mike and Ron and Shiela and Gary, who sincerely tried to give the best treatment they could and who did not deserve the kind of condemnation Kate was giving to doctors in general, but she expresses the attitude of many who have good reason to suspect their doctor's advice.

Competent Advice

Western medicine is superbly capable in emergencies and surgical intervention and often accurate in diagnosis. As well, treatments are often appropriate and effective. Western medicine is, at the same time, capable of causing illness and worsening conditions. Who advocates for the safety and reliability of the treatment prescribed for women? How can a woman find out whether the advice she is getting is reasonable?

Consultation

There is an amazing amount of knowledge available to doctors both from their university educations and ongoing from their professional organizations. Women want doctors to reach into that forest of knowledge and point out which stand of information is relevant to us so that we can find out what we need to know. The doctor needs to understand our problems and give the diagnosis and treatment in a consultative manner. Not only do we want to feel a part of the diagnosis and treatment process, we want actually to *be* a part of it. It does seem obvious that the patient is the most important part of this process, but women tell me they don't feel that way, nor are they treated this way. We are treated, for the most part, as if we were plastic people, faceless, without personality or emotions, placed in 15-minute time slots for the convenience of the doctor. We want much more than that. Women want an honest, mature, respectful, straightforward, defined relationship with our doctor so that we can know what we can expect from him or her.

Doctors' Acceptance of Their Role

Women are also dealing with a patriarchal medical system of competition and one-upmanship. The competitive, driven, compulsive personality that got them into medical school in the first place may keep some doctors from admitting their weaknesses. Such personalities make superb technicians but not holistic practitioners. To be comfortable with a broad view of health and healing the holistic practitioner must be able to tolerate ambiguity. They cannot know everything. Some practitioners want an answer to all problems and need to feel in charge and competent at all times. The illusion of omnipotence is necessary for some. Women want doctors to face this restrictive attitude.

It would be more useful to everyone if doctors realized that they were part of a medical system that provided good service and good information in a narrow area of health care and that others were needed to provide services and information in other areas. We would all benefit if we could see doctors as important as only *one* source of information, *one* health resource, not the only resource. Once a doctor understands his or her place in the health and healing life of the patient, he could ask for resources and assistance for those problems that are outside his competence.

While doctors do appoint their representatives to health boards, hospital boards, and various medical advisory committees, there are few who go to women's organizations and offer to help. A local women's health center takes medical students into their treatment clinic and shows them how to do a comfortable and respectful pelvic examination. The staff requires male medical students to strip and put their feet up in the stirrups, exposing their genitals as if they were receiving a pelvic exam. This forever imprints on the brain of the new doctors the humiliating position doctors routinely require women to assume. This kind of exchange of knowledge can only improve relationships between doctors and women.

It may be that economic competition will force changes in the ways doctors treat women. In the area where I live a male doctor takes 2 years to get a full practice; a female doctor takes 6 months because women prefer women doctors. It may be that with the increasing number of female doctors, male doctors will change their attitudes and methods so that they are seen to be more respectful of women and more caring. With the change in male doctors, females doctors will also change to actually become more empathetic instead of just being perceived to be so.

It would be truly wonderful if doctors as a powerful lobby group moved with women's groups to get the resources women need. Working with other resources could increase the doctor's satisfaction with his work and would certainly increase women's satisfaction with the health care system.

10

What Women Want from Society

Women want a great deal more than we get, so we protest, object, and demand a health care system that is more useful to us. We do more than that; we offer ideas and solutions so that we can change the way society views us and the way the health care system treats us. We want to be served by health care workers who value us and who give accurate and appropriate information in a comfortable, safe, healing environment.

Equality

Women hate the inequalities of race, age, and sex. We often feel discriminated against, as if we are somehow a foreigner in the medical community, tolerated but not valued. We see a moral philosophy that puts more value on men than on women and more value on some women than others.

Race

First Nations women, Native Americans who are the aboriginal people of North America, see themselves as being doubly handicapped by society, first because they are women, and then because they are native. Aboriginal people in Canada have a higher rate of infectious and respiratory disease, twice the infant mortality of nonnatives, and a much lower life expectancy.[1] Madeliene Dion Stout, Director of The Centre for Aboriginal Education at Carleton University in Ottawa, Canada, said:

> In my language, Cree, Kitmakesowin means poverty and poverty is a health issue for us. We as native women become a poverty statistic. More of us bear children and we have more children than nonnative women do. When nonnative women are retiring, we are having children. We have higher numbers of stillbirths and pregnancy-related problems. We have higher accident and suicide rates. In the middle years, we are more likely to die from cancer. We have higher death rates from respiratory conditions. Kitmakesowin housing is commonplace for us. We have low literacy rates, employment rates, and low levels of income.[2]

Black women in the United States have similar problems. According to the Boston Women's Health Book Collective:

> Racism is a serious threat to health and in some instances creates more barriers to obtaining needed care and to survival than does social class.[3] For example, even allowing for social class, black babies still die at higher rates than white babies living in the same geographic area, due mainly to low birth weight among black babies, which is almost entirely preventable . . .[4]

> Although people of color need medical care more often than white people do, they frequently get less. For example, black people are less likely to get the most modern specialty treatment and follow-up care for cancer and do not survive as long after diagnosis. Similarly, even though hypertension is 82% higher among women of color, they do not receive any more treatment than white women.[5]

Predictably, the *patients* are blamed for these problems—not the system. My own nursing experience has shown that aboriginal people often are given incompetent diagnosis, misinformation, and substandard treatment. In the village I visited in the Arctic, a woman had all her teeth pulled by the traveling dentist in January of that year. It was now July and her dentures had not yet arrived. When they do arrive, her gums and supporting bone structure will have shrunk, and the dentures will be unlikely to fit. She is 39 years old and she looks 60. She had no idea that the dental care she got wasn't practiced in the south. She had no one with whom to compare her problems or from whom to get advice—except the dentist who removed her teeth. She had no choice of dentist, no options for care, no way of making an effective complaint. No one should have to accept that kind of "care." I have never seen anyone in my southern society who was without teeth for six months. In this modern age, that treatment is cruel. The policies of Canada and the United States in the past have made sure that many aboriginal people and many black people, because of their color, live in poverty, and poverty makes health choices difficult.

Age

Aging women are less likely to receive adequate care than aging men and are more likely to be put into institutions.[6] Maddy, 51, said:

> I think the medical profession needs a rattling around. Just about every other culture in the world respects their elders—but us.

It is amazing that our society has developed a health care system that pays so little attention to the needs of women of all ages. Somehow women are seen as second-class men who have to be fitted into a high-tech system. When women do find services that are women-centered, such as the Salvation Army women's hospitals, feminist health clinics, or the Kentucky Frontier Nursing Service for Mother and Child, we feel safer.

Medical Research

Too little research is done on women's health problems and too many erroneous assumptions are made about women's bodies, such as the notion that treatment for heart conditions should be the same for women as it is for men when few studies have been done on women. Studies are not even done on female mice because female mice have too many complicating factors, such as hormonal cycles, that interfere with the research, and they usually cost more than male mice.[7] Most studies are done on men because the results are more predictable and easier to test than studies done on both men and women. I checked through the MedLine list of studies for 1992 and 1993 to see if this fact was changing. There were more studies done that included women in the last year, so perhaps this problem is being addressed; however, it will perhaps not be solved in a way women are going to accept. Ullrich, Yeater, and Dalal in the *West Virginia Medical Journal* presented the results of their study done on women as if men's bodies were the norm.[8] What we want from these studies is an average or normal *for women*. Women have different body fat proportions; we have menstrual cycles and a differing ability to absorb drugs. In a 1988 study of 22,000 men, physicians determined that men could lower their risk of heart attack by taking one aspirin tablet a day.[9] No one knows whether women also could probably be protected from heart disease in this manner because no women were tested even though heart disease is the most frequent cause of death in women over 50.[10] Dr. Nancy Futreel, a neurologist at Creighton University in Omaha, Nebraska, has found that both sex and age make a difference in test results. She found that older female mice do not do as well as male mice on antistroke drugs. This tells us that the drug trials on male mice that form the basis of drug recommendations for men should not be assumed to be adequate research for drug recommendations for women. Dr. Jeri Sechnzer of Pace University in New York City found differences in AIDS and depression research.[11] Yet gender differences are ignored by most "scientific" studies in the interests of creating solutions to men's health problems. This is not useful to women. Women want research that does not treat our natural hormonal functions as a nuisance for researchers, but instead treats them as relevant and important.

Gender

The attitude that men's bodies are "normal" and women's bodies are somehow irritatingly deviant from normal is reflected in the way women are treated. Dr. Jerilynne Prior, an endocrinologist in the Department of Medicine at University of British Columbia, Vancouver, Canada, said:

> Physicians have been trained in the disease model, and doctors are obviously part of a culture that view women's bodies as not quite right.[12]

When we ask questions about our health in an effort to understand our bodies and our health choices, we often are treated as if we are foolish or neurotic and as if our bodies are somehow substandard.

Gail, a woman from Saskatchewan, reported to me that her daughter's support group of men and women with Chronic Fatigue Syndrome had compared their reception at the doctors' offices. The men had received much different treatment. Their complaints were believed and investigated immediately. The women reported trivialization, disbelief, lack of effort to investigate, and sometimes years before a diagnosis.

> It was so hard to face the fact that the medical profession would treat women as if they were neurotic just because they were women. My daughter went through so much just to get a diagnosis: the put-downs, the psychological testing, all that. And the men in her group had none of that humiliating garbage. It makes me mad.

While women are not sure that society designed the health care system for men, we are sure it was not designed to suit women. Women have felt used, abused, and ignored by a health care system that directs but does not educate. There is some suspicion by women that we are diagnosed as sicker than we are and are medicated and treated unnecessarily in order to fuel the health care system and provide economic support to an industry. We suspect that we are used by the industry, particularly when we are in pain, without advocate support, poor, nonwhite, or old.

Correct Interpretation of Facts

Even some women who are victims of assault and battering have come to see themselves as the cause of a medical problem called "wife-battering syndrome" (and listed as a condition in the Diagnostic and Statistical Manual of Mental Disorders, 3rd ed.). They are not treated as if a fist came from an assaulting man and hit them in the face; they are treated as if something within themselves caused that fist to move into their face.

Typically, women who first approach the doctor for help with the painful results of battering are given drugs and psychotherapy to try to understand how they can accept and live with the violence. A quote taken from *The New Our Bodies, Ourselves* shows the all too common response of doctors when a woman wants help after a spousal assault: "I was given little pills to relax me. I was 'just too nervous.'"[13]

Battered women are probed for personality faults and chemical imbalances that create the situation in which they are battered. The male perpetrator remains outside the medical environment. He does not go to the doctor. A local study by the staff of the Women's Center estimated that 1% of abusive men enter treatment.[14] The abuser has no condemning file in a doctor's or psychiatrist's office labeling his deviant personality, no drugs in his system that might prevent his violence, and no record that he is being treated for a "psychiatric disorder." There is no effort by the medical community to create a socially hostile environment for his actions. The woman, the victim, must absorb the blame and the interference of the medical community. She is often given drugs and then blamed for her reliance on those drugs. When comparing the medical histories of women who have been beaten, we can see the initial drug treatment, then the evolution of the doctor-prescribed drug therapy leading to the drug abuse that the doctor now treats. The doctor then redefines the wife-beating into self-abuse or drug abuse and even says that the woman wanted to be abused.[15] After treating the woman with drugs, then viewing her as self-abusive, the doctor often decides that the woman is psychiatrically disturbed. Western medicine effectively takes a victim and creates a patient without ever coming close to helping.

This pattern of creating a disease out of a coping reaction is common to the treatment of obesity, eating disorders, anxiety, unhappiness, and the many and varied difficulties of maintaining health that surround women's lives. The aim here does not seem to be to help women to live healthier lives but to slot them into the health care system as consumers.

Safety with Doctors

Men still are seen as arbitrators of morality, given their positions of power as judges, church ministers, and legislators. Doctors, male and female, often see themselves as experts and consultants in maintaining this male-dominated morality and system of social order. This attitude creates an immense distance between the doctor and his patient, leaving many women feeling they have no voice, choice, or power.

As I said in Chapter 9, many women have a justified fear of doctors. We are told by the media to complain to the doctors' association (usually the College of Physicians and Surgeons or the local Medical Association), who will investigate and deal with the offending doctor. Women who do try to get such associations to stop an abusive doctor often find the association more committed to protecting the doctor than to protecting the patient. Occasionally, it is dangerous to complain. In my community, a doctor was convicted of hiring a killer to murder a young woman. She was going to testify against him to the College of Physicians and Surgeons on a sexual abuse complaint but was murdered before she could do so.

Dr. Thomas Handley, of the British Columbia College of Physicians and Surgeons, said that women who complained of abuse were "part of a tremendous social upheaval related to women, which has brought a tremendous number of issues out of the woodwork."[16] This appears to be a smooth sidestepping away from the issue. By concentrating on the socialized reasons why women are now more likely to *complain* about abuse, Dr. Handley is avoiding the problem—doctors are abusing women. This doctor-protective attitude is extremely frustrating to women who are trying to get safer care. Women see the problem not as a problem of increasing complaints by women but a problem of abuse by doctors.

In Ontario, Canada, the College of Physicians and Surgeons had 114 investigations into sexual misconduct in 1992.[17] How many women who were abused, molested, or fondled did not register an official complaint? There seems to be so little done to improve the situation of physician sexual abuse that the Chief Coroner of the Province of British Columbia, William MacArthur, advised women to take their complaints of sexual abuse to the police rather than to the College of Physicians and Surgeons:

> I don't believe the college [of Physicians and Surgeons] has taken them [women] as seriously as they should have. I think there is something really wrong when a woman goes to the college, complains about sexual abuse by her doctor, and is left dangling.[18]

The police, if they are receptive and helpful, still have to investigate a problem that has no witnesses; as one police constable told me, "It's usually the doctor's word against the patient's, and you know how powerful doctors are." For some women, it would be enough that the police seriously investigated the abuse, but most women would not even make the complaint.

Many men in other professions in our culture—teachers, lawyers, accountants—abuse women, but doctors seem particularly wicked in their abuse since women are physically at risk in the doctor's examining room. Young women who are not sure what a doctor is supposed to do in a physical exam are especially vulnerable.

The role of the doctor in Western medicine must be examined critically and changes made before doctors can be used efficiently and safely by women. Most of the women I interviewed did not trust doctors' advice. It is no wonder that so many women look for health information outside the traditional Western medical model.

The fear of abuse from doctors is probably more widespread than those who work in the medical community realize. There seems to be an agreement among medical practitioners that very few doctors are abusive. They have a kind of self-protective, head-in-the-sand attitude as well as a lively fear of false accusations. Many women have been abused by doctors through everything from sexual abuse to indifference—molestation, fondling, trivialization, ridicule, unnecessary drugging, unnecessary surgery, cruelty. They don't want to have to get information from male doctors. They want something better.

Available Information

Women mine their communities looking for education, ideas, and support. Many use their public libraries, bookstores, and health unit libraries to research problems. Others use mental health counselors, private counselors, psychiatrists, community health nurses, societies organized around specific diseases, relatives, and friends to find more information. In some areas community health nurses take on the role of health educator and mentor. Typically, though, the community health nurses are used by young mothers and very few others. Older women in menopause seldom call the health nurses for advice. Older women search for advice among their friends, in health magazines, in books at the library, and at classes sponsored by women's centers and hospitals.

Maddy, 51, a homemaker who has had a difficult time during menopause, suffering from mood swings and depression, said:

> I go out and look for it [information]. I go to the bookstore and the library and learn—I'm like that. I'll go out and look for whatever I have to know. I've found that doctors don't know anything about menopause—even specialists don't know as far as I'm concerned. They treat you like, "Oh,

another woman paranoid. Kids must have left home and she's got these aches and pains." They don't take it seriously—menopause.

Many women read to get information. All the women I interviewed could read, although I know that not all women can.

There are many magazines put out by groups who are interested in women's health education. Most of these magazines are not managed by nurses, doctors, or members of the Western medical community but by interested lay health enthusiasts. A few are published under the auspices of a medical group, such as *Update* by the Women's Health Resource Centre in Calgary's Grace Hospital, *The Johns Hopkins Medical Letter*, the *Network News* from the National Women's Health Network, and the *Wellness Letter* of the University of California at Berkeley's School of Public Health. In addition many private clinics publish newsletters that they send to those on their mailing list. Addresses of some information sources appear at the end of this book.

Women are not waiting for the medical community to show them options. They are reading and consulting nurse practitioners, physiotherapists, chiropractors, and alternative sources. They realize they need the expertise and skills of Western medicine, but they are looking for a safer and more comfortable environment in which to learn about themselves.

Other Women as Educators

Women want a system that provides an understanding, knowledgeable *woman* who has time to listen to us and who is capable of showing us new information and new ways of dealing with our problems. This experience with a knowledgeable woman would contribute to our own abilities to be competent and even more correct in our decisions. We want a system that validates our experiences, values our understanding, and uses our shared experience to improve health care for everyone. Too many women feel isolated. When Brita first started taking her children to the doctor she was very passive and fearful, but she has learned to demand health information. She said:

> I'm tired of having 5 minutes with the doctor to tell him that Susie has a fever and have him give me antibiotics and that's that. Why does she have so many fevers? What can I do to head off a fever before it gets so high? Should I change her diet? Is this stress? Should I change her classroom? Is there something else going on besides infection? I want to get better at understanding this problem; I don't just want antibiotics.

I met older women who wanted to offer their knowledge to other women but had no way of doing so except within their circle of family and friends. One woman, Doreen, a former nurse, had looked after her elderly father and learned ways to keep him happy and comfortable for years. She learned many techniques through this experience that had not been taught in her nursing education and probably were not generally known. Why was there not some place for her to offer this valuable information to others? There seems to be a tremendous pool of knowledge in the community that is never used. Women who have researched a particular health problem have valuable information to offer others. They often have tried many resources in their communities and arrived at the one source that helps, or they have read many books and written away for information that helped them to understand their condition. Why should all that work, effort, and expertise be ignored? These women would be happy to add their bits of information to the general knowledge of women. We are neglecting not only a valuable source of knowledge in our communities but also a tremendous source of emotional support. Women want wise women in their communities to advise them; they want "crones."

There is no place in the present health care system for the emotionally unsupported woman who seeks to resolve her problems with medical diagnosis and treatment for her emotional ills. Doctors fear that neurotic women will besiege the health care system, looking for salvation from their emotional problems. "Women like that are a waste of time," a busy surgeon in my former town said; and, indeed, women with these problems usually do not need the kind of solution they get at the doctor's office, especially in the 10 minutes allotted to them. Doctors deal with such women without helping them.

Perhaps they need crones, elders, wise women who could give them compassionate support and practical advice. Now, some women go for years looking for another test, another diagnosis, another examination for problems that include emotional distance, socialized uselessness, and lack of definition or production. With a wider range of resources, a broader base of health counseling, and a mentor system or support system within health care, these women would be more likely to find help instead of palliative, cursory attention or ineffective, even dangerous, treatments.

Then there are the many women who have been diagnosed by doctors as emotionally unstable simply because the doctor doesn't know what is wrong with them. The diagnosis is outside the doctor's knowledge and, therefore, according to the doctor, doesn't exist. Women have gone for years with doctors who trivialized their physical complaints, ignored their symptoms, and labeled them neurotic and who were only convinced that the woman did indeed have a physical illness when *another doctor* diagnosed it. The women's own descriptions and reports were not accepted as real.

Women are looking for a health care system that values us, respects us, and gives us the opportunities to educate ourselves. We need the doctors to be a part of that education system—but only a part. We want a system where women are active participants, mentors, and advisors and where women can challenge, discuss, and change health care.

11

The Cost of Health Information

Most women want accurate, competent advice and realize that somehow, in some way, they must pay for it. Free information is always available: your mother gives it to you, your friends at work give it to you, total strangers on the elevator give it to you. There is free information on television, radio, and the Internet bulletin boards and at low cost in magazines and books. We are, in this information era, smothered in information. The trick seems to be in getting accurate, reliable information exactly when you want it at a price you can pay.

A Moral Right

Quality usually costs money; because we are conditioned to pay for this, we may accept the idea that we have no right to health information unless we *can* pay for it. It is at this point that our commitment to the free market system runs into trouble with our sense of compassion and fairness. A United Nations Unicef report released September 22, 1993, told us that 20% of American children and 10% of Canadian children live in poverty.[1] Does that mean they have no right to immunization that will prevent polio or to penicillin that will cure pneumonia? Shouldn't their broken legs be set? vision saved? heart defects operated on? Most women can't sanc-

tion a system that does not allow at least the children to have
medical care. If we feel morally compelled to see that children get
medical care, what do we feel about the rest of society? At what age
is health care *not* a moral right? And who decides this?

Insurance

Women in North America live under different systems of
payment for health information and medical care. Women in
Canada live under an almost 100% insurance plan where their
biggest concern is whether they will receive unnecessary treatments and surgeries simply because their insurance pays for it;
that they will be "cash cows" for a medical industry. In the United
States, many live without any insurance, praying every night for
health because they could not get treatment if they were sick.

"What do you do about medical insurance?" I asked a 42-
year-old single mother of two teenagers in Oregon.

"I stay healthy," she said.

She smiled at me as if that were all there was to say about an
impossible situation. She is not stupid. She built her own computer accounting business and now employs three people. She
understands costs, expenses, and contingencies. She is only telling
me that she has no way of dealing with medical bills. If one of her
family gets ill and needs medical care, she'll use all her assets to
pay for it and be left destitute. She simply hopes it won't happen.
If the new Oregon legislation that grants basic medical care to all
residents passes, she'll have some security. Otherwise, she hopes
that she is lucky and "stays healthy."

In Canada, the universal medicare system is threatened by
political opinions such as those of Ralph Klein, the Premier of
Alberta, who advocated user fees. Some Quebec politicians also
would like to see user fees introduced into the health care system so
that patients would pay for some of their care directly. Defenders of
Canada's universal system such as Greg Stoddart and Robert Evans,
authors of the report on user fees for the Premier's Council on

Health in Ontario, express the fears of many when they say that user fees will benefit the rich and create more hardship on the poor. Some attempts have been made to implement user fees. Seven doctors in British Columbia and several in Alberta tried it, though such fees are illegal under the Canada Health Act.[2] Laws are there to be tested, of course, for all kinds of reasons. Profiteers such as hospitals, clinics, and doctors who have technical equipment and expertise like the magnetic resonance imager (MRI) want to change laws of regulation and payment so that their high-demand services can make them more money. Then there are some idealists who see private enterprise as the only route to excellence in health care.

In the United States the private health care system is being revamped by the President, the First Lady, and Congress, who are trying, for reasons of compassion and cost efficiency, to provide for the 37 million Americans not covered by medical insurance. The goal of the bill presently before Congress is to guarantee comprehensive insurance coverage for all Americans by 1998.

We do not know yet what that means to a woman. Does it mean that she can have routine Pap smears paid for by insurance companies? Open-heart surgery? Renal dialysis? Vitamins? Massage therapy?

Such coverage looks like a glimpse of hope to the many who are presently without health care. Some are afraid that those presently without health care insurance will be forced into a substandard kind of care. Does that mean that a doctor will be assigned patients and patients will have no choice of doctor? Those who make a living in the health care system fear that they will be forced to take a government determined fee and make less money. These fears are speculative since we're not sure what proposals, if any, will become law.

The Canadian Way

It comes as a shock to Canadians to discover that many Americans envision Canadian health care as a system of dreary doctors' offices with bile-green peeling paint, hard chairs, and antique equipment; long lines of waiting patients; and substandard medicine. Canadians, generally, see their health care system as the best possible system, with modern hospitals; superb ambulance service; high-tech equipment; and comfortable, available doctors' offices as well as state-of-the-art drugs and treatments. Neither view is accurate.

A woman in Canada makes an appointment with the doctor of her choice, usually in her neighborhood, but she may go to any doctor she chooses. Occasionally, for special examinations, such as life insurance physical examinations, she is required to use a particular doctor, but she is expected to return to her own doctor for all other health care. A woman in the Canadian health care system goes through the process of accepting or rejecting the doctor's advice as she wishes. She can go to another doctor; she can ask for a referral to a specialist of her choice. She usually goes to the hospital that the doctor chooses since the doctor must have privileges at the hospital to admit her. If she wants a particular hospital, she has to choose a doctor who has privileges there. For all this, the provincial health insurance system is billed. All patients who are residents of the province have insurance. The insurance pays the doctor the same amount for each service no matter who the patient is. Occasionally, particularly when doctors are lobbying for an increase of fees, a small number of doctors will try to bill patients an extra amount directly. This government-insurer system works well: not only does the patient get the medical help she needs, but so do her sister and her daughter and her neighbor. Everyone has the same access to medical care.

It sounds wonderful, and it is—but it is not perfect. In spite of the available-to-all health care, the best Canadian medicine is concentrated in cities. Specialists live in areas of high-density population near universities and big hospitals. Canada is 1½ times as big as the United States, so distances between cities are great. If a woman needs to contact a specialist, she may have to travel to the big cities, which are almost all along the southern border. Travel may take days, as specialists' care is not available in most parts of the country. Rural health care may be competent, but women often have little choice if it is not. Women suspect that doctors' attitudes are shaped by their dependence on the insurance companies, and women worry that provincial governments and the medical industry are more concerned about cost efficiency than individual care. If 3 weeks of high radiation is more cost-effective than 6 weeks of lower radiation in the treatment of breast cancer, will the government only pay for 3 weeks even when 6 weeks may be a better treatment? How closely are doctors' recommendations aligned to government spending?

Most women are happy to have this universal medical plan. A family of three or more in British Columbia in 1994 that makes over $19,000 a year pays $72 a month for medical insurance. A single person pays $36. Those with life threatening diseases pay the same as those who are robustly healthy. There is a sliding scale of reduced payments related to yearly income until anyone who makes less than $11,000 a year gets free medical insurance. It is exactly the same medical insurance coverage whether the fee is $72 or nothing. It entitles you to the same benefits, the same services, the same doctors, hospitals, specialists, therapists, and treatments.[3] In Alberta, those over 65 pay no premiums, single adults under 65 pay $30 per month, and a family pays $60, although employers often look after this cost. No other provinces charge fees.

The British Columbia provincial health care system does not always pay for the services of a dentist or psychologist; the reason for these exclusions is, no doubt, safely hidden in some government archive. It will pay for a psychiatrist, who is an MD, but not for a psychologist, who is not. In general, any specialist, including a psychiatrist, must be recommended by a family doctor. So a woman must go to her doctor, get a referral to a specialist, and then go to the specialist. She may choose the specialist; doctors usually offer the names of more than one. Some people have additional insurance plans, usually with their places of employment, that cover dentists and psychologists. When I asked women if they had ever not been able to get medical care because they could not afford it, they answered "no;" they could always afford the care they wanted, with the exception of counselors, psychologists, or dentists.

It is a fair system that gives access to all, and generally it works very well. It is expensive and is paid for by taxes, but it is slightly less expensive than the U.S. health care system: according to 1990 statistics from the World Bank, Canadians spend 9.1% of their GNP on health care and the United States spends 12.7%.[4]

It has a few problems. Women find that they often are less demanding of their doctors because they are not paying them out of their pockets for the visit. If they were signing a check, some women would demand more answers. Women feel that doctors do not feel obligated to answer questions or respond to their needs because the doctor's first loyalty seems to be to the government health insurers. There is a sense that the doctors feel obligated to defend themselves only to the one who pays the fee.

Because they live in a market economy society in the rest of their lives, it is hard to adjust to a socialist system in health care, but women find that easier to live with than the idea of being without health care insurance or being without enough health care insurance to look after themselves and their families.

There is, of course, the frustration of not being able to buy elective surgery, experimental surgery, or treatment when you want it. Surgeries and treatments are usually done according to the severity of patient need. Of course, implicit in the idea of patient need is the administrator's value judgment about whose need is greater and whose quality of life is more worth preserving. There are occasionally scandals involving administrators of some programs who try to privately control their departments. The system is not always as fair as it first seems. For instance, in one *in vitro* fertilization lab in this country, the administrator refused to help lesbian couples have a child because he personally did not approve of them. I recall instances where the racial prejudice of a few doctors prevented some people from getting the services of a hospital. The system is designed to be fair, but the people who administrate it can prevent equal access to all.

Those with greater finances can make more choices outside the Canadian medical system. A woman waiting for surgery who wants it done immediately can pay to go to the United States and have it done there. Those who cannot afford that option have to wait their turn at home. This is a peculiar situation. On the one hand, Canadians have the security of a universal health care plan. On the other, they have the luxury of accessing expensive high-tech medical care that comes out of the American capitalist health system without having to pay for the education and development costs that such a system requires. American hospitals and doctors don't object to Canadian patients because Canadians are paying for the services. But the American taxpayers have contributed to that service in university educational subsidies for doctors and the maintenance of the hospitals in which the doctors work. I have seen no studies that show whether the amount of money a Canadian patient leaves in an American town is enough to offset their cost to the country.

In Canada, there is no one whose family finances need to be ruined by a health condition. Financial concerns around illness may be about loss of wages or loss of opportunities while ill but rarely about the cost of the care, with the exception of medications. Medications taken out of the hospital are not covered by all provincial medical plans, so the cost of drugs can be a problem, although drug prices are set by provincial pricing regulations.

A woman facing illness in Canada is worried about many things: finding good information, getting competent advice, finding a skillful surgeon if that is necessary, and staying in charge of her care; but she rarely worries about who is going to pay for the health care she receives. The governments worry, the doctors worry, the hospital administrators worry, but the patient expects to get the care she needs without concerns of cost.

Longer Life

According to the U.S. Health Care Financing Administration,[5] the United States spends $751,771 *million* on health care.

Canada, according to a calculation based on the GNP and the World Bank 9.1% designation, spends $45,690 million which is the rough equivalent of 33,840 million U.S. dollars.[6] The United States has approximately ten times the population of Canada; allowing for that difference, the United States spends 55% more than Canada does. In spite of all that money spent on health care, the increasing longevity in North America over the last 100 years has not been due to the increase in technology and treatment of illnesses but to the increased use of public health measures such as better hygiene, sanitation, and immunizations. Good water and sewer facilities equal better health. These undramatic and unromantic measures are cost-effective in terms of human life. We can be dazzled by the wonder of our high-tech medicine: the way doctors can attached a severed arm, replace a kidney, and repair a heart. But our most efficient health measures in terms of longevity and disease prevention are in the field of basic public health.

Community health is a government responsibility in both countries. In Canada, children's immunizations are free. Public health nurses give nutritional advice and help parents with early childhood illnesses and conditions. The emphasis on free, available health care for children results in an increase in the rate of infant survival and the increased health of children. After all, the cost of preventing polio is a good deal less than the cost of treating it. The cost of one dose of injectable polio vaccine in my Vancouver area is $5.84. A child needs four doses in his or her life, which is $24.96. The cost of treating polio, with doctors' fees, nurses' wages, hospital costs, intensive care equipment, and the care during convalescence, is more than a thousand times that. The funds for those measures ultimately come from the same pocket—the taxpayers'—either directly in private insurance as in the United States or indirectly in taxes in Canada.

Many states and counties in the United States are well aware of the importance of public health measures and try, often successfully, to create at least small areas of socialized medicine in their communities so that all children have clean water, adequate sanitation in their homes, and free immunizations. When I worked in the state of Washington 30 years ago, county health departments promoted immunization and still do so. Public health nurses throughout the country are very concerned about the number of babies still not immunized and about the need to educate women and promote health care information and to help women gain greater competence in using health information. Many county and city governments have taken the responsibility for health care in ways similar to the Canadian government. Even hospitals are supposed to be committed to health care for all. I saw a sign in a hospital in Kentucky that said that all patients would be treated regardless of their ability to pay. The chief operations officer of that hospital told me that sign was supposed to be displayed in all hospitals in America. While this Kentucky hospital did accept everyone, we know that in other hospitals the sign is a fanciful ideal. People are turned away because they can't pay; they are asked to leave their hospital beds when their insurance runs out; they are denied treatment and care when their insurance is not adequate. In most areas, private medical insurance is an important component of good medical advice and good medical care.

Canadians, on the other hand, know that insurance is rarely a problem for them. Everyone is entitled to insurance coverage; therefore, care is rarely decided on the basis of adequate or inadequate insurance. At the same time, Canadians know that they can be lost in the grand plan of physicians, hospitals, and government insurance providers when treatment and delivery of services may be decided on the basis of the greatest good for the greatest number instead of the needs of this patient. Women who want microsurgery for the removal of gallstones don't want to be told that this hospital and this doctor are set up to do surgery the old way and therefore they must have it the old way. If a women is aware of the different surgical techniques, she can ask for another doctor and another hospital where microsurgery is done, but she needs to be aware of her options. Neither the doctors nor the hospitals seem to feel any obligation to give her a choice. Because hospitals are usually government financed and not private, there seems to be little competition for excellence in care, service, and comfort. Hospitals do not market their services to attract customers and do not compete for patients the way they do in the United States.

Doctors and hospital staffs in Canada are fond of blaming the amorphous government for their own mistakes. One woman heard from her daughter's doctor that the reason he delayed the Cesarean section was that the government had said that he was doing too many cesareans, so he had decided to stop for the rest of the month. She said she couldn't remember being so angry and told him:

> Grow up and get real! You're responsible for your own decisions. When you can sit for 20 hours with your asshole dilated 10 centimeters, you can make decisions like that.

He did the cesarean. It's that kind of reasoning that scares us.

Still, it is hard for hospital staff to work in situations where the government will not pay for enough staff members, demands justification of minute expenses, and sometimes ignores safety standards. It seems to women that they are pawns in a giant medical game that benefits doctors, governments, and insurance companies and that the only way for them to get individual attention is to scream for it.

The difficulty in comparing the United States with Canada lies in the great variety of services and medical accessibility in different parts of the United States. Some state governments and some county governments provide public health measures that are second to none in the world, but some do not. There is unequal access to medical care; insurance companies are allowed to dictate who should get medical care and who should not, and the sick, the handicapped, and the infirm are often abandoned. The actual state of health care in communities across the country is a patchwork of superb and mediocre, competent and substandard.

The Kentucky Experience

In 1925, in Wendover, Kentucky, Mary Breckenridge, a nurse midwife trained in England, experienced in health delivery in postwar France, and well-connected to endowment funds and wealthy donors, started the Frontier Nursing Service to answer the needs of mothers and children in the Appalachian hill country. Too poor a district to attract physicians, this hill country has enthusiastically supported the health service provided by its highly educated nurse practitioners and nurse midwives and its home health workers. Since then, this compassionate and people-responsive group of women has provided excellent care not only to mothers and children but to the whole population. A nurse practitioner with a Masters of Science in Nursing degree works out of a rural clinic. She does routine and essential diagnosis and recommends treatment. She is in line to receive prescription writing privileges (Kentucky will be the 44th state to create this legislation) and soon will be able to give even more treatments. She refers to such specialists as internists, pediatricians, surgeons, and midwives. No one in this district is turned away or has their medical care limited because of poverty. What Medicare and Medicaid do not pay for, private donors do. I saw a poor mountain man with a pacemaker and a retarded, poor woman in her own home with a wheelchair and daily home health service. The expectation of the people in this community is that when medical care is needed, it is given.

In areas where there is little money to be made by doctors, such as rural Kentucky or the slums of the inner cities, nurse midwives and nurse practitioners are establishing a reliable, competent health delivery service. Also, in some sophisticated areas nurse practitioners are demanded by patients because they are seen as knowledgeable, competent, practical, and compassionate. They charge approximately 85% of a general practitioner's fee. For these reasons, nurse practitioners are often preferred by patients for initial primary care.

Doctors tend to see patients as physical entities, separate from work, their family, and community. They also tend to see the patients' bodies as divided into separate systems (circulation, digestive, reproductive), so the doctor may investigate your stomach ulcer while ignoring your menstrual problems—as if one system was totally unrelated to the other. This concentration on the part of physicians may create experts in certain areas of the body, but it makes patients feel as if they are a collection of parts. This goes against most women's understanding of their bodies and makes it difficult for them to talk to the doctor or accept that the doctor understands or can advise them on their problem.

Nurses are often better able to understand the health problem from the point of view of the patient. They have been taught to value compassion and patient-centered care, and they are often out in the community in patients' homes, where they can see the problems.

A nurse I know told a doctor after a postpartum visit:

> There's no sense in nagging me to teach breast-feeding to that mother until I get the propane leak fixed in the house. If everyone in there is alive tomorrow and not blown into the sky, I'll teach breast-feeding.

Nurses seem able to see the patient in the social context of their lives, to see what makes accepting medical advice difficult, what would help, what is possible, what is most important to the patient at this moment.

Nurse practitioners seem to be more a part of their community, more "of the people" than doctors. Kay, a nurse practitioner in the hills of Kentucky, told me:

> When you live in the community, people see you and they learn to trust you. They know that you are a person just like they are and they can tell you care about them. In a way, they are willing to give you too much trust. They say "My doctor is a practitioner." I say, "I'm not a doctor. I'm a nurse practitioner." And they say, "Yeah, well you doctor me." I think the doctors hear that and shudder.

The Lure of a Specialty

There is a movement among physicians in the United States to become more specialized. More and more doctors are gravitating to specialties and leaving general practice. There are family practice specialties as well, but doctors tell me that because there are many lawsuits and because the malpractice insurance is high, they prefer to be in a specialty where they have limited responsibilities and high fees with which to pay their insurance premiums. An anesthesiologist in Oregon in 1993 paid $79,000 for one year's insurance, a substantial reason to be in a position to charge high fees. In some areas this move to specialties is leaving the space for nurse practitioners to establish a practice. Nurse practitioners are not as likely to be sued as are physicians, not only because nurse practitioners communicate better with their patients and are seen to be more understanding and less adversarial, but also because they are not perceived as being wealthy. If nurse practitioners increase their fees to the level of physicians, that perception may change.

Women Advisors

Women generally prefer to go to women advisors. They feel safer, more likely to be heard, less likely to be abused. Having said that, I have noticed that the women I interviewed did not consider women physicians any more likely to listen and be compassionate than male physicians. Kate, the forthright critic of doctors, said:

> Women are taught in the same system as men. Just because you're seeing a female doesn't mean you're getting better care.

The preference for women is for women who are not doctors. That makes a nurse practitioner, if she can maintain the spiritual and emotional understanding that has been part of her practice in the past, the choice most likely to satisfy women patients.

A New System

The Canadian system of universal access to health care and the U.S. system of differing access to health care rely on the doctor as the center of the health delivery system and the central focus of health information. Women in both countries are frustrated with that and are making efforts to change it.

While Canadian women seem to be putting their energies into national women's information services, women's center data sharing, and public health or community-financed information centers, American women are, with the innovative and intrepid spirit that characterizes Americans, setting up private information and women-centered services. The National Women's Health Network in Washington, DC, is a private organization dedicated to providing women with information about their health. There is an annual membership fee that pays for a newsletter. The same is true of many private women's centers throughout the country. These grassroots organizations are vital in bringing the concerns of women to the attention of the medical community. They are also vital in raising the consciousness of women about their own problems and showing women that the concerns they thought were private and isolated may well be of national interest. This politicizing of private concerns is what creates public awareness and often motivates change. It has tremendous potential for creating a new vision of women's health. The new information network on computers will make a national voice more possible.

By communicating with each other and debating issues and problems such as unnecessary hysterectomies, unnecessary estrogen replacement therapy, and the use of questionable drugs such as Depo-Provera, women can protect themselves from the avaricious and marauding profiteering of the medical industry.

Many women who are educated, used to researching problems, aware of communication links, and able to evaluate information can use the many resources throughout our two countries. But women who are used to getting information by word of mouth, who trust information only when they trust the information giver—and that is most women—want a *person* from whom they can get information. It may be that the answer to getting good health information lies in establishing reliable health information centers in communities where free information is given the way it is in public libraries. If women want this service badly enough, we will find ways in the Canadian system and in the United States to get the funding to adapt what already exists to include a health information service, or we will create one. Such centers could have on-line data information and a library of books and videos and could be staffed with nurses and trained laywomen who can respond individually to women's health concerns. In this way, in both countries, we may be able to develop a source of information that is independent of the medical and drug industry, that is responsive to women, and that can include holistic and alternative medicine that may benefit women. It could also give women a place to exchange ideas, validate concerns, and get support. Women need other women who can hear them.

12

Healing in Different Cultures

I found it impossible to study all the cultures that make up my community of Vancouver, Canada. I live in a cosmopolitan, urban community of Chinese, Japanese, Caucasian, Vietnamese, Punjabi, aboriginal, and black people, among others. I have not lived in these distinct communities, and it would take several lifetimes to be truly knowledgeable about all of them. Subcultures and blends of cultures mix and move through the larger North American society: Scottish with Hispanic, French Canadian with Inuit, Southern Creole with black, and Polish, Hungarian, and Finnish with Irish. We have also, after several generations, a hardy brand of American and Canadian culture that defies definition.

Different Health Systems

All of us are used to Western medicine—the advertising, the drugs, the doctor-knows-best attitude, and the total reliance on a doctor's opinion by insurance companies—so it is difficult to appreciate a different view as valid. All cultures give a kind of obvious deference to the great god of Western technological medicine, but underneath that often lies a strong belief in a different system. Enduring cultural practices blossom in many pockets of North America. Aboriginal people such as the Navajos retained their midwives while the rest of the country outlawed them. They managed to hold onto a women-centered, women-managed, safe, and effective system of birthing, while the rest of the country opted for a doctor-centered medical experience. It is only recently that midwives have been accepted back into the dominant white culture, not because the aboriginal philosophy forced a change or because patients wanted midwives, but because midwives cost less than doctors. At least the practice of midwifery lasted on the reservations and in the Appalachian mountains, allowing midwifery to spread to the rest of the country when the economic climate permitted.

I tried to experience the medicine of other cultures—cultures other than my white, Scottish-English-Irish Western medical culture. There is a large Chinese community around me, so I made three appointments with a Chinese Qi Gong doctor and had three treatments that consisted of lying on a table fully clothed while the doctor shaped air with his hands and spoke to himself in his own language. While I do not know what effect this may have had on my body, I found the experience relaxing and nonthreatening. It left me feeling as if my body could handle any problem it encountered. The "master," according to his wife who spoke English, was trying to balance my qi (chi) so that my body would be healthy.

Cultural Meaning

An isolated experience of medicine from a different culture is probably useless. Such medicine exists in a web of meaning that takes years of study and exposure or a familial acceptance since birth. A cultural community gives meaning to certain kinds of medical treatment within that community, creating a "system" of treatment that cannot be separated from the culture. Perhaps it is enough to know that other systems of health and healing exist.

While I could experience a treatment from a practitioner in another medical system, I couldn't receive the meaning from the treatment the way a woman of that culture could. It is hard to tell how the effects of the treatment differ, but I can guess that it would certainly involve the 30% placebo or "good faith effect." No doubt many treatments remain the same: an antacid given by a Chinese herbalist may exact the same effect on the body as an antacid given by a Western MD. Certain aspects of treatment by different cultures may, on examination, prove to have the same biochemical basis as treatments of Western medicine. Still, it is important to look at the big differences, the ways in which other cultures view health and disease, to try to discover if other cultures offer a healthier way of life, a more practical useful response to illness. Maybe there is something better than Western medicine?

The Nature of Disease

Cultures differ in their concepts of health and disease. Western medicine describes the body as a battleground where disease is an invader that must be fought. Other cultures, such as the Chinese and many aboriginal cultures, see the body as a healthy part of the earth that must maintain a balance with nature. We are beginning to understand this better when we work to protect our ozone layer and maintain our rain forests, but we don't seem to be quite ready to see our individual bodies as existing in a state of harmony. The increased interest in immunology may be the way Western medicine tries to understand harmony and balance, attributing to the immune system a regulatory function, a balancing function, an intelligence, and a mythology: "the immune system is a map drawn to guide recognition and misrecognition of self."[1]

This seems a concept more familiar to Chinese medicine than to Western medicine. Perhaps we are beginning to assimilate other cultures' beliefs.

We are taught in Western medical school to be aware of the difference in cultural attitudes to medicine. Usually, this urge to be aware is underscored by an arrogant belief in Western superiority. Rarely are medical students taught to evaluate the cultural practices of their patients, to *learn* from them, and to *change* to accommodate them.

Cultural Hubris

In an urban center near Vancouver, Canada, a hospital has posted "Husbands and Grandmothers Only" signs in their maternity ward. The hospital is anxious to restrain the visitors of their East Indian patients whose culture celebrates the birth of a baby with visits from many relatives and friends. Here, at this hospital, the East Indian cultural community is required to conform to the standards of the hospital and to reflect the dominant Anglo-Saxon culture that decrees the birth of a baby to be a clinical process involving the mother, the child, and the hospital—and, possibly, the father. Happily, most families ignore the rules and invade the hospital, wearing saris like brightly colored birds and flocking around the new mother with chatter and good wishes. "Every event in your life is a family celebration," a young East Indian woman told me. She wears Western clothes except for feasts and parties, has a Western university education, a responsible job in a large insurance firm, eats at McDonald's occasionally, and watches Hollywood movies. "Sometimes, I'd like a little more privacy, but, for the most part, being surrounded by love and concern is only good for me."

Is there a relationship between the lonely North American experience of childbirth and incidence of postpartum panic? Common sense would tell us that the East Indian example, where new mothers are surrounded by grandmothers, mothers-in-law, sisters, and aunts who share in child care and with whom they can discuss experiences, should contribute to a happier adjustment to motherhood than the isolated regimen that is recommended by the hospital. In spite of this common sense, the hospital staff is trying to force the East Indian community to change to the less effective North American way. Our culture shows an amazing arrogance.

Ayurveda

East Indian people may consult trusted folk medical practitioners who practice Ayurveda if they have an Ayurveda doctor in their area. This system of medicine revolves around a belief in a life force that regulates the body and that must be kept in daily balance. A combination of foods, herbs, meditation, and regular habits results in a balance that promotes health and healing.

Chinese Medicine

My friend Judith lived with me for a few months while she received treatment for breast cancer in our city. She followed the radiation, antiestrogen regimen of Western medicine, but she also allowed a Chinese doctor to treat her affected breast with Qi Gong—the hands-above-the-body treatment. She said that the breast felt harder immediately after the treatment. When I palpated it, it *did* feel harder. She believed she was assisting her body to deal with the cancer by using the Chinese medicine, but she continued using Western medicine.

She also consulted another Chinese doctor who held a Western medical degree. He prescribed herbs that would help "boost" her immune system and help restore harmony and balance in her body. He also prescribed "Women's Precious Pills," which were supposed to counteract some of the side effects of the antiestrogen Western drugs she was taking. We shopped for her treatment in the Chinese district of the city in a store lined with jars and bins containing herbs and plants. Obviously, a whole community of people use a distinct system of medicine here. A whole community shopped and argued and discussed ailments and ambitions and based their ideas of disease and health on a philosophy that was different from mine.

Judith reported to me after her visit to the Chinese medical doctor that he believed cancer to be always in our bodies and that problems occurred when the immune system was weakened. His efforts were directed toward improving the immune system, not in "killing" the cancer. To that end she was prescribed and took pills and plants. When she thought of the radiation, surgery, and chemotherapy that had first been recommended to her by Western medical doctors, she said, "The choice with them [the Western doctors] was to be fried, cut up, or poisoned. Chinese medicine looks a lot more attractive. It seems to respect your body's ability to look after itself." While she appreciated the Chinese ways and used them, she did not have faith in them alone and had radiation treatment. Chinese practitioners do not suggest that their patient take only their medicine. They advise continuing the cancer treatment prescribed by Western doctors. They do not have the solution for cancer or AIDS.

I interviewed a Chinese doctor, Dr. Y. Lee, who had an office at the back of his herb store. He sat relaxed at his desk while the smells of a thousand herbs wafted around us:

> I don't treat cancer alone. I work only as a complementary physician to the Western doctors in those cases. I recommend my patients use the radiation and chemicals the Western medicine advises, but I add herbs to help the body maintain its strength. Other than cancer, AIDS, and diabetes, I diagnose and treat everything else.

Dr. Lee had studied 5 years of Western medicine in China as well as Chinese herbal medicine through continuing education. He is a certified member of the provincial Acupuncture Association. He told me that there were three types of Chinese doctors: traditional doctors who studied 5 to 6 years, Western medical doctors who studied 5 years, and medical doctors practicing both Western and traditional medicine who studied 5 years of Western medicine with additional continuing education in Chinese medicine. I asked him how he got the information he needed from his patients in order to diagnose, since he did not do physical examinations or tests. "I get it in stories," he told me. "They tell me what's wrong in stories."

Stories

I thought how wonderful it would be to give a medical advisor the *story* of a problem. Most women understand their illness in stories such as, "I woke up yesterday burning with a fever and it seemed to get worse after lunch until I wanted to take off all my clothes and lie on the cement. I had to cancel my interviews and I was so tired that night I couldn't even eat supper and I'm worse today. I had to cancel all my work for today, and what's that going to do to my bills at the end of the month?" They tell the story of their illness this way rather than giving the doctor a list of facts, such as "My fever is 100°F and has been that high the last 6 hours; I have fatigue and no appetite."

Western doctors pick out facts from the patient's narrative and write them down in a list of symptoms: "Fever, 100°F last 6 hours. Fatigue. Anorexia." They ignore the story, the context in which the symptoms exist. While I expect there are incompetent, impatient Chinese doctors, the process described by Dr. Lee of listening to his patients seemed to allow the meaning of the illness to influence the diagnosis.

The Promotoras

The *promotoras* are indigenous healers in the Mexican-American communities of the southwestern United States. They practice a folk medicine that pays attention to the meaning of illness in the community. Public health nurses in these communities have learned to work with the *promotoras*, to adjust treatments and health information so that it is acceptable to the people they serve.

In the poorer area of Tucson, Arizona, four women who work as health unit aides told me that they would like to blend their health information with the beliefs of the culture they serve. One worker told me:

> What we really need is a black health nurse for the black people and a Hispanic nurse for the Hispanic people and a native nurse for the native people. We need *real* examples and *real* people the patients can talk to.

Perhaps one of the most useful tools of folk medical practitioners is the fact that they are part of the indigenous community.

Aboriginal Medicine

The aboriginal culture was the only culture that allowed me some long-term exposure because I had friends in that culture and had worked in aboriginal communities and because I am related to aboriginal people. I had heard of the healing circle, the concept that each person is a composite of mental, spiritual, emotional, and physical entities and that all must be in balance for healthy living to be possible. Western medicine has strongly overlaid this traditional concept with the conviction that folk medicine was pagan and ignorant and Western medicine was morally superior and correct. Aboriginal people have struggled for years to adapt to a kind of medicine that does not suit them and in which they are second-class citizens.

I knew that access to good health information was different for women in aboriginal communities, but I wanted to know how these women saw the differences. I remember the difficulties that the women in Native Indian communities had with the health care system when I worked as a public health nurse in the Cariboo country of British Columbia, but I didn't go back there to do my research. I went further north.

In 1991, I lived for a week with an Inuit family in Canada north of the Arctic Circle in a small community on Baffin Island.

The family who boarded me was a traditional family. The father was a hunter and the mother cut up the meat and sewed the caribou hides into clothing. They spoke no English, although the mother and two of the children understood it, so the teenage daughter acted as my interpreter. The whole family was warm, accepting, and wonderfully kind. After a few days with this family, the women of the community realized that I was a nurse as well as a writer and came to me with their health questions.

One woman had lost a son to Reye's syndrome 6 years earlier. She told me that the doctors had told her that her older son might also die of Reye's syndrome. She wanted to know if there was anything she could do to prevent it. I was appalled and couldn't speak for a moment. Her son was not in any more danger than anyone else. This women had carried this unnecessary fear for her surviving son in her heart for years. I tried to control my anger against a careless health practitioner who had allowed her to suffer like this. I carefully explained to her the nature of Reye's syndrome, the need for a certain kind of virus infection, the need to have the virus *and* aspirin. If she did not give her son aspirin, he would not get Reye's syndrome. I explained the difference between aspirin and acetaminophen (Tylenol).

She told me that when her late son had first become ill she had taken him to the nursing station. The nurse gave him aspirin and told her to continue it. I knew that the medical profession had not been giving aspirin to children for fevers for 20 years because of the danger of Reye's syndrome. This nurse gave bad advice and the boy died. I returned to my little bedroom in the house on the beach later that night and stared out at the water of the bay. It was midnight; the sun was still giving us daylight; the children were playing under my window; the sled dogs were barking; it was still, tranquil, and beautiful. I thought of the casual cruelty this woman had endured. I tried to deal with the rage that was shaking me. How many more women had been treated like this? *Were* being treated like this? How many times had this kind of pain been casually tossed out to women like Miari?

The women of this remote community asked me quietly about their mothers, their sisters, their friends. They had one information source, the staff of the Red Cross Hospital and Clinic consisting of a *qulunaat* (white) nurse and visiting doctors. If the women of the community could not get information from the staff, if the staff person was incompetent, abusive, or even just aloof, they were reluctant to ask questions and had no other source of information. They had telephones, so they could phone "outside" for information, but this is a community that has few people with skills in finding information in the mainstream world of telephones, libraries, faxes, and computers. The people felt awkward in the world of books, paper, and reports, particularly materials written in English, and there were few books of information in Inuktituk because theirs is primarily an oral language.

Many of the women did not speak or read the language of the health care givers, so the language was difficult for them to understand. Their culture also accustomed them to a language more slowly paced than that of the health care givers: their verbal interchange gives significance to silence and pauses that allow the other person to give a sign of acceptance. There is a comforting emotional pace to their conversation. The heath care workers did not fit into the rhythms of the indigenous community in language or culture and so the women did not ask questions or search for more answers with these workers.

Further south in the Northwest Territories, I spent 8 days in Yellowknife. I slept on the floor of the women's center, ate my meals with the staff and visitors, and traveled out "on the land" to drink tea with Dene (aboriginal) women in their tents, listening to women speak about their experiences in their communities and in this part of the country. The Dene women told me that they struggle with language barriers. Even if their English is excellent, it is usually their second language, and they still must deal with medical jargon. Often their health care is given, they told me, in a perfunctory and casual way. They see this as a problem of racial prejudice, a conviction of caregivers that their white race is *de facto* superior. Their inability to communicate, demand choice, or verbally defend themselves results in misdiagnosis, neglect, lack of explanations, erroneous suppositions, and abuse and the subsequent mistrust of the medical profession.

In Yellowknife, the doctors in the hospital were performing abortions in 1992 without anesthetic and often making pejorative remarks while they were doing this, such as, "Well, this really hurt, didn't it? Let that be a lesson before you get yourself into this situation again."[2] The aboriginal women felt this had a racial basis, although nonaboriginal women were getting the same horrendous treatment. Nonaboriginal women banded with the aboriginal women as did the feminists with the antiabortionists to protest this abuse of women. The doctors were required to provide anesthetic.

The aboriginal women also feel vulnerable in their small communities when there is only one doctor. If he or she is abusive to patients, they have few options: they can travel to another community to seek other medical help (if they can afford to), they can accept the abuse (which many do), they can have a witness stay with them in the doctor's office, or they can avoid medical treatment altogether. Sometimes the medical insurance plan will not pay for women to travel to another center for advice. For instance, there is only one gynecologist in Yellowknife, a man. If a patient prefers a female gynecologist, she must pay her own travel expense to go to another center, probably Edmonton, which is 500 miles away.

Many women in the north have been sexually abused. I heard story after story from the women. The staff of the women's organizations are well aware that sexual abuse of boys, girls, and women is widespread. They see it as a community problem of both men and women.

I sat in a restaurant late in the evening with a worker from the Women's Center who had, at 10 PM, just finished for the day. She said:

Sexual abuse is endemic here. There were two girls in the graduation class of the high school last year who were *not* abused. The boys get it as well when they are young. It's a product of oppression and poverty and the ripping away of the old social values. It's so prevalent that the justice system is useless. You can't jail a whole community. One 15-year-old girl was charged last year with abusing a young boy. It turned out that she had been abused by 15 of the local men, including the Catholic priest. Sexual abuse is a social problem that goes deep. The women are meeting about it now, talking about it, setting up healing circles, trying to deal with it, but the men aren't ready to face it yet.

Sexual abuse seems to be at the root of addictions, alcoholism, violence, and school dropouts. It seems related to the hopelessness of the life in small northern communities made worse by the Christian religions that disbanded the social contracts and disciplines of the aboriginal people, their rituals, and their healing ways. The aboriginal people are slowly trying to reclaim their culture so that abuse will move outside the norm.

Some of the old ways survived. Because the aboriginal tradition was an oral one, it was not completely destroyed by the missionaries. "If we'd had a written culture," one women told me, "the priests would have burned it." An oral culture survived, generation after generation, not strongly, sometimes only tentatively, but in many areas it did survive.

The Healing Circle

While most people talk about the healing circle as a personal philosophy of health and wellness, Dr. Judith Bartlett, an energetic aboriginal physician and Medical Director of Health and Welfare, Canada, in Winnipeg, Manitoba, talked about the possibilities of redesigning the medical system to suit the "Indian Way." The potential for this idea is enormous. She emphasized that the design for a health organization using the healing circle as a model is not a proprietary concept. Anyone who wants to can use it. The community of native people she works with are willing to share the idea.

Dr. Bartlett suggested that the regions be divided into north, south, east, and west and that representatives from each area serve on a committee for a period of 2 years. After that time the representatives would change, the wheel would shift, and new representatives would meet and carry on the work. This would prevent a hierarchy from establishing itself and provide for fresh perspectives. Each area would always send, in addition to the representatives from various disciplines and organizations, a young person and an elder. This would keep the committees grounded in the realities of the community.

Inside the wide circle is a smaller circle that represents the committee of the larger circle, which again changes every 2 years. This shifting, flexible, representative model could well replace the directive, hierarchical model now typical of health organizations. The healing circle is a concept of health care that is practiced in many aboriginal communities including Pascela Yaqui community in southeastern Arizona. A public health nursing supervisor for that community told me that they have respected medicine women who still practice but that it takes years to be knowledgeable enough to be a medicine women. She said:

> It's too bad, but I don't think we'll have medicine women for very long because they are old now. The young women don't want to study for so long; there is so much to learn. Soon there will be no one who can take over the medicine women's job.

This supervisor had a university degree in nursing; she had chosen the Western medical model over the traditional, yet she had not totally abandoned the old ways and was looking for more education in traditional herbs and medicine.

First Nations Women and Wellness

To work toward a concept of wellness, 700 women met at the First Nations Conference on Women and Wellness in Vancouver, Canada, in February 1993. Similar conferences take place in dif-

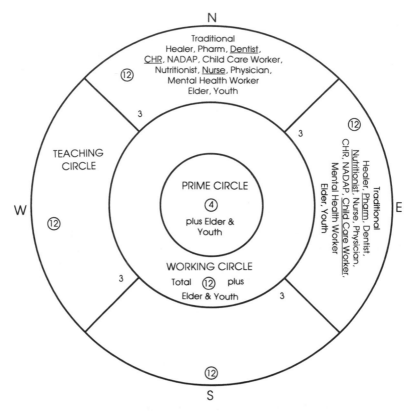

Drawing of the model of the Healing Circle.

ferent areas in the United States. I was one of six or seven white women attending. There were no acts of exclusion, no prejudiced remarks, no body language rejecting me, but I looked much different from the majority and I noticed it. It was a strong emotional experience, one that native women experience often. The women met to discuss their problems with health, with traditional medicine, with Western medicine, and with addictions and alcoholism.

They discussed the philosophy of the healing circle, the four parts of wellness—mental, emotional, spiritual, and physical—that must be in balance to achieve health. They talked about the pain, the oppression, the abuse, and the poverty; the promise of the future; and the path to self-sufficiency and health.

There are many women who have knowledge of traditional aboriginal medicine—the herbs and potions that have been useful for centuries to promote health and cure illness—who also have achieved a university degree in health sciences, including nursing, and who combine their traditional ways with Western medicine. These women are able to evaluate the traditional medicine and use it. After all, if a poultice is hypotonic (concentrated) and bacteriostatic (kills bacteria), it doesn't matter if the ingredients come from a tree or the drug store; they use their Western medical knowledge to accept aboriginal medicine. These women are more comprehensive in their health care than strictly Western-trained nurses and are therefore more likely to affect the health of the communities in which they work. They are more inclined to place ancient ritual in a positive psychosocial context and to encourage their patients to use what is practical. The cedar boughs in the hospital room represent health and healing and may *promote* health and healing in the mind and body of the patient. They may also promote a change in attitude in the hospital staff if they understand that the cedar is hanging in the room to promote healing and not just to "look pretty." The Western medical sanction of traditional healing is a positive change from the missionary's condemnation of pagan ways and is doing much to encourage healing in aboriginal communities. Nurses and doctors who are aware of and who encourage many of the old ways are often able to understand the social context of illness and the role illness and health play in the community.

Responsibility for Health

Aboriginal people's recent experience with the health care system has taught unhealthy reliance on Western medicine. The

Western model of health care encouraged giving up individual responsibility and assigning care and health to the nurse or doctor: if you are sick, get the nurse to "fix" you. More culturally attuned medical staff members are becoming aware of the need to reassign responsibility for health back to the patient, back to the community. Dr. Bartlett said:

> The people think that the doctor and the nurse and the health clinic own the disease and that it is their job to get rid of it. We have to change this so the people realize they are in charge of their own health.

Communities are beginning to understand that the responsibility for health care rests with the whole community and that the solution to health problems lies with the people. Nothing else will work. Thankfully, some tribal administrators and government officials are also beginning to see that change must come from the inside.

There is increased understanding in the public that the aboriginal ways may have benefits to all people. Western medical people are starting to pay more attention to other aspects of the healing circles, giving more credence to the mental and emotional aspects of life as components of illness. Doctors are beginning to realize that it is perhaps impossible to treat the physical symptoms of anorexia until the individual has healed the spiritual wounds caused by the sexual abuse in their past. Doctors treating cancer now are asking if their patients are living with anger. Western medicine is beginning to see the necessity of addressing the emotional life of the patient before the treatment can make a difference.

Women as Healers

The women I met at the First Nations Conference are determined to set up a system of health care and health information that uses the advice of their elders and the ancient herbs and potions along with Western medicine. They are trying to strengthen women's position of healers in the communities and to get support for the concept of the healing circle, where a balanced life supports health and healing. They see commitment, concern, and consensus as the tools of change.

The Importance of Culture

Culture creates differences in how healers are viewed by a community, how healers view themselves, the meaning of illness and health, the meaning of treatment and medications, and the compliance or noncompliance of the patients with the health care worker's advice.

To assume that Anglo-Saxon Western health care is universally and constantly superior to the health care of other cultures is blind and foolish and destined to condemn us to what we have. Healing comes from the culture the way scent comes from a flower, intrinsically bound and recognizable. To deny the contribution of culture to healing is to ignore the context in which health care is given, the web of meaning culture gives to the body, illness, the body's place in the community, the place of disease in the community, and the necessity of that community. To try to ignore all this is to try to grow flowers without leaves, stems, or roots. Healing is nestled in an interdependent environment of individual and community, beliefs and science. Perhaps we must understand the meaning it has in other cultures before we can understand the meaning it has in our own.

13

Finding Health Information

Ask and you shall receive. The just-give-it-to-me-straight-and-give-it-to-me-now attitude of Pat, the energetic, confident mother of two, seems to get amazing results. She says she wants to know, and, with repeated questions and increasingly complex answers, she does eventually find out. One of the best ways to get health information is to have the attitude that we have a right to that information and to believe that we can find it. We don't necessarily have to be belligerent, abrasive, or rude. Our style may be politely firm, sweetly tenacious, softly persistent, or cooly angry; we all develop our own style. Many women have been conditioned to wait to be told information and to trust that they will be given any information they need. What is obvious is that, in the medical industry, a passive attitude gets you nothing. Asking questions is the path to information. Finding information requires determination, conviction that we have a right to it, and perseverance. Attitude is important.

The Information Age

We read in magazine articles and hear on the radio and television that we are living in the "information age" or, more recently, the "multimedia information highway age." We are bombarded with information we often do not want—flyers, junk mail, telemarketing, and even fax junk—and so find it doubly frustrating not to be able to get the information we *do* want.

We need to look at the health care system as an industry made up of many components, capable of being useful to us but designed to serve itself and its practitioners. Health information is one of the components of the industry that is seen by some practitioners as a marketable commodity. They sell information. If we understand that, we can look for information from someone who does not expect to be paid for each bit of information but who receives a salary independent of how much information they give. Librarians usually work in this way as do community health nurses or doctors who work for salary. We also may get the information on a fee-for-service basis when we offer to pay for it. There are exceptional practitioners who offer advice regardless of monetary return. They may bill you for a 10-minute consultation and give you 20 minutes, but most will give you only as much as their billable time allows.

Industry Roles

Women who understand the role the health care practitioner plays in the medical industry, women who make demands of their practitioner within that role and who have no other expectations of him or her usually get what they ask for. In order to have this method produce results, we need a clear idea of the roles of different health consultants—doctors, nurses, physiotherapists, and pharmacists—in our system of health information. We need to understand what the doctor and the specialist are supposed to know and then ask each for their advice. We need to ask a dietician for information on food, not our doctor, and the pharmacist for information on drug dosages and side effects, not the dietician. That way we limit our questions to the specific area of expertise of each health professional. This means that there is no one practitioner who can direct and manage our care. We have to stay in charge. Many women do not take the time to understand what each health care professional can tell them and what they can't. Few women have Pat's confidence that they have the right to any information they want.

Film

At the Women's Health Centre in Vancouver, Canada, a six-minute video that every patient must view instructs the viewer on how to present herself to a doctor, what she can expect, and how to ask questions. It tells women to ask questions of their doctor and expect answers and gives the viewer some examples of ways to do this. The information is presented in a lecture form and probably will not inspire many women to change their ideas of a doctor–patient interview. It is not a multimedia, interactive, dynamic learning tool, but it is, at least, a small effort to give the patient the right to make changes.

Other centers have videos or pamphlets that give patients information on what they can expect from the clinic or center. An introductory video helps the user of the center understand the limits of the service. It also gives the patients confidence to ask for the services the video has led them to expect.

An introductory film in a doctor's office can create a better understanding of the limits of the doctor's services and, simultaneously, create confidence in the patient about her right to ask for the services the video tells her are available there. The patient assumes that if the video is in the doctor's office, the doctor knows what the video is saying and approves of it. The patient then can expect the doctor to fulfill the promises the video made—that the patient will be heard, respected, and informed.

Health resource centers often have videos on different diseases and conditions. Libraries also may have such videos. Associations organized around certain diseases are good sources of health ideas. Check the endorsements in the video credits to find out *who* approved this information. If this video on healthy living is sponsored by a tobacco company, you might expect there would be little emphasis on the dangers of smoking, even though lung cancer is a threat to many women. If the information in the video is not accurate, it still can give the viewer a starting point in her search for information. She can check with other sources and educate herself. Perhaps virtual reality experiences will help educate us about health and healing in a more dramatic and understandable way than books and videos. The next 10 years may bring us interesting experiences with CD-ROMs and the fascinating possibilities of fiberoptics. New ways of explaining difficult subjects will allow many of us greater understanding.

Pamphlets

When I was working as a community health nurse, I was often frustrated by the many, many health information pamphlets that gave cursory information and then told the reader to "Ask your doctor." Since the women I served were often a day's travel from any doctor and some of the information they did get from some of the doctors was less than adequate and sometimes dangerous, I *longed* for pamphlets that said, "for further information read the following books or phone the following numbers." But no; for years, the pamphlets continued to say, "Ask your doctor."

Credible Sources

Women look for information from many sources. In doing research for this book, I asked women where they looked for health information and how much they believed the information they got from different sources. I asked them to rate the information they received from their doctor, specialist, community health nurse, hospital nurse, dentist, teacher, mother, father, brother, sister, friend, relative who is a health worker, health magazines, Ann Landers, TV documentaries, Oprah Winfrey, and books. The results indicated how much these women believed the information they got from different sources and gave some idea of where these women would look for advice. It also gave a fair idea of whose advice would motivate them to act.

The women I interviewed ranged in age from 16 to 77, were from all socioeconomic classes, and were of many races. They represent no one but themselves, but they do give us an idea of what a diverse group of women think. I asked them how much they believed the information they received from their doctor. If a rating of 10 meant that they truly believed what he or she said and a rating of 1 meant that they did *not* believe it, what rating would they give him or her?

Most women placed the information they got from their doctor at 6, well below the rating they gave books, community health nurses, dentists, hospital nurses, and TV documentaries.

"He doesn't give me enough."

"He doesn't read enough about my problem."

"I'm just a billing number."

Community health nurses were rated the most credible health care worker, with specialists next, then doctors and dentists. Hospital nurses did not enjoy the same confidence as community health nurses and were seen to be only slightly less credible than doctors.

Many women believed the information they saw on television documentaries; 57% rated them 8 to 10, but some were very skeptical, suggesting that film is highly manipulative. They felt that filmmakers can ignore important facts and emphasize others until it becomes hard for the viewer to be sure of information. More than half of the women felt that television documentaries on health were well researched and credible, but others felt that the credibility varied with the producer. They thought that they did not have a chance to check on the sources the filmmakers used and that they may be getting superficial or skewed information.

Eighty percent rated the Oprah Winfrey Show at 6 or less. Ann Landers was a little better, ranging from total disbelief to admiration for her research; her credibility stretched from −3 to 9.

There was also no consensus on advice from mothers. Some women would trust the information they got from their mothers, other women would not; others would listen but not give much credence to it. No one trusted the information they got from their fathers or brothers, with the exception of one lone woman.

I asked women how much they would believe the health information that teachers gave to their classes. Teachers are being asked in some districts to do a great deal of health teaching. While a few women qualified their answers by saying it would probably depend on the education of the teacher, teachers fared little better than fathers and brothers, and most put the teacher's credibility (on health information) at the low end of their rating scale. They would believe almost anyone else before they would believe a teacher. Teachers, I am sure, would maintain that it is not their job to teach health information. What women said was that teachers should not teach health information because they do not accept such information from teachers.

Books—medical textbooks, books of facts, and health information—were the most trusted source of health information. Women usually freely chose the books they read and therefore culled out what they would not believe. They also checked bibliographies and footnotes for credibility. In many ways, they had more control over the information they absorbed through books than through any other media. Most women rated the information they read in books between 7 and 10, with the majority in the 8 and 9 range. They believed the health information they read in books and pamphlets before they believed the advice of anyone else. Most trusted their own ability to evaluate the information in books. Luckily, most libraries are free. Libraries in hospitals are usually inaccessible to the public; libraries at women's centers and women's health resource centers can be important sources of women's health information.

In some areas such as Hollywood, Eugene, Akron, Boston, New York, Washington DC, Vancouver, Toronto, and Winnipeg, women are banding together to form health collectives and resource centers that serve only women. When men and women are served at the same center, women often feel unsafe and unimportant. Some centers deal only with some aspects of women's health. Planned Parenthood and the Federation of Feminist Women's Health Centers are organized to deal with women's reproductive issues and concentrate on providing education and service in these areas. Many others, such as the Women's Healthcare Plus in Guilderland, New York, and the Santa Cruz Women's Health Center in Santa Cruz, California, are set up to accommodate a broader range of health issues. Some are set up with phone lines, lending libraries, and a monthly newsletter as a health information source, giving the women of that area a place to ask questions and find answers.

How to Research

Wherever you live and whatever your circumstances, you can improve your ability to get health information by organizing your method of searching. Make a list. Write down your health problem and then write down the things you need to know to make a decision. Take this list of questions with you to the health care worker's office. Even women who seldom use lists will find that taking time to think out their problems and write down the questions will make a visit to a doctor or health consultant more productive. Women who are compulsive list makers (as I am) may find that the process of writing down their questions makes them focus on the most important questions and keeps them from getting sidetracked into other issues during the doctor's interview.

Few Quick Answers

Our health problems may not have simple answers. This is frustrating in a culture that wants instant answers, fix-it solutions, and daring and decisive actions. We don't respond well to the idea that health problems may be intricate, difficult to diagnose, or responsive only to long-term conservative treatment. We may have to look at diet, lifestyle, stress, genetics, and emotions as well as physical causes of a problem. That kind of investigation takes time, a good deal of effort, and a new understanding of the condition. Rarely will you find the health information you need about a problem in one spot. You may have to educate yourself so that you can understand the information you do find and not feel overwhelmed by the amount of information you need to understand your body and its problems. It's quite usual to be shocked by a diagnosis and not hear anything the doctor says after that point. You could find that the doctor or health consultant gives you a list of facts in medical language that you misinterpret or don't understand. Medical personnel use "SOB" when they mean shortness of breath, not son of a bitch, and "gross" when they mean big or major, not disgusting. The use of such jargon, while not designed to be offensive or exclusive, certainly is both. You need to realize that most people don't like medical jargon. It is even normal not to like it. Ask for an interpretation.

Remember that comprehension is not impossible. It just may take some time to interpret the language in words you can understand and to reassemble the information so that it makes sense. Refuse to be overwhelmed by information. Take in the information you need either by memory, in notes, or on a tape recorder; if the health consultant is not willing to clarify it, take your information to an approachable, knowledgeable person who is.

While information overload may be confusing for some, it's not a common experience. Far more common is the experience of *not* getting enough information. Very often women don't realize that they haven't enough information until they leave the doctor's office. As Brita, the quiet, self-effacing mother, said:

> He sat half-turned away from me, writing the prescription, and I forgot everything I was going to ask. I felt like I had used up the time he could spare for me and I was supposed to leave.

During the visit some women may be concerned about their own safety in the office and about maintaining their dignity. While finding the health information may have been their motive for making the appointment, once in the room with the doctor other issues become both important and distracting. It may be only outside the office after the appointment when the woman feels safer that she remembers what she did not ask. Write down your questions beforehand, and refer to the list while in the office.

When looking for health information, you need to think about who else has your health problem. Do you have a health problem that many people have, such as diabetes? If so, look for an organization that serves people with this problem. The Diabetes Association's address and telephone number should be listed in your phone book or at your local library. Contact someone from the organization and ask for information. Associations organized around a particular health problem very often have good, current information. They also may have a newsletter that will give you information on new medications and treatments and a support group or mentor who can listen to you and who can help.

If you can't find anyone who has your problem, check the library for books on the subject and read. Bibliographies at the back of the books can give you ideas for further reading. You could also write the author in care of the publisher and ask her or him for sources of information. For a speedy answer, send a self-addressed stamped envelope with your request.

Write an outline in a step-by-step fashion of how you are going to find information. Give yourself a deadline; as my friend Judith who had to decide what kind of treatment she was going to take for breast cancer said, "I could research forever and never *do* anything."

Try to see your process of getting information, your decision about treatment, and your goals for your health care as a process over which you have control. Give yourself decision points in this process.

Here are two sample plans:

Sample I.

A. Recognize symptoms:
   1. Decide to consult (e.g.)
      a. mother for family history
      b. doctor
      c. books
B. Discuss information with others and try to understand what is happening to my body and what treatment options I have:
   1. Decide to accept treatment (e.g.)
      a. from herbalist—evaluate in 1 month
      b. from doctor—evaluate in 2 weeks
      c. from massage therapist—evaluate in 1 month
   2. Decide to change lifestyle (e.g.)
      a. no coffee
      b. walk three miles every day
C. Evaluate treatment, 1 month later:
   1. Decide which treatment is effective and which is not
   2. Decide if I am experiencing any bad side effects
   3. Decide if I need to consult any other person, who and when
   4. Decide which option I will do and for how long

Sample II.

A. Recognize the symptoms:
   1. Decide to consult (e.g.)
      a. general practitioner
      b. books
      c. friend with similar symptoms
B. Discuss information with others:
   1. Decide to look for further options
      a. from specialist
      b. from friend's doctor
      c. from Women's Health Resource Center

2. Decide to accept treatment
   a. from specialist—evaluate in 1 month
C. Evaluate treatment:
   1. Decide if treatment is effective
   2. Decide on next step
      a. continue treatment
      b. consult other sources for more options
      c. abandon treatment

If you design a decision chart that shows you obviously in charge of your own health, you will make the best decision you know how to make, with the greatest amount of dignity. Each decision chart will be different for each person and for each problem. By building in evaluation dates and decision dates, you will break the problem down to manageable segments and allow yourself time to make good decisions. You will see your health problem as a series of smaller problems and not one overwhelming unmanageable one. Also, if you design a positive outcome into your plan, you are more likely to *have* a positive outcome.

The Problems of Immigrant Women

The process of getting health information is often different for women who do not speak, read, or write English. Many women can read and write in their first language, but not in English. Many can read and write English but have trouble speaking it, and some cannot read or write in any language. For those who are not fluent in English, translators and advocates are important. Some people use their school-age, English-speaking children as translators but find this embarrassing and sometimes impossible when their complaints involve their reproductive system.

These problems also apply to women who speak in idiomatic English, a dialect of a poor district or ghetto, or heavily accented English. They must also approach caregivers as if they spoke a different language. Communication is important. A report on the problems of immigrant women in Alberta said that "The greatest difficulty for both caregivers and clients was that of language."[1]

Some cities offer immigrant women services that include an advocate or translator: a worker goes with the woman to the doctor or public health nurse's office and interprets for her. Very often such translators work as volunteers and may be new immigrants themselves and not skillful in English. Sometimes the translator is a friend who is embarrassed to be a party to the intimate details of her friend's life. When you consider how difficult it is to understand diagnosis and treatment recommendations when English is your first language, it would be a monumental job to understand it when the langauge itself is difficult. The Alberta report said:

> If immigrant women were to be taught English, surely that would overcome many barriers. They could choose the doctors they want to go to. They could articulate their problems and that could remove most of the negative feelings they get from interacting with physicians, provided the women can locate physicians in whom they have confidence.[2]

The answer to the difficulties of translating is to have paid, professional translators whose code of ethics prevents disclosures and whose professional silence immigrant women could trust. A women is unlikely to talk about the problems of battering, abuse, alcoholism, or drug abuse when a child or friend is the translator. Birth control and abortion issues will probably not be discussed, and any issue that the woman wishes to keep private will either not be discussed or discussed only superficially.

Immigrant women are often not prepared for the medical definition of health care in their new country, nor are they prepared for Western medicine's almost exclusive answer to health problems with treatments and drug therapy. They may have come from a culture that had a tradition of women as healers, of preventative medicine, and of folk remedies for minor problems and may find the drug interventions and Western fix-it approach frightening. There is no room in the Western medical health care system to include the folk medicine of other cultures. Immigrant women are expected to drop their traditional methods of healing and adopt the Western style.

They are unlikely to get help for stress from the Western medical system unless their body decides that reality is too painful and they become mentally ill; then they will get medication. But, at the anxiety stage, when they need to be heard and supported, when they need practical advice, they are often isolated.

Often an immigrant service recommends doctors who speak the language of the immigrant. The common language may solve their communication problem, but the doctor may not give the best medical advice the woman could get. Her choice is then limited by her langauge. The doctor in these circumstances is not competing for her business on the basis of his competence but on the basis of his fluency in her langauge. This is not the best way to choose a doctor, but it is often the way she must choose. Immigrant women sometimes feel as if they are living in a refugee compound in North America, where the free society exists outside the barriers of language.

Women who speak halting English have a difficult time getting health information because, although they can explain their health problems to the doctor, they can't debate, question, or ask for clarification in the few minutes allotted to them. The fee-for-service time constraints of most doctors' practices will not allow the time these women need. As well, the women are often frustrated by many doctors' assumption that, because they do not speak English well, they are therefore stupid and incapable of understanding. "They give directions in a loud voice," one woman told me, "as if I could only obey orders." The problems of English as a second language are complicated by the medical jargon that many doctors use, which is not taught in an English language course.

Many immigrant women may be handicapped for a long time in their new country because they are home with children, not in the work force, and don't have the opportunity to learn

English. They also don't have the information network that women who work outside the home develop about health care and health information.

All women, new immigrants or old residents, need a friend who will listen to them, understand them, and help them. When trying to get health information, a woman needs to join with a "sister," someone to whom she can report her efforts, her options, and her successes and failures. A "sister" can help her plan her actions: whom to ask for information, how to get information, and what to do if she is prevented from getting that information.

Dr. Elizabeth Maunsell, assistant professor at Laval University, Canada, presented the results of a study on 224 patients that shows us that women with breast cancer who had a close confidant had a 16% better survival rate after 7 years than women who did not have a confidant—that is, a 72% survival rate compared with a 56% rate.

"This is quite a dramatic difference," Dr. Maunsell said. The survival rates were even higher for women who had at least three confidants, including either a physician or a nurse.[3]

It seems that not only is a "sister," a confidant, necessary for encouragement and support, she may be necessary for physical health.

A female lab technician told me: "But women only need to ask, and they'll get answers." She worked within the health care system where she could casually, without appointment or much planning, ask the informed, highly educated people around her for information. When we consider that women in our culture are socialized *not* to ask questions, the lab technician's advice, while in some ways effective, is impossible for many. This is why a woman will probably need a sister-friend who will support her and help her, who will remind her that she has the right to information and that she deserves to get it.

Finding information may be as simple as asking for it, but only rarely. Most of the time requesting information is complicated by having to know what questions to ask and in what words so that the questions will be heard, by picking the right source of information, by finding a safe environment in which to ask the questions, and by feeling entitled to the answers. Women who band together in groups, at women's centers or even casually in social groups, are more likely to learn how to find information than those who are isolated. Finding information is not as simple as it first seems.

14

The Ideal Health Information System

I asked every woman I interviewed:

> If you were "Goddess for a day," and you could make any changes you wanted in your community to improve women's ability to get health information, what would you do?

Their eyes lit with pleasure and they smiled; usually they looked thoughtful for a moment, and then they told me how they would change the world, if they could.

The Ideal Center

Most told me that they would establish a center, a place where women could either call for information or walk in and get help from the staff and library there. Jean, a 39-year-old single mother, sat in a Chinese restaurant with me and told me what she wanted:

> I'd like to see a women's resource center that is well organized, keeps updating information, and keeps in contact with support groups so information flows both ways. I'd like to see it advertised in the community and with a phone line for those who can't read.

They wanted a place in the community that belonged to them, a place where the information was trustworthy and useful. Such a place should have the atmosphere of the old village well—a casual meeting place where everyone was welcome—yet would still contain the latest technological and research information, medical facts, and journal articles so women could get accurate information. They insisted, also, that this center include information on alternative medicine.

Lisa, 30, worked as an advocate in a women's center. She had experiences with doctors, hospitals, misdiagnosis, and unnecessary surgery. She saw women who were confused, abused, and frightened, and she wanted a better system:

> I would like health centers specifically for women. I think no longer can we allow men to diagnose us or decide that we need this taken out or that changed. I'd like a really woman-centered place where young girls could go and have a truer understanding of their body and how it works. There is so much about our bodies that we often don't know. It's scary to be as ignorant as we are.
>
> We need a room where we can go and exchange information and maybe do research at the same time and try to better understand ourselves. We've been defined by men for too long.
>
> We need to go to a center where we can say, "This is my body, and you [the health care worker] are my consultant." I think women need more than a diagnosis; they need to have prayer—not in the religious sense but in the spiritual sense of good will toward others or good will toward ourselves, maybe therapeutic touch, traditional [aboriginal] medicine, folk remedies that seem to be gifts from one person to another.
>
> I think this kind of center would be very important to women's mental health. Now women go to a male psychiatrist and he says, "Here, have a tranquillizer, dear." That isn't even close to healing.
>
> This center could be not only a place to go when something hurts, but a place to go when everything feels good but you want to learn.

Lisa believes that women are not given the spiritual or emotional support in our medical system that they need. She also is dismayed at the kind of psychiatric care she sees women accepting. She thinks psychiatrists define normal as that which is natural to men and abnormal as that which is not natural to men. She wants women to establish their own definition of normal and their own remedies.

Some women see a fundamental flaw in the Western medical system, which accepts "facts" and recommendations about women's health coming from men's interpretation of it and men's definition of what is normal for women. They find bias and misinformation at the research level, and they think that the medical system where men write the textbooks about women's bodies, interpret the research data as if it applied to women, and make recommendations about treatments that satisfy men's view of what women need does not serve women. Until women do the research on women, write the textbooks, and make the recommendations, there is little hope, they say, of unbiased or practical medicine for women.

Anne, 36, had several episodes of strep throat, psoriasis, and influenza. She tried many different doctors and finally found help and satisfactory advice from a homeopathic doctor. She would like to see an information center where every woman is accepted:

> I see a women's center as a place that's comfortable for you just to chat. So you don't have to do anything if you don't want to. No pressure.
>
> I think we need a holistic clinic where you have a massage therapist, a naturopath, a reflexologist, a nutritionist, whatever you want. They'd all work together and refer patients to each other.
>
> You need a place that's inviting so you feel good there, a place where you can network with other women. I think you need a place where you get a sense of belonging, a feeling that other people support you. If we have a place where we can feel comfortable about getting better and keeping in touch with ourselves, I think we can build a community, a community spirit. There would be change and growth at a place like that, and the women would create it and participate in it.

Most women agreed with Anne and wanted a center in their community where they could casually walk in and feel comfortable and accepted. They wanted to feel that there would be no pressure on them to be different or to meet the needs of the health care workers, to feel that the center belonged to them because they are women.

Dora, 35, has had extensive contact with the health care system. She had an eating disorder, her two children had physical and emotional problems, and her husband had a kidney transplant. Because she had to make so many important decisions about her own health and her family's health and she had to understand so many medical reports, she took a course on medical terminology. No doctors seemed to be able to communicate with her in plain English. She wants a more user-friendly information system:

> I would like to see a health library with videos, with obscure pieces of information from all kinds of sources. I'd like to have people who are knowledgeable there, who can help me find the information I need, help me access it. I'd like to have films shown, meetings in the evenings, discussions of certain problems with personnel who know what they're talking about and are prepared to offer themselves to you without any reluctance. I'd love to see that.
>
> It would be interesting to see what effect this would have on the community. It might be a catalyst. As it grew, more women would begin to realize their options, to realize that they did have choices.

The Gatekeepers of Information

Over and over women said that they did not get enough information from a doctor, that they were not heard, and that doctors did not take enough time to get a complete picture of their health problems.

We have a big problem. Presently, doctors *are* the gatekeepers of health information for much of our society. That is the way our health system generally works. Women don't see a solution—at least not a solution to this problem—that involves doctors and that depends on the cooperation of doctors or on improvements in medical education; they see solutions in the hands of women. They see women's health information centers, information phone lines, team consultants at health centers, and cooperative women's centers as practical answers to the problem—all of which can be organized and delivered to the woman without the involvement of doctors.

Women see a health information center as a resource that helps them do that. They want the counselors at the women's health information centers to recommend safe and reliable medical consultants. One counselor told me:

> We try to make good recommendations, but we don't always know who *is* good. It may take several women reporting back to us before we really know if a doctor is a good referral or not. And, in time, we get to know the doctors that call us for information and who want to work with us.

Some women may want an advocate to go with them to the doctor's appointment. Others want a counselor to rehearse with them what they are going to ask the doctor and to help them understand what he or she advised. Generally, women want the health care worker at an information center to make them feel more protected.

An Established Center

Teresa, a 41-year-old conference organizer, told me about her views on a women's health center:

> I never had much experience with the medical profession, and years ago when I had some back problems I saw, for the first time, a specialist. I found him to be very impersonal. I thought to myself, "How can you be like that?" but then I realized that I'm just a job to him. That's the way it is and that's how doctors have become.
>
> So, when I went down to the Women's Health Resources, I guess I was expecting that they too would be very analytical and very cool. I found that they were really caring people and that they were women who had similar experiences as me. It was quite comforting. It's funny, because a lot of my friends at first thought I was with a bunch of feminists. I certainly don't consider myself a feminist. It's just that this is my health I'm dealing with and I need other women. I changed all my doctors from male to female. I can relate to women doctors better. It's interesting that my career background was all with men. It was predominantly male. So I think it's kind of

a process for me to change to being with women. I've always had a lot of women friends, and they have been very important to me. So it was just natural to go to a woman doctor. It became natural. I used to believe the old stereotype that "A woman doctor is not going to be as good as a man." That's how I used to think.

Teresa now volunteers at the women's health information center. She feels she gets better information than most women because she has a network of contacts from this center who can advise her. When she had back pain she checked out her doctor's advice with the physiotherapist at the center. Her doctor had referred her to an orthopedic surgeon. The physiotherapist at the center advised that she see a neurosurgeon first. Teresa said:

> I felt I would be better informed about what was wrong with my back if I saw a neurosurgeon, because even if he couldn't fix it, he could tell me exactly what was involved, and I could make my own decisions [about whether to have surgery or not].

Teresa thought that the women's information center that she used was very important in her search for health information in this case. She thought that it could be better located in the city, in different parts instead of only one place:

> I'd like to see community resource centers. I'd like to see them more centered in the community. I know a lot of people won't drive, so if the resource center was more central to the community, more women would use it.

Community Centers

In Pima County, Arizona, health resource centers are starting in schools. This makes them available to the neighborhood, responsive to local health problems, and more "user-friendly." While not designed necessarily as woman-centered, they are usually staffed by women and used mainly by women. In rural areas, schools are often used for temporary health clinics since they may be the only community center in the area.

Many women agreed with Teresa (and the nurses of Pima County) and thought that a health information center needed to be seen as a part of the community and available to all women. If there is a women's health information center in the community, women need to educate each other about its purpose; some women still see health centers and public health nursing centers (which can be good sources of information) as resources for the poor—that is, resources for others.

As Gilda said about her local women's center:

> It sounds like a terrific center. I might go there now. I never did before because I had a different idea in my mind of what a women's center was. I was dead wrong. I thought they were a bunch of flaming feminists.

Gilda, the woman who had been so depressed after her daughter's birth, had thought that the women's centers were political centers whose purpose was to lobby the government. In some areas this may be so; in some centers the need to make changes politically may be the most important purpose of the center. This concept intimidated her, as it does many women who don't trust any kind of politics. She wanted a women's center that focused on health, and she needed to be aware of what her women's center or a women's health center could do for her.

If, as Teresa suggests—and Teresa is in a good position to know since she volunteers at such a place—the women's health information center is centrally located in the community and supported by the women of the community, it will still need good public relations. Women need to adopt good marketing techniques and "sell the center." All the women of the area should know that the center exists, and all should know how to access it. They should also know how to be part of it, how to influence what happens at the center, and how to make such a center responsible to the community.

Communication

When I worked in the rural and wilderness areas of British Columbia as a public health nurse, I visited some communities only once a month. The women usually gathered in a school with their babies and exchanged information. They also asked me for information. If I was late (washed-out bridge, tire-deep mud, ice on the road, tire chains wrapped around the drive shaft), they spent the time talking and asking each other for advice. We didn't call it a "network," but it truly was one. While this informal and temporary health center was useful and better than nothing for women with children, it didn't serve childless women, and I didn't realize at that time how important it was. I can only say that I was young and had a lot to learn about how women needed to communicate with one another.

Women told me that they wanted accessible phone lines or computer access lines so that they could phone for information without having to expose their identity or without having to take the time and energy to get out of their houses and go to the center. Seniors would find the phones very helpful. Non-English-speaking women want to phone someone who understands their language. Generally, women want to access the center in any way that will allow them to communicate.

Michelle, 75, a retired community health nurse crippled with fibromyalgia and struggling with diabetes, yet still impressively energetic, said:

> We have to remember that doctors don't accommodate the seniors' needs. They set up appointments, spend 5 minutes with you, and then fly out. Seniors have no one who will answer health questions. They pick up information at the pharmacy or from the *Reader's Digest* or they overhear it in the halls. Some people just don't have any research skills. They don't know who to ask or even when to ask.

Many older women find it hard to be aggressive in a culture that doesn't value them. Many have been socialized into passivity. (Not Michelle, though. She said what she thought.) For many women, the physical frailty of old age makes aggressive behavior difficult because it takes more effort and energy than they can afford to expend. And for some, clinics, centers, and sources of information are too far away from their homes to serve them.

Michelle said:

> If I can get to St. Paul's [Hospital], I get a reasonable reading on my blood pressure because they have a little room set up where I can lie down for a half an hour so I'm settled before they take it, and my blood pressure is accurate. Then the cardiologist drops in for 5 minutes, and you'd better have your questions ready because 5 minutes is all you get. But I've got to travel all that way to St. Paul's and then there's no parking there close enough for me. So that's finished. I can't go there any more.

It may be that, with the increasing older population, more attention will be paid to the needs of old women because they will be seen as a source of income for the health practitioners. Presently, elderly women are not an economic force because most old women are poor.

Maddy, 51 and a homemaker, had thought about the place of older women in the health care system:

> I would like to see seniors involved in this health information center. I think that seniors are put out to pasture. My mother is a very bright lady and she's gone through a lot of experiences and I think a lot of these women instead of feeling that at 50, 55, or 70 they're old, can feel useful. Boy, they've got a lot of knowledge packed in their heads. They could open up a world for the rest of us. They can tell us things we'd never find out from our doctors. I had this doctor tell me that they basically entertain the elderly because they've written them off as dead. "Well, hello," I said to him, "guess where you're going to be in 30 years?"

In addition to phone lines, some older women would like a home visitor to come and give them health information. There may be some services by senior centers, health units, and senior bureaus already in place in some communities. The women's health information center should cooperate with the already-established organizations, keeping in mind what the older women say they want. They want choices, the way all women want choices.

Women of all ages wanted to talk about their health and their health problems in a different way than the present medical system allows. They wanted to relate their health problems to the context of their lives, in story form, that would include the meaning of the problem. Most women wanted to receive health information and health advice in the same kind of story format so that the information would contribute to their understanding of the problem. This is not to suggest that women want romantic fairy tales; they don't. But they want their particular life story, their circumstances, genetics, family life, emotional life, and spiritual life to form part of the story of their physical illness, and they want the health information they receive to recognize that.

The Facts

They want bare facts as well, to interpret themselves or have someone interpret for them so they are better able to understand their health or illness story.

My friend Judith took her cancer laboratory reports and spread them out on my kitchen table beside several books on breast cancer that she had fetched from the library. She showed me where her test results were on the scale of good to awful. She read the prognosis for such results and the recommended treatment, then compared her results to the charts in the books and found out what type of cancer she had, what the usual treatment was, what side effects were common—and they were considerable—and what probability of success she might have taking certain treatments. She put that information against the advice of three doctors and her experience with Chinese medicine.

Judith understood from her reading that no one was promising her a cure whatever she did. She only had more or less chance of success with different treatments. She listened to everyone's advice but made her own decisions, needing to understand the story of her illness as completely as she could so that she would make the wisest decision possible. To make that decision she needed facts that contributed to her story and also the courage to trust herself.

Dora, a 35-year-old mother of two and insurance salesperson, said:

> I go with the facts. It's much easier to deal with the facts rather than testimonials. Testimonials can be so emotional, and every situation is different. I think the facts are the way I feel most comfortable. But then I don't just have a list of facts. I store them in my mind, then I build my knowledge of the problem bit by bit, because sometimes the facts can be contradictory and you have to figure them out. Nothing is really cut and dry. I collect the facts and then I listen to my gut feelings. I take other people's advice and I store it and then when I get enough information, I decide.

What the women told me was that they had differing and private ways of learning and that they wanted to be able to find information and make decisions in a way that acknowledged their individuality. They wanted the medical facts, to put those facts into their life stories, and to do what they decided was best. At the same time that each woman saw herself as only one person in a community of women, she also thought about ways in which health information could be more accessible and good decisions about health more likely for *all* women.

Linda, 45, an accountant, considered my question about what she would do in her role of Goddess-for-the-day. She said:

> I'd like to see a medical information database center where you could phone in and say, "Can you give me some information on this or that?" and the information would be totally up-to-date. The center could refer you to books on the subject and they could tell you where to find them, where more of this literature is available. It's pretty hard to find some things unless you have some help.
>
> I think people need a place other than the doctor's office where they can go in and discuss their lives. Maybe there isn't anything really wrong with them, but they just don't feel quite right. They could talk to someone at the center, take a look at their life and what they need to do to improve, and maybe check out their eating and exercise habits. I think as a people we

have to talk more about ourselves, start really taking care of ourselves, watching what we eat, being a little better about what we're doing.

I'd like a comfortable place to go where I wouldn't feel there was a stigma attached to going there. I'd like some place to go that I could sit and be with somebody and not feel that I had to go flying out of there, some place where I can be comfortable and maybe even sit in a comfortable chair and read some material and then go talk to someone with my questions.

After a year and a half of intense listening to women's ideas, I saw in my mind the kind of health information center that I thought would serve these women. I haven't seen it yet in any place I've visited, but there are some that are close to idea.

The Vision

I envision a central information center, a data bank, a resource center, a place where women can get accurate, current information and advice. The data bank could be in another city— probably on Internet—but picked up by computer in the women's centers of smaller towns. I see a community health nurse or a trained laywoman educated in community concerns and resources and experienced in working with women in their homes and in their community helping women interpret the data from the center's information pool so that it has meaning in their lives. She would work for the health information center, helping women get the information they need, helping interpret the information, answering their questions, researching for them, helping to prepare them for a doctor or specialist visit, debriefing them after the visit, pointing them in the direction of more knowledge and more independence, assisting them to educate and empower themselves, supporting their decision, and putting women in touch with other women with similar problems.

There would be room for "crones," the wise women of the community, to give their knowledge and advice. Women who had researched a health problem could bring their information to this center and have the center's staff evaluate it and prepare it for inclusion in the center's pool of information. Such a center would offer seminars and workshops on subjects of interest to the women of the area. One center could offer a workshop on menopause, another on temper tantrums in children, and another on endometriosis. There would be childcare services so that women could attend and transport for seniors and those with handicaps.

The center itself would be comfortable, homey, and open. There would be no high counters or rows of numbered files. It would have the open and useful design of a good library. It would try to make everyone welcome: the wealthy junior league sophisticate and the unemployed 17-year-old living in poverty, immigrant women, native women, union workers, and self-employed women. The various life experiences of those who use the center would add to its diversity and increase its ability to help most women. There may seem to be a huge gap between insured women who can get health care and uninsured women who can't, but they share many problems. While insured women may have the problem of being overtreated, uninsured women may have the problem of being undertreated. They both may not be *fairly* treated and could research health information side-by-side.

The data bank would contain information on disease, diagnosis, and treatment but also alternative and complementary medicine, traditional and ethnic. Lists of resources would be evaluated by an advisory committee who rated the resource from useful to dangerous. Notes on the resource could be enclosed with a testimonial on its efficacy and practical use from women who have used that resource. Women could access all different types of information and make their own choices. Professional women would do research from the centers, helping to define the health problems of women and helping to create solutions.

The extent to which medical doctors would be included in this health information system would vary with communities. I see no doctor working for the clinic unless it was on a salary basis under the direction of a board of women directors. I do see referrals to doctors in the communities. Those doctors more likely to work with a women-centered, women-directed health center philosophy would no doubt get more referrals than those who did not. Eventually, women's health services would include doctors who understood the goals and aims of the women of the community. Such a reciprocal community could create a richer, safer, more useful healing environment where women depended on respectful and compassionate assistance when they needed it and where the health care practitioners were accountable to women.

This seems to be such a sensible idea but, as Lisa said wistfully as we finished our interview and were reflecting on how the present health care system affected women: "Sometimes, I think, there isn't much common sense around."

15

Some Examples of Close-to-Ideal Centers

I looked for a women's information center that already existed and that could stand as a model for others. It seemed to me that, if there was a great need for such centers, someone else would have realized this and done something about it. Developing a local center, designing it to fit the community, establishing it, and owning it are ways strong women create their own healing communities; I knew that. Perhaps there were women who could teach the rest of us how to do this? I wanted to find a center that was already established and had already achieved what other communities only dreamed.

I found several: the Women's Health Resources in Calgary, Alberta; the Federation of Feminists Women's Health Centers in Renton, Washington, and Eugene, Oregon; the school health clinics in Pima County, Arizona; the Health Center in Winnipeg, Manitoba; the Women's Health Collective in Vancouver, BC; the Mid-Columbia Medical Center in The Dalles, Oregon; the St. Charles Medical Center in Bend, Oregon; and the community clinics of the Frontier Nursing Service of Kentucky. They were all primarily women's centers, but they were all different. Some were associated with medical clinics, some with national reproductive health services, some with private hospitals; some were independent, self-sufficient entities. All of these centers had workable ideas, dedicated staffs, and loyal community support. I corresponded with but did not visit other information centers in New York, Montana, Connecticut, Florida, Washington DC, California, and Newfoundland.

Calgary, Alberta

The Women's Health Resources in Calgary, Alberta, is housed in a small bungalow on the grounds of the Grace Hospital, a Salvation Army Hospital. It contains a library of books, pamphlets, and videos. The counselors interpret information and, with invited lecturers, present afternoon and evening health education workshops on topics related to women's health.

The Grace Hospital Board of Trustees, along with determined staff members, created Women's Health Resources in 1986. The board, including some very strong women, conducted a study in the community and found an obvious need for a resource of this nature. Some board members traveled to other centers, looked at other resources, and determined the policies of the present center. The board also established funding to allow the center to set up and operate for 2 years until it was able to operate without "parent" funding.

From the clear vision of the board came the definite statements of purpose that shaped the service of this resource. The board took the broad view of women and health and saw that their definition of health had to include the environment in which women live and the circumstances that surround their lives. They sanctioned the holistic approach women want. The philosophy reads like a satisfying manifesto. Among the policies the board devised are:

- The acceptance of women's development and changes as normal and not unhealthy.
- That women should be protected from unnecessary medical intervention in normal, natural life processes.

In line with their commitment to a women-centered resource were the beliefs that all health care, including Women's Health Resources, should:

- Test and validate holistic, nontraditional approaches to healing.
- Advocate public policy changes to increase the number of women in positions of influence in health care and public policy positions.
- Advocate change in the education and training of health care workers so they understand the needs of women.
- Advocate the increase of women in clinical research.
- Advocate more research of women and for women.
- Work with women to make the information from practitioners more understandable to their patients.
- Assist women to see choices in their health care by making health information and education available to them and by promoting a system that empowers women to take responsibility for their own health decision.[1]

I flew to Calgary to interview Kathy Grand, Director of Community Services for the Grace Hospital, and Liz Longmore, Program Coordinator for Women's Health Resources. They are a complementary pair: Kathy, dark haired, energetic, extremely organized and an analytical thinker, and Liz, tall, friendly, and soft-spoken. They were both intensely committed to Women's Health Resources and well aware of the viability of such a center in other communities. During the interview I thought fleetingly that if someone would just give these women a couple of million dollars to implement resource centers like this one across the country, women's health would be transformed.

We sat in the empty lounge area in the early evening while Kathy told me about the need for the center:

The women of our community lacked information. It wasn't that they thought there was inadequate treatment in town—in fact many of them were overtreated—but rather they didn't feel they were partners in their own health care. They got "You couldn't possibly understand" and "Don't worry your pretty little head about it." That's not women's style. Their role in the family, historically, has been nurturer, health care provider, organizer of health care services. They decide who goes to the doctor and when. And it is those management decisions they wanted assistance with. Not treatment.

It was not that the center developed in a climate of "bad" medicine but that here, as in most of North America, women were not able to get what they needed from the system.

Kathy said:

I think that what makes this program unique is the consulting option. We don't just offer a book to read or a pamphlet or a reading list. What we do is follow up. We want you to do some reading. Fine and dandy. We want you to come with some knowledge. But we want to discuss this. Perhaps rehearse what you are going to say to the doctor.

No one needs a referral or an appointment to the center; information is available to anyone who wants it. Granted it is more available to white middle-class women and is seen to be a service for them; but then most of the community is white and middle class. This is definitely not an excluding policy of the center. In meeting the needs of the community, they tend to meet the needs of the majority of that community. The center tries to be accessible to everyone—they have begun a rural outreach program—but the staff is aware that in serving one part of the population they may alienate another. They would like to see more native women, immigrant women, and women with disabilities use the services, but these populations of women are hard to reach from the hospital grounds. Perhaps satellite systems within already-established organizations such as the Immigrant Women's Association or the Native Women's Association could open an access line to these women. They also do not give counseling on reproductive technology or abortion but refer women with these concerns to other organizations in the city. This is partly because competent agencies already exist and partly because the

Salvation Army philosophy does not encompass these subjects. A model agency would include these areas of concern.

Kathy told me about the kinds of problems the women bring to them:

> Initially, I think, women came here with a medical diagnosis. They walked in here and said, "I have diverticulitis [inflammation of the bowel]. My doctor tells me I need a certain kind of diet. I have no idea what a high fiber diet is. He's given me this sheet but I can't figure out what I do with it."
>
> That's a very direct, simple example of how we could sit down and talk with her with some expertise about a high fiber diet and help her build that information into an action plan.
>
> What we're finding now is that women are coming in with multiple difficulties. There may have been relationship difficulties as a result of some complex physical situation, perhaps endometriosis. They've been to see every possible practitioner they can think of. They have been shifted from physicians to nurses to fitness instructors to pharmacists. Whoever. In their opinion they have exhausted the system. They have come to us as a last resort. "My pain is still there. It is having an impact on my family. It's having an impact on the quality of my life. I'm about ready to give up. I've thought of suicide a few times."
>
> Situations like that are far more complex in terms of what these women are willing to divulge and what they feel we can help them with. There is such a need if some skilled person will just sit there and listen.

This consulting aspect of the center is enormously appealing. Women do need a center where they can walk in and talk with a skilled worker about their health. Over and over, women told me, "I want a place where I can *go* and a *woman* I can talk to." It seemed to me that what this center had was an incredible sense of family, as if the place was staffed with concerned aunts who were available to help and guide the women who came. Kathy agreed:

> Historically, it was the women who taught the younger women the health practices of the community. It was the women who delivered the babies. We've taken a lot of this community responsibility and put it into institutions. Women have been disempowered around health care issues. A lot of women are socialized into ignorance. They don't have the knowledge they need about health care, and knowledge is power. They need to be able to ask the questions they need to ask and feel assertive enough and comfortable enough with themselves to risk asking those questions.

The center is a substitute for the old circle of available aunts and probably an improvement on it because it uses skilled workers as confidants—nurses, psychologists, and nutritionists—as well as houses current information in books, videos, and pamphlets.

I was concerned that the doctors in town might see a health information center as an alternative to medical consultation and a threat to their business. While it would be possible to establish a center without the support of the local medical industry, it would be difficult. Few women want to brave controversy, criticism, vigorous negative lobbying, and public condemnation.

Kathy thought that initially some of the doctors in Calgary did oppose the center, but now most are cooperative and often send patients to them for information. There are still some doctors who feel they "own" the patient and must "control" the information the patient receives. As women increase their knowledge and their demands as they broaden their view of health and healing, they will consult doctors as partners, not masters. Doctors in this partnership environment will be more attuned to the nature of their role and, one assumes, less authoritarian. Some women snorted in disbelief when I suggested that such changes were possible, but we can hope. We only have to look back 30 years and see what kind of choice women had for childbirth and the choices they have now to see that changes that include doctors are possible.

Kathy and Liz see their center as a place where women do not just get information, they receive education; it is a place where women come to learn more and more about themselves. Many women use their local libraries to get information about health; libraries are places that women feel they can get impartial, broad information. However, few women expect the librarians to be health consultants. I suggested to Kathy that it was very difficult for anyone to evaluate the medical information that is available to them in magazines and health books and through doctor's offices. She said:

> But we actually don't have enough information out there. There is not enough research. We know there isn't enough research in women's health.

There is absolutely no conflict about that. What we now have is a tremendous amount of information coming out around various areas in women's health, and we need to know what is legitimate and what is not, what is promoting a certain program or a certain product and what is really useful. There has to be some ability to go to someone credible to look at the information.

We know that information on both sides of a question tends to set up controversy. There's a lot of medical controversy. I'm not saying there is anything wrong with that. I'm simply saying that the consumer is in the middle of it. It's very difficult for them. Look at the estrogen replacement therapy controversy. Some are all for it. "Every woman after the age of 45 should be battered with hormones so that she remains young and vital and whatever else she's supposed to be." On the other side is the theory that women do not want to interfere or intervene in a natural process. Then there are women who are really suffering and who could benefit from knowing the scientifically based information and the options around what they might do. These women go back and forth to professionals trying to get a thorough discussion. They can get a thorough discussion if they have a knowledge base—which they can get here—and then go out and experiment with some therapy and at least feel they are in charge of it. We are trying to promote health responsibility.

Here we allow women that time to talk about their health. We offer discussions with other women. We offer resources to help them decide. We offer them strategies. And if it comes to a decision that relates to a medical treatment, we refer them back to their physician with new knowledge so they can have a more productive discussion and get answers to their questions. This allows them to make better decisions. They feel more comfortable; the doctor usually feels more satisfied.

One of the most important things the center does for women is to encourage them to appreciate their experiences as real and meaningful.

We used to have a joke here. We used to say we were going to put a neon sign outside that flashed and said, "You are *not* going crazy!"

It sounds like a weird thing, but we were half serious. Eighty-five percent of the women who come here have been told, or it has been implied, that all their problems are in their head. People have been doing that to us [women] for years now.

Eighty-five percent of the women that come to Women's Health Resources in Calgary have been told their health problems are "in their heads"? That seemed incredible until I reflected on the way the women I knew had been treated in the medical system. If women's concerns are not being received with respect, are not being treated as real, and are being diminished, trivialized,and ignored by the health care system, then of course women are going to look to the health information center as the one place they will be heard.

I have given this Calgary center a lot of space in the book because it seems to be one that can act as a model for many more. It has defined goals and policies that could direct other resource centers; it has a flexible, responsive, independent flavor that should give longevity to the organization and practicality to its work; and it is community based and designed, community responsive, and community used. With the addition of counseling for women in reproductive technology and abortion, a center designed on this model would be ideal for women.

Bend, Oregon

Other organizations have set up systems of health information. The St. Charles Medical Center in Bend, Oregon, is a private hospital with a department for the diagnosis and treatment of endometriosis. Like many centers in the country, it deals with a defined medical problem. But unlike many, it incorporates into its treatment plan the recognition that most women with this diagnosis have had years of frustration with the medical model and years of being ignored and trivialized by doctors. They estimate that 75% of the women who come to them have been told that their suffering is "all in your head."

Sister Katheryn Hellmann, the President of St. Charles Medical Center, is a compassionate visionary who sees whole-person healing as essential to her hospital. On my tour of SCMC I saw ways in which the staff tried to give patients a sense of participation. I saw efforts to incorporate the healing circle, with attention by all the staff to the beauty of the surroundings and the patient's interaction with art, music, and the spiritual life of the hospital community. The healing conference I attended in Bend, sponsored in part by SCMC, emphasized patient-centered, whole-person care. This attitude is percolating in hospitals, clinics, nursing schools, and communities all over North America. Let us hope that it will bubble up and over the entire medical industry.

The St. Charles Medical Center Endometriosis Clinic has a strong educational component that starts at the initial contact, when a brochure describing the center, including an explanation of the diagnosis, the treatment options, the professional background of the surgeons, and the policies and practices of the clinic, is sent to the inquiring woman. In the grand American tradition of superb sales technique, all the customer wants and needs to know is explained, including the costs. In addition, if a woman calls the center and talks to the coordinator, Nancy Petersen, she gets an understanding, supportive, professional woman who has personal experience with the disease and who is committed to education and choice. Anyone who talks to Nancy is going to feel informed, supported, and accepted.

While the center advocates one type of treatment, the information a woman reads in the brochure is sufficiently broad to make it possible for her to "comparative shop" for other treatments. If all medical centers would adopt this open and explanatory promotional approach, women could educate themselves, compare treatment programs, and make informed choices. They could take their information to their health information center and discuss it with the health care worker there. They could compare several packets of information. Presently, rather than get a pack of information before a visit, most women find it difficult to get their few questions answered by the doctor. Some women have surgery without even knowing why it was necessary.

The Dalles, Oregon

Hospitals are beginning to understand the fear patients feel when they are confined and to care about it. The Mid-Columbia

Medical Center in The Dalles, Oregon, is a Planetree Hospital. It embodies the philosophy developed at the California Pacific Medical Center in San Francisco of a "supportive humanistic environment that fosters compassion and comfortable, home-like surroundings including entertainment and art that nurture and heal; including choice and personal control and access to information."[2]

The patient is the focus of the healing environment here. Patient understanding and choices are crucial to planning, treatment, and care. One nurse spends all her time preparing patient education material. She visits the patient on admission, asks what he or she wants to know, and prepares an individual information package at the education level the patient requests. If you want to know, you are encouraged to ask.

This is a dream of a hospital. A grand piano graces a three-story atrium where a cascading waterfall curtains one wall. Patients sit in a library-lounge on the second story and look out over the atrium through the glass walls to the beautiful Columbia River country.

I toured the hospital and was impressed with the flexibility of the care. Staff are encouraged to ask questions, make suggestions, and constantly improve patient care. The decor is relaxing old English, with warm wood trim and chintz covers on sofas and windows. Patients talk to nurses and doctors in the nursing station or in the patient libraries on each floor. Families are part of the healing team, and one member, chosen by the patient, is designated the care partner. Massage therapists and other complementary therapists are also invited into the hospital to help care for the patients. The hospital has an atmosphere of a good hotel—comfortable, supportive, and committed to customer welfare.

Vancouver, Canada

The Planetree Hospital contrasted sharply with the busy city hospital in Vancouver, Canada, where I spent a day watching too few staff deal with too many patients. The hospital is modern, with excellent equipment and some of the same family-partner programs and patient-centered approach as the Planetree Hospital, but with a far heavier nursing patient load. The high-tech of the medical industry is obvious here. The patient fits into the efficient industrial community of carts, tubes, shiny rods, and smooth counters. However, nurses manage to give each patient a bulletin board, as much personal space as possible, and patient-centered, compassionate care. Even with their amazingly heavy work loads, I saw nurses take the extra time the patient needed to be heard, give patients as much control over their care as possible, deal courteously with visitors and rude physicians, and respond to even unreasonable patient behavior with understanding. Women create this atmosphere of healing both inside and outside the hospital and sometimes under tremendous personal pressure.

When women are patients in such hospitals, they want information, and they don't want to have to stage a revolution in order to get it. Nor do they want to feel like a hostage who has to please her captors in order to escape suffering. They want the hospital staff to treat their questions about illness as reasonable and their efforts to stay in charge as normal and admirable. Hospital care should be evaluated on the independence and knowledge of the patient as well as on how the disease is progressing or receding. If women's health centers are strong and influential in a community, they will affect the way that hospital staffs treat patients. Nurses trying hard in a restrictive hospital system will be grateful for this community support.

The Planetree Library

Good hospitals should have a community information program. One hospital in my area believes it has a community program when it sponsors a health education lecture once very 2 months. Other hospitals have a broader view of patient education. The Mid-Columbia Medical Center in The Dalles, Oregon, has an outreach information center in the downtown area of the city called the Planetree Health Resource Center. Here, in an attractive yellow Victorian house, the public is encouraged to come and find the health information they need. Resource centers like this are one of the ways women see of redirecting health and healing back into the hands of women. This center is open to men and women, but it is the women who investigate, question, and search for answers.

This library uses a professional librarian to search for information in books and periodicals. She accesses Internet to find information her clients need. She does not interpret, evaluate, or discuss the information she finds, but she *can* find it, and that is the first step in a woman's search for information. Some health information libraries offer a mail service for which they charge a fee.

Other Information Sources

There are many areas of North America that are remote from good libraries but not necessarily isolated from good information. More and more people in remote areas are able to connect with information sources by computer—if they have one or if they will use one. In rural clinics nurse practitioners are often still the one information source for the area. If rural clinics can be resource centers where patients request and receive information, it is possible to organize, by computer, access to information for most people. From health clinics all over North America public health nurses visit homes, bringing health information with them. They could offer addresses and phone numbers of other information centers and so give individual responsibility and control of the research to the patient. Some public health nurses are actively trying to facilitate patient independence, while some are still committed to providing traditional "service." If public health nurses were educated to see the advantage of making independent researchers out of most patients, they might, through the public health system, promote more health information centers.

At the same time I am advocating more information centers, I realize that the amount of information available to us is often overwhelming. In a bookstore in London, England, in 1993, I asked to be directed to the section on learning disabilities in children since a friend had asked for help with her son. There must have been 2000 different books on learning disabilities. Luckily, I had a recommendation from an expert in early childhood education (whom I met on a hike in the Lake District), or I would have been totally intimidated. This is how many feel when faced with books of health information.

Guidance

It may not be enough to have a choice of information and have access to it. We may need trusted guidance. The fact that we may not understand all the information we can get does not mean that we should not have it. We can look for translators and advisors. We aren't the only ones who can misinterpret information; doctors also misinterpret information. One woman told me that a new doctor, on examining her abdomen, commented that she had had major surgery:

> I sat right up and stared at my belly. "Where?" I asked him. If I'd had major surgery, it was the first time I'd heard of it. He pointed to the pink line left on my waist from my too tight panties. He thought the elastic line was a scar.

Anyone can misinterpret. That does not mean that we should not seek to know. Women need the information from several different sources: doctors, specialists, popular books, pamphlets, videos, textbooks. We need to interpret that information so that it makes sense to us.

Some efforts have been made on a national level to create a center for women's health information. The National Women's

Health Network publishes a newsletter that is available on sub-
scription. Medical computer data banks are often available
through libraries, but the abstracts compiled are written in medical jargon that most people would need a translator to understand.
Across Canada, women involved in groups concerned with
women's health issues have formed the Canadian Women's
Health Network. They want to share information and make
changes in women's health care. One of their goals is to make
communication among women more efficient and accessible. In
their long-term plans, they envision a shared databank of well-re-
searched, critical information on women's health issues that will
be available in language understood by most women. Once information is on computer across Canada, it should be available to
anyone who logs in. The Vancouver Women's Health Collective is
working on a system that would make information on health
available to all women's centers in the province via computer.
While these systems are very valuable, most women would want
the information interpreted. Information from computer data
sheets usually is too impersonal, objective, and remote for most
women to incorporate into their lives. Women need someone to
discuss information with, to help them evaluate it, to find meaning for that information in their lives, to help them plan a course
of action based on that information, and to help them role play
their confrontations about that information, to support their decision when the decision becomes difficult to carry out.

As women told me over and over, they want the health
information center to be available to them in their own communities—outside the medical system and staffed by women who can
be advocates in the medical industry and translators and teachers
of health information. Women generally are not happy with cold
facts and need an emotional and spiritual component to health
and healing to make it work in their lives. Any system that ignores
this part of women's reality will not be effective.

16

What One Woman Can Do

If many women make small changes in their lives, they will affect others and eventually will transform the whole society. Many women see a future of giant leaps of independence; a profusion of choices; accurate, competent advice; and educated women as caring, helpful advisors. This is a wonderful view, but it is also overpowering. When faced with the wide-screen view of the changing attitudes, new ideas, and new behaviors in the world of healing, some women are afraid. They fear change and feel incompetent. Not every woman is called to be the Joan of Arc of health care. Luckily, it is not necessary for everyone to start a revolution. We can make modest, individual alterations that are important. Small changes are a first step to a paradigm shift.

The First Step

The first step is difficult because it requires at least some change in yourself. It is easier to fall back on the way you have always thought and always acted than to vary it. Remember the first time your were nervous about a new experience that now seems routine? Perhaps the first time you drove a car? It seemed hard to do then what you now do easily. The greatest effort to making change will probably be in deciding to do it.

Kate, the community activist who insists on better health education for women, believes that it is very important to change in small ways:

> It'll never happen with big groups that are in the news; not in registered societies. It'll never happen that way. Are you kidding? Women who are powerful, taking care of themselves? We'd be arrested; we'd be too frightening. Women aren't allowed to have power; they aren't allowed to take care of themselves. Society likes to shame women, make them vulnerable. There will be lots to keep women from forming groups to take care of themselves. The only way change will happen will be in little groups, with small changes.

While Kate saw the organized medical industry and the established habits of society as the biggest obstacles to a different system, it may be that the habits and fears of individual women are even bigger.

We may have trouble making changes because we have not looked at our own beliefs and attitudes but continue to operate out of beliefs we haven't examined or challenged. We may act out of habit, indifference, or social conditioning without ever examining why. There is a great deal to learn about ourselves if we take the time to look at the way we think.

Place your attitudes toward health and healing against a few "rules."

Rights

You Have a Right to Information about Your Health

You have a right and an obligation to understand all you can about your health and your healing options. You know your body best, or you can come to know your body best. Everyone else in your healing environment is a consultant, not a director.

While laws differ, the laws of both Canada and the United States lean toward the rights of the individual over the rights of a group. There may be laws in your area that support your right to stay in charge of your health.

We have been conditioned to believe that the lab results, the specialists' reports, and the X-ray reports, belong to the doctor who ordered them. According to *The New Our Bodies, Ourselves*: In most states, patients have a legal right to see, obtain, or have access to their hospital records, but "Physician's records are the doctor's property although states vary in requiring physicians to make them available to the patients." [1]

Some states and provinces declare that you have the right to see your test results but that the physician owns his or her copy. In most instances you can ask for a photocopy of those results or sit in the office and copy them. Ask your doctor what his or her policy is. You do not want a doctor who will not give you your own information.

Some women are content to let the doctor look at the results and make decisions based on them; they will not ask to see reports. Not asking to see your reports is one way in which you give away responsibility for your own health. Look at the report, ask for an explanation, and take a copy of the results with you.

You Have a Right to Ask for a Second Opinion

It is usually easier to ask for a referral to a specialist than to ask for the second opinion of another general practitioner. It is, of course, more expensive. If you live in a small town, it is also easier to ask for a specialist referral because your choice of family physician may be limited or nonexistent. If your doctor is the *only* doctor in town you will have to go outside for another opinion. While you may never ask for a referral or another opinion, it is important that you know that you may. Some women get more information on car repairs than they do on their own surgery. Ask questions whenever you need to know something and from whomever you think can help. Consult your network of friends, your alternative medical sources, your library, and your health information center.

You Have a Right to Know What You Are Consenting To

You need to understand the purpose and effect of any procedure and the expected results and risks. If you need to use an interpreter in order to understand this, you have a right to the interpreter.

When you are given a consent form to sign, take the time to read it or have someone read it to you. Do not give consent to a doctor or a hospital to decide what is best for you. Put a line through what you do not agree with; write in what you want to add.

A young man I know accompanied his wife to the surgery while she was being prepared for a cesarean section. The nurse handed him a form to sign. He read it.

"I'm not signing this," he said. "You can't do whatever you want to my wife."

But we need your permission or we can't go ahead with the C-section.

Look, you have to get permission from my wife for anything you want to do to her. If she's in no shape to give it to you, you have to get it from me. I'm not going anywhere. I'll be right here.

I'm sorry, sir. We can't do the surgery without a signed consent.

He looked at the form. "Okay. I'll cross out this, and I'll cross out this, so you won't have a blanket permission, and then I'll sign it." He did.

That's fine, sir. We just needed to have the form signed.

Generally the person who gives you the form to sign is not concerned about *what* you are signing; their job is to get your signature. If you cross out items or write in items, they may not be at all concerned about it. They only want your signature. If many people change the wording, the forms will change.

You Have a Right to Refuse Care

You are not usually immoral, foolish, or criminal if you refuse care. If, after hearing about the expected results and risks of a procedure, medication, or operation, you do not want it, you have a right to refuse it. Be sure you have as much information as you need to make a good decision. Some health care professionals will advise tests that may satisfy your curiosity and theirs but will not make any difference to your treatment. Remember that it is your body and that you will have to live with the consequences of your decisions. Find out what use the results of any test will be. If a test makes no difference to your treatment, you may decide not to have it, especially if you find there are health risks to the tests.

Attitude to Health

Your attitude toward yourself and toward health care makes a big difference in your ability to get information and in the way you are treated. Develop a healthy attitude toward your body. Respect it, admire it, treat it well, and learn to understand it.

Many women who have dieted for years do not trust their body's hunger signals. When I researched the book *Looking Good: Teenagers and Eating Disorders*, I learned how women train themselves to ignore signs of hunger and to trust a written diet. They substitute their body's natural regulatory process—hunger and feeling full—to an external process—a diet sheet. Those who rely on their internal feelings of hunger and fullness regulate their food intake with their own feelings. In the same sense, women need to rely on signals from our bodies and learn to recognize signs of fatigue, stress, and irregularities; to learn when our bodies need rest, food, stimulation, and exercise and when they do not; and to trust that our bodies will work well for us. Once we are firmly convinced that our bodies are remarkable and admirable, we can more easily demand respect and care from the health care system.

Health

What is this "health" that we are anxious to achieve?

- Is it an athletic body, a functional body, a body that works without pain?
- Is it a body free of drugs, alcohol, coffee, aspirin, and cold remedies?
- Is it a body that is energetic most of the time?

An 80-year-old woman may define health as a regular heart pill, no arthritic pain, and the ability to walk a mile a day. A 50-year-old may define it as no hot flashes, no fatigue, no colds, and no antihistamine tablets in hay fever season. And a 22-year-old woman may think that she is healthy as long as she can run 5 miles before breakfast and work all day without fatigue.

Take a moment and think about what health means to you. Once you know what health is, you can then decide to maintain that state as much as you can. Kate, with her unique view of the health care system, said:

> Health is self-care and self-love. Health is not just physical, it's emotional and mental. I think it means doing less 9 to 5, enjoying life, having time to yourself, reading a book, going into the forest. To me, that's health.

With your own definition of health in mind, compare all the medical advice to the state of health that you have decided suits you. If you are advised to take pills, exercise more, have an operation, or take megavitamins, try to judge the effect of such activities on your state of health. When you think about health in this way, you are in charge of it. It is vitally important that you accept responsibility for your own health. Except in situations of emergency, you are the one most concerned with your health, and you are the one who is responsible. The health care professionals are useful to you, invaluable even, but not in charge of you.

Our usual attitude to ourselves often decides what we can ask for or demand. We all need high self-esteem, for it creates abilities that allow us to achieve. Many women with low self-esteem do not believe that they are capable adults. Because they do not feel capable of caring for themselves, they give that responsibility to others, and when they are ignored or harmed by others, they feel they deserve such treatment, that "nothing can be done" or that "it's just too bad." A woman with high self-esteem expects better treatment and, while she may have to fight for it, usually gets it. I am not suggesting that high self-esteem will transfer a poor healing environment into a better one. I am only suggesting that high self-esteem will help a woman to get what she wants from any system.

Using the System

Since the health care system is presently not easy to use, we need to develop ways of getting what we need. The following might help you get what you need:

1. Do not agree to a course of treatment you know is harmful.
2. Ask why a treatment or surgical procedure is recommended.
3. Ask if there are other options.
4. Say that you want to think the advice over and will return.
5. Ask if the health care professional has more information on videos, in pamphlets, or in books.
6. Ask what you can expect to happen. What are the expected results? What are the risks? Get them in writing.
7. Decide whether you will accept the treatment or not.
8. Remember that the health care professional does not know your body as well as you do.
9. Advice is only advice, and, while it is often good, it is sometimes very bad.

10. Find a public health nurse or a relative or friend who is a health care professional and check the advice with her or him.
11. Develop a network of reliable sources with whom you can check information or from whom you can get information.
12. Remember that healing is more than curing a symptom, and it is often within your control.

Asking Questions

Our attitude to others affects our health care. Our attitude to the health care professional may govern how much information we receive. If we ask questions or ask the health care professional to elaborate and expand on his answers, we will usually get more information than is freely offered.

Sheilagh, 29, disabled as a teen and in a wheelchair, mother of a 1-year-old son, is our local example of how to get information. "I'll phone the office ten times in an afternoon until they give me the information I need," she said. "You have to *demand* information or you don't get it." Sometimes a health care professional only needs to know that we are interested in acquiring information to offer it and sometimes we have to crack their resistance and demand it.

There are some women who prefer ignorance, who leave control of their health in other's hands, and who are unable to take responsibility for themselves. Health care professionals know that some people do *not* want to know information for reasons of fear, anxiety, habit, or social conditioning. You need to distinguish yourself from the timid few and label yourself as an inquisitive patient.

Understanding the Information

Health information can be too much, too soon, and too overwhelming. Most people cannot take in and absorb frightening or shocking information the first time they hear it. They must return in order to understand a difficult diagnosis and often find it easier to return with an advocate, a person who will ask questions for them and interpret answers or just give them moral support.

Connie, the 56-year-old woman who had survived cancer, said:

> His [the doctor's] mouth was moving and I knew he was talking but I couldn't hear a word he said. All I could think was "Cancer."

Most of us need time to adapt to the new, threatening information; time to sort out what we need to know; time to absorb the problem. But, with the exception of such dramatic times when the diagnosis is severe, most women can understand information if it is conveyed in plain language. The trouble is, we often get information in medical jargon. If the doctor says you have a high level of high density lipoproteins (HDL), you need to know: Is this bad? Is this good? What is an HDL? What does it mean when you say I have a high level—anything at all? Are the tests usually accurate? Would it be different if the test was taken on a different day? Does this mean I always have a high reading or only sometimes? Am I in good shape for my age or not? Most tests are only part of a picture and sometimes they can be wrong.

Networking

Once we have the information, we need to develop networking strategies that allow us to use our contacts for our benefit. Women need each other. When a women has health information to absorb and understand, she needs to talk it over with another woman who has had similar experiences. Some health care professions provide a "sistering" system for their patients. Some health units also offer names of caring others. Women usually find this support person within their own social network.

A "sister" can listen to a woman's health problems, recommend a good health care professional, help role-play her visit to the doctor, and help prepare a list of questions that the woman can ask on her visit. Such a "sister" can help decode the health information the woman receives. The secret is to find a "sister" who is reliable, educated, full of common sense, and able to give good advice.

Getting Answers

It is hard to insist on information that is not freely offered, but it is dangerous not to have the information you need. It's amazingly difficult to get detailed and honest answers because sometimes there are no answers. Often there are at least two points of view to health questions: the health care providers may see the question embedded in a narrow "curing" industry, and the individual woman may see it in a broad way of living. Many women who are intimidated by a system couldn't consider making changes in that system.

Gilda, who had been so depressed after her first child's birth, said:

> I couldn't really ask my doctor for help. I always felt like I would be a failure if I had to ask. But then, he could see I was in trouble and he never suggested any help. I didn't do anything and he didn't do anything.

Many women find it hard to challenge the system. However, they may be willing to modify the way they react to it. If a woman changes the way she sees herself in the healing community, she may view the health care system as one of many aspects of her healing life along with lifestyle behavior, alternative medicine, nutrition, spirituality, and emotional health. When she alters the way she views health and healing, she may alter the way she reacts to the health care system. As she changes herself, a small part of the health care system changes around her. Many people with similar attitudes can make a difference.

Starting Small

Small groups can make a difference. A few women, gathered together, can exchange information, get a speaker, advocate for each other to good health care, and create a healing environment for each other. In such a group trust and commitment are high, and women are able to seek information and demand services they would be unable to get individually. A community health nurse, a frontier nurse, or a public health nurse who is educated in preventative medicine and who has knowledge of the medical model can consult with the group to add information, but the women only *consult* with such health care workers; they must stay in charge of their health in order to create a strong, useful network that serves them—not the medical industry.

Divided or isolated, women can be intimidated, managed, and held hostage to medical threats to their children: "She'll be sick all her life if her tonsils aren't removed." "It's too dangerous for your baby to deliver without ultrasound, monitoring, and an episiotomy." When women are part of an information group they can evaluate advice more easily than they can when they are isolated and alone. It doesn't matter if the group is a casual neighborhood coffee group, a health committee of the Women's Institute, a women's health center subgroup, or a Feminists for Health collective. Women need to exchange information with each other, ask questions of each other, and get recommendations, evaluations, and support for each other.

Cost of Information

Some people have Medicare or Medicaid that gives 100% health insurance coverage. Some have "basic" health insurance but no coverage for treatments. Some have little if any coverage. I would like to assume that anyone can access information because money is not preventing them from doing so, but I realize that this is not true.

Free information is vitally important for many. Libraries, health units, and many government offices can and do offer free information. Private companies give away promotional information. Mass market magazines with articles on health issues are usually available in libraries. Most societies organized around diseases or conditions have information available. If you need advice about arthritis, you can phone or write the Arthritis Society for their recommendations. There are pamphlets available in doctors' offices, but check to see who is publishing them. Often pamphlets are produced by companies with a vested interest in persuading you to use their drug or take their vitamin.

How to Make Some of These Changes

When you decide that you are going to make changes in the way you create a healing environment around you, you may want to alter the way you deal with your doctor. The following outline may help you teach yourself to get more information from your doctor.

Guide to the Doctor Visit

1. Get a personal recommendation from friends, colleagues at work, or even casual acquaintances such as sales clerks and hair dressers. Let it be known that you are looking for a doctor in your area who is respected and respectful.
2. Give the doctor a written copy of your medical history or send it in ahead of your appointment.
3. Decide before you go into the doctor's office what problem you want to discuss. Keep it to one, two, or three at the

most, and decide what you expect from the doctor on each problem.

4. Ask the doctor whether he or she will educate you with each visit so that you will become more and more knowledgeable about your own body.
5. Find out how much time is allowed for your visit. Do you think it is enough?
6. Ask the receptionist when you book the appointment about their standard practices. Do you meet the doctor with your clothes on, or must you strip before the interview? Would they change their procedure to suit you? It is intimidating and threatening to have an initial interview when you are naked.
7. Ask what the usual practice is for house calls. Does this doctor do them? Is he or she part of a group of doctors who respond to emergencies?
8. Notice if the doctor's waiting room is patient-centered. Is the patient's comfort considered?
9. Do you have to wait long? Is your time considered important? Does the receptionist tell you if the doctor is late and why he or she is late and offer to re-book you?
10. Does the doctor take time to listen to your concerns? Does he diagnose and treat quickly on the first symptom you present?
11. Do you feel as if the diagnosis and treatment are superficial?
12. Does the doctor ask you how you feel about the diagnosis or treatment?
13. After the visit write down what you learned and what you understood of the doctor's explanations and advice. If this brings up more questions, write them down for the next visit or for your own investigations.
14. If the doctor's advice is contrary to your common sense or if it frightens or threatens you, do not agree to the procedure, test, or treatment that he or she recommends. Tell him or her that you will consider the advice and return.

15. Take the advice to your network of advisors and to another
    doctor for a different opinion.
16. Stay in charge.

There are many community organizations that can give you
health advice. For instance, if your doctor advises that you have
a mastectomy to "get rid" of your breast cancer, you can phone
the Cancer Society nearest you, give them your diagnosis, and ask
for literature that gives their recommendations for treatment.
They may also have counselors available. You can ask about the
mortality rate of patients who have mastectomies and those who
have lumpectomy and radiation. Take time to get all the information you can.

Medicine is not an exact science. Sometimes medical science
does not know the answers to your questions and cannot give you
a cure. Be clear about your expectations from your doctor. Be sure
the doctor is clear about what he or she can do for you. Do not
accept the opinion that if the doctor can't help you, no one can.
There may be help for your problem in areas in which the doctor
has no education. Remember you are getting his or her opinion
based on what he or she knows. Doctors cannot be experts on all
aspects of healing.

We can make changes in the way we find information, the
way we look for it, and how we use it. If every woman assessed
her attitudes to getting information, assessed her ability in her
community to find information, and made an effort to improve
the way she got it and the way her family found it, we could shift
the healing environment around us until it truly serves us.

17

The Next Generation

In time, we may have health information centers for women in all communities: urban, suburban, and rural. If we do succeed in creating useful, practical centers staffed by nurse practitioners with midwives in nearby clinics, with libraries of books and videos, with counselors who can listen to our concerns, with support groups of women who also deal with our particular problem, and with advocates who can help us through the medical system, we will still need to create consumers who know how to use such centers.

Positive Examples

We need to raise children who can stay in charge of their health and who know how to get information; that means parents will have to be a positive example. When we change our own approach to health care, we change our children's approach as well. If you cannot see yourself smashing a boulder into the sea of life and creating huge waves of change, see yourself as throwing a pebble in a small pond and watching the ripple spread in circles. Even small changes in attitude and actions can affect friends, families, and perhaps even the whole of society. We can make a difference, and we need to make a difference. It is important to create attitudes and expectations in our children that allow them to use the health care system with competence.

The Responsible One

In some families the mother is the one person who is in charge of the family's health, so all problems of pain and sickness are given to her to solve. She is expected to do all that is necessary to keep the family healthy. In such families one person, if not the mother or wife, then the father or perhaps someone outside the family like the doctor, is designated to be responsible for the health of the entire family. If children grow up in a family where their mother, father, or doctor is given charge of their health, if they grow up with little understanding of the decisions made about their health or no sense of participation in the decisions, they are likely to continue in this attitude as adults. As much as they may trust their mother, father, or doctor, it is both foolish and dangerous for them to give away control of their health.

Understanding Our Bodies

We need to raise children who see their bodies as reliable and good. Much of our health teaching is based on the idea that our bodies are fragile entities that need constant monitoring for failures and breakdowns, and much of the health advice available to young people is marketed negatively: "Are you too fat? Are you too tired? Are you too weak?" Children are being taught that their bodies are unreliable and useless without additional vitamins, additional exercises, or additional diet formulas. Rarely are children taught that their magnificent bodies work well under most circumstances and that they can keep this state of health for years through simple methods of good nutrition, exercise, and enough rest. Children are not taught to trust their bodies' ability to withstand disease but are given cold tablets and antibiotics at the first sniffle as if their bodies were unable to function without help. There is little talk about how medicine *helps* the body cope in serious situations; the child is convinced that the medicine alone is responsible for health.

We have an example of teaching that *can* change attitudes. About 20 years ago we started to teach young children in elementary school about the dangers of drinking and driving. The educational program, usually started by public health nurses and taught in the schools, ignored adults for the most part and concentrated on children. In a short time, less than 5 years, the attitude toward drinking and driving had turned until most people considered drinking and driving "not cool." A great change occurred in social attitudes, which created changes in law. This was a huge positive social step in a short time.

Language

It is possible to make a similar social change in the way children view their bodies. One of the ways we can teach children a healthy attitude toward their bodies is to change our language. Small shifts in language could help children have faith in their bodies. As caretakers, health professionals, and parents we can watch our language. We can say, "If you sleep and drink fluids, your body will take care of you and get rid of that cold," and not say, "Sleeping and drinking fluids will cure a cold." It is not the fluids that cure the cold, it is the body. We can say, "The antibiotics will help your body fight the infection," not, "The antibiotics will cure the infection"; "The doctor will give you advice that can help you deal with this problem," not, "The doctor will fix it."

Participating in Treatments

Children need to learn that they can influence their own health. There are many programs in elementary schools and on television that teach children to avoid sexual abuse by staying in charge of their bodies. "Good Touch and Bad Touch" and "Say No" programs teach children that they should trust their feelings and allow no one to invade their body space. As an extension of that program we can begin to teach our children about medical choices and begin to strengthen their autonomy. While parents do make medical decisions for their child, they need gradually to transfer the responsibility for deciding on treatment and medicine to the child as the child grows.

When we tell our children that "The doctor knows best" or that "The chiropractor knows best," we are encouraging them to give away their autonomy. Children often object to painful experiences—few people really *enjoy* dentist visits—but children can be gradually given autonomy in the area of their health care in the same way they are gradually given autonomy in traffic safety. No one would allow a 2-year-old to choose when she is going to cross a busy street, but if parents are still holding her hand at 12, they have not taught her well. If they are still telling an 18-year-old that she should do whatever the doctor says, they are stunting her development. She should comply with the doctor's advice only if she is informed about the problem and the solutions, understands the doctor's advice, and thinks it is reasonable and in her best interests, but she should not blindly do as she is told.

An 11-year-old girl I saw in the hospital had broken her finger playing soccer. The doctor had hurt her when he examined her and the girl was crying in the waiting room while she waited for the results of the X ray.

"I don't like that doctor. He hurt me," she said with indignation. Her mother sat beside her.

"Yes, he did," she said. "I don't think he thought it was broken. Do you want another doctor? I'll arrange it."

"Is this one any good?" Her mother was a nurse at this hospital so the daughter's question was a serious effort to assess his competence.

"Yes, he's the best; all the nurses in town go to him, but I will get you someone else if you don't want him."

She thought about it. "How can I keep him from hurting me again if I keep him as my doctor?"

Her mother gave her something concrete to do. "Tell him he has to let you know what he is going to do before he does it because he hurt you the last time he touched you."

"Okay. I'll keep him then."

Later, back in the Emergency Room, the doctor approached the girl.

"Well," he said, "the X rays say that finger is broken."

The girl put her left hand in front of her right hand, shielding her finger. "Exactly what are you planning on doing to me?"

The doctor stopped and stared at her.

"You hurt me before," the girl continued. Her mother looked on but said nothing.

"Oh," the doctor said. "I am sorry. I didn't think it was broken."

That wasn't good enough for the girl. She waited.

"I promise I'll be gentle this time," the doctor offered.

"You have to tell me what you are going to do before you do it." The little girl stated her terms.

"Okay," the doctor agreed.

The girl nodded and held out her hand. The doctor was very careful. The little girl stayed in control of her care.

Being an Example

While we may be able to change our children's attitudes toward their bodies with good teaching, we could do it best by example. I know, this is much harder than telling our children what to do. If parents are inquisitive, self-reliant, and competent researchers, their children likely will mimic them. If parents do not understand their own bodies, if they continually look for a magic pill and neglect spiritual and emotional needs, their children will probably do the same. The old adage, "The apple doesn't fall far from the tree," applies here. Children generally adopt their parents' attitudes.

Pressures on Children

Children also learn attitudes about their bodies and their health at school. Most children, even as young as kindergarten, are subjected to pressure about body appearance from the media and their peers. The media tells them that to be thin is to be intelligent, popular, and personable. When I researched the book *The Body Image Trap*, I found that appearance replaced character in many children's value system. The better you look, the better you are. Advertisers seem to envision children as robotlike Barbie and Ken dolls moving from classroom to classroom with perfect bodies in perfect clothes. I was asked by a reporter from *The Baltimore Sun* to comment on the classes for 6- to 11-year-old girls sponsored by a local department store. The classes were called "Pretty Me" and taught the children make-up, skin care, fashion, and deportment. The thought of lively, curious 6-year-olds being taught to disguise themselves and present an image to others made me wince. Luckily, children seem more impulsive, honest, and resilient than advertisers realize and do resist some of the pressure, but enough advertising moves into the social world of children to make many children embrace passive behavior and compliance.

Illness in this world of perfection becomes a personal failure, a blight; women want to "fix" illness the way they can fix an unattractive hair style. When one is sick, one goes to a doctor to get "fixed." The doctor owns the solution. We seldom teach children to find their own solutions to their health problems, to accept some responsibility for them, and to learn to understand their bodies' needs.

Staying in Charge

The ability to understand our physical needs grows as we listen to and satisfy our bodies. If parents provide children with the opportunity to be in charge of their bodies, children will become more confident in their decisions about their health care, more capable of making such decisions, and far less likely to cooperate in any treatment or procedure that would harm them.

The Education of Girls

We want to raise children to become adults who see the care and treatment of their bodies as their responsibility. We want adults who will not give that responsibility away. There is some work being done at the elementary school level in White Rock, a district near Vancouver, Canada. The therapist from the local health unit, who has worked for years with women and girls with eating disorders is trying to show fifth grade girls how to retain the inquisitiveness, self-determination, and active participation in life that they had at 8 years of age. By 15, many young women have lost those qualities and have replaced them with passivity, people-pleasing behavior, and conforming attitudes and actions. Sandy Friedman, the therapist at the health unit working in the "Girls in the 90s" program, said:

> By then [adolescence], girls think it's normal to apologize for what they eat and how they look. They lose track of who they are and what they feel. Instead of saying, I'm angry, I'm nervous, or I'm vulnerable, they say, I'm fat, or ugly, or stupid.[1]

In their efforts to please others and be accepted by others, young girls often lose a clear definition of self. They cannot give a description of themselves that sounds individual. At 8 years of age they say, "I like to skate, play ball, and make pictures." At 13 they say, "I like to make other people happy." Girls change their language to include many qualifiers, such as "I think " and "I don't know," and become much more concerned with adapting to others than in becoming themselves. According to studies, including those of Carol Gilligan of Harvard University and Lyn Mikel Brown of Colby College, this lack of self-esteem and lack of definition is a result of social conditioning of girls in our society. It creates adults who are easily led to agree to give up control of their bodies and to agree to unnecessary surgery, unneeded tranquilizers, or crippling medications as they try to please the authority figures in the medical industry. Perhaps we need to change the way girls are socialized into womanhood in order to produce young women who are self-directed, self-defined, accepting of their bodies, and definite about the limits of intrusion of others into their bodies.

Young girls in our society use their bodies. Eight-year-old girls skate, swim, play the piano, hike, play baseball, run, skip, jump, and fly through the air on swings. By the time a girl is 15 she has curtailed her physical activity, until she rarely moves quickly unless she is in some kind of organized sport. In a few short years, she is trained to fit into a social role of an inactive observer of life. She learns to look good, not to be productive and active. In these years, she has also discovered sex, either as an onlooker or a participant, and the world of relationships. She often spends her time testing relationships with parents, boys, and other girls in manipulative ways that do not come out of high self-esteem or feelings of control. Her passive life makes her use the tools of the oppressed: manipulation, deviousness, and avoidance.

Such a passive personality, concentrating on appearing perfect, is not confident about her body. She is constantly looking for imperfections: "I'm too fat," "My hair is too dull," "My nose is too big." At a time when she should be learning how to be independent and productive, she is learning how to be accommodating and dependent. A passive, dependent personality is easily molded by the medical industry because passive people are not sure of their feelings, don't trust their bodies, and are confused about what they need. Gilligan and Brown in *Meeting at the Crossroads* said:

[Adolescents] are in danger of losing their ability to distinguish what is true from what is said to be true, what feels loving from what is said to be love, what feels real from what is said to be reality.[2]

Explaining

Do not deny your child's perception of her body and its problems. Investigate those problems with her. If your daughter, at age 7 is upset because she is afraid that all the blood in her body will run out of a cut, as if her body were a plastic bag that could not survive a tear, don't trivialize her fears or her questions. Explain how the blood runs in veins near the surface of her skin and how her body is able to seal off tears and cuts. Give her explanations and reasons so that she can deal with her fears herself. Use opportunities like this one to instill confidence in your child, teaching her how capable and well organized her body is to deal with injuries like cuts and bruises, and make her questioning a positive experience so that she will ask again and feel entitled to ask.

Again, Being an Example

Our daughters and sons will tend to adopt our attitudes, especially if our attitudes and methods get positive results. When you go to a health care worker with your child, take that opportunity to teach your child how to ask questions and get answers. Don't carry on a conversation with the doctor about an 8-year-old child and exclude that child. Encourage the 8-year-old to have a question ready for the doctor and to ask the question herself. Don't allow the doctor to answer the question by talking to you; encourage the doctor to speak directly to your child. Talk over the visit with your child afterward. Ask if she has any more questions and help her find the answers. She will learn that she has a right to information and that it is possible to find that information.

Give your child choices. If she does not like the health care worker, ask her if she would like to see a different one and help her choose that worker. If she doesn't like the treatment, ask her why and see if you can adjust the treatment to take care of the problem and satisfy her. As much as possible, let your child at a young age be part of the decision making about his or her own health. This does not mean that all choices on health care are left to the child.

If you have decided that your 10-year-old daughter will have a rubella (German measles) immunization so that she can protect her future children from the dangers of rubella *in utero,* you may explain your reasons to her. If she doesn't want the immunization because she "hates shots," you can give her information about the nature of the pain involved and help her devise ways of dealing with it (take a deep breath and slowly recite a poem) while you still make the decision about whether she is to be immunized. You owe your daughter an explanation of why you have arrived at this decision so she can deal with it, and you owe her an explanation of the process she needs to go through in order to reach decisions of this kind; but I am not advocating that you indifferently allow your children unlimited choices in health care procedures and treatments. I am advocating involving her in those decisions until you have relinquished responsibility to her when she is ready for it, sometime in the teen years. By 15, most young women know how to make their own health decisions. The goal of parents is to help their child become independent so she can make good health decisions by herself.

Women don't want their daughters to have the same experience of health care that they have had.

Kate has a daughter and a son for whom she wants a supportive community; she spoke to me about daughters:

> When a young girl wants to learn about her body, she's shipped off to the doctor, who tells her nothing. She is supposed to look for information from the doctor? This kind of process will only make her feel isolated from other women and teach her that her body is something to be ashamed of, or it's private; you don't tell anyone about it. So she goes for 5 years thinking the bumps on her legs are cancerous because she doesn't have anyone to talk

to? How does she get someone to talk to? It's not going to be the doctor. We've got to give her something better than that.

We don't want our daughters to be sexually abused by doctors, to have surgeries they do not need, or to have frightening childbirth experiences, dangerous drugs, and the trivializing, paternal, patronizing experiences many of us have had. We want them to consult women doctors about their problems and receive respect, attention, and competent information. We want them to be able to be in tune with their bodies, notice when something is wrong, and walk into a health center and find the information they need to investigate the problem. We want them to receive encouragement in their search for answers, to find emotional support for difficult problems, to find appreciation of their situation and their abilities to cope with the situation, and to choose the best option.

We don't want them to feel intimidated, confused, beleaguered, or assaulted; we want them to feel competent, as they are in other aspects of their lives, to find information, see options, make choices, and discover what is best for them. To achieve that, they need to know how to get information and so do we. Most young girls in North America are taught computer skills in school that include the ability to find information. We can hope that those skills will create good researchers in the next generation of women, women who with information feel more in charge of their lives.

Networking

It is often easier to join a women's health information group if there is one in your area than to work alone. You can take your daughter with you to see women exchanging information and working together to get good health information. She can see how such a group can help individual women create a feeling of competence and develop methods of dealing with the health care system. If there is no health information center in your area, you could start your own. Investigate your local library and health unit to find out what information is already available. Start looking for more material and more resources through public health sources, women's health network resources, and health magazines. Meet with a few friends or your women's group and establish a supplemental library; write for information.

The Computer

As our communities become more and more computerized, we should be able to tap into more and more health information through national health information systems such as the MedLine on Internet. The danger with computerized information of any kind is that once wrong information has been entered into a system it may be passed into many other systems and moved across the country very quickly as "fact" and "truth." No one source of information should be considered the authority on health. We need to compare information from several sources. There are often no sure answers to health questions, so we must evaluate what we learn, ask for advice, and weigh all information.

A First Nations woman told me that in her culture in the past a young girl celebrated her first menstrual period with a party with her female relatives. Her mother, aunts, and older cousins met with her for several days and talked to her about what it was like to be a woman. They told her how to deal with her menstrual periods, what kind of birth control to use, what men are like, and how to keep herself independent and free from coercion and domination. They had a lively, comfortable, informative group meeting, assuring the new woman that she was accepted, understood, and part of the community. She then had a supportive group of relatives to consult for the rest of her life. This woman's tribe was reinstating this practice, and she had hopes that it would create bonding among the women so that they could get strength, support, and information from each other. I would wish this kind of sisterhood, this kind of love and support, for us all.

Epilogue

There seems to be no end to the research I could do for this book. People continue to phone me with more ideas for better care. I read articles in newspapers about new organizations providing health information, new kinds of affiliations of health care workers, new legislation, and new experiments in health care delivery. The average consumer in Canada and the United States is becoming more aware that health care is both a multifaceted helping industry and a many-headed monster. We are beginning to see that we cannot allow health care to be "done to us." We must be a partner, an informed consumer. Women are beginning to understand that their problems are important and are often shared by many. They are beginning to see that the solutions to these problems must be in their hands. They can look back into history and see that women have been caring for women with competence and efficacy for thousands of years and feel that they have the right to demand that this competent, compassionate care continue. At the base of appropriate care, safety, and choice is their ability to get good health information. Whatever women can do to make health information more accessible will increase their chances of competent care. I hope that by reading this book you understand the need to find as much information as possible about your own health and that you become part of a movement to create a new, safer, woman-centered health information system that will serve us all.

Notes

Chapter 1. Women in the World of Health and Healing

1. Marilyn Suzanne Miller, "Cancer for Christmas," *Globe and Mail* [Toronto], 15 Jan. 1993: A13.
2. Michael Kesterton, "Social studies: Violence against women," *Globe and Mail*, 18 Jan. 1993: A14.
3. Susan Faludi, *Backlash: The Undeclared War Against American Women* (New York: Anchor Books, 1991), 365.
4. Marlene Mackie, *Gender Relations in Canada: Further Explorations* (Toronto: Butterworths, 1991), 201.
5. Dr. Maye Cohen, "Health care for women," an address to a conference at the University of British Columbia, 16 Oct. 1992.
6. Bernie Siegel, *Love, Medicine and Miracles* (New York: Harper & Row, 1986); xi.
7. John M. Smith, *Women and Doctors* (New York: Dell, 1992), 20.
8. Smith, 20.
9. Elaine Showalter, *The Female Malady: Women, Madness and English Culture 1830–1980* (New York: Penguin Books, 1987), 205.

Chapter 2. Women in Medicine: A Historic View

1. Riane Eisler, *The Chalice and the Blade: Our History, Our Future* (San Francisco: Harper, 1987), xiii.

2. Kate Campbell Hurd-Mead, *The History of Women in Medicine: From Earliest Times to the Beginning of the Nineteenth Century* (Haddam: The Haddam Press, 1938), 22.

3. Hurd-Mead, 6.

4. Hurd-Mead, 21.

5. Hurd-Mead, 68.

6. Hurd-Mead, 5.

7. Hurd-Mead, 40, according to Soranus of Epheus.

8. Hurd-Mead, 54–55, from Von Siebold, "Geschiachte der Gebortshulfer," 1901, 163.

9. Hurd-Mead, 50.

10. Hurd-Mead, 60.

11. Hurd-Mead, 168.

12. Judy Chicago, *The Dinner Party: A Symbol of Our Heritage* (New York: Anchor Books, 1979), 160-b.

13. Hurd-Mead, 350.

14. Howard W. Haggard, *The Doctor in History* (New Haven: Yale University Press, 1934), 246.

15. Hurd-Mead, 491.

16. Hurd-Mead, 516.

17. Catriona Blake, *The Charge of the Parasols: Women's Entry to the Medical Profession* (London: The Women's Press, 1990), 43.

18. Blake, 193.

19. Blake, 34.

Chapter 3. Different Problems at Different Times

1. Marlene Mackie, *Gender Relations in Canada: Further Explorations* (Toronto: Butterworths, 1991), 246.

Chapter 4. Walls around Us

1. Bill Moyers, *Healing and the Mind* (New York: Doubleday, 1993), 177–193

2. Gloria Steinem, *Revolution from Within: A Book of Self-Esteem* (Boston: Little, Brown and Company, 1992), 124, from *Short-changing Girls, Short-changing America* (Washington, DC: American Association of University Women).

3. Steinem, 124, from Karen D. Arnold, *Values and Vocations: The Career Aspirations of Academically Gifted Females in the First Five Years After High School* (College of Education, University of Illinois at Urbana-Champaign, 1987).

4. Carol Gilligan and Lyn Mikel Brown, *Meeting at the Crossroads: Women's Psychology and Girls' Development* (Cambridge: Harvard University Press, 1992), 86.

Chapter 5. Walls around Information

1. Barbara Matacotta, "Therapeutic touch, a gift of healing," *Healing: The Journal of the Health Care Project* (Sacramento: The Health Communication Research Institute, 1993), 28, from Nurse Healers Professional Association, *Therapeutic Touch, Teaching Guidelines: Beginner's Level* (New York: NHPA, 1992).

2. Forest P. Chisman and Associates, *Leadership for Literacy: The Agenda for the 1990s* (San Francisco: Jossey-Bass Publishers, 1990), 4.

3. Statistics Canada, *Adult Literacy in Canada: Results of a National Study* (Cat. # 89–525E), 12.

4. Paul Taylor, *Globe and Mail*, 28 Oct. 1991: A2.

5. B. Singh Bolaria and Harley D. Dickinson, *Sociology of Health Care in Canada* (Toronto: Harcourt Brace Jovanovich, 1988), 109.

6. Nancy Roberts, *Breaking All the Rules: Feeling Good and Looking Great No Matter What Your Size* (New York: Viking Penguin, 1985).

Chapter 6. Why Doctors Don't Give Health Information

1. Ivan Illich, *Medical Nemesis: The Expropriation of Health* (New York: Pantheon Books, 1975), 43.

2. D. Stewart, *The Five Standards for Safe Childbearing* (Marble Hill, MO: MAPSAC Publications, Spring 1981), 118.

3. H. Browne and G. Isaacs, "The Frontier Nursing Service," *American Journal of Obstetrics and Gynecology*, 123:14–17, 1976.

4. "Sixty-seventh annual report of the Frontier Nursing Service, Inc. for the Fiscal Year May 1, 1991 to April 30, 1992," *Quarterly Bulletin of Frontier Nursing Service* 68:34, Summer 1992.

5. "Summary of first 10,000 confinement records of the Frontier Nursing Service," *Quarterly Bulletin of Frontier Nursing Service* 33:45–55, Spring 1958.

6. Metropolitan Life Insurance Company, "Report on the FNS of Hyden, KY," 9 May, 1932.

7. E. Steele, "Report on the fourth thousand confinements of the Frontier Nursing Service," *Quarterly Bulletin of Frontier Nursing Service* 16:4–13.

8. B. Levy, F. Wilkinson, and W. Marine, "Reducing neonatal mortality rate with nurse-midwives," *American Journal of Obstetrics and Gynecology* 109:50–58, 1971.

9. C. Slone, H. Wetherbee, M. Daly, K. Christensen, M. Meglen, and H. Theide, "Effectiveness of certified nurse-midwives," *American Journal of Obstetrics and Gynecology*, 124:177–182, 1976.

10. Ursula Franklin, *The Real World of Technology* (Concord, Ontario: Anansi, 1990), 18.

Chapter 7. Alternative Practitioners: Complementary or Fringe Figures

1. Leslie Miller, "Alternatives meet the mainstream," *USA Today*, 22 Jul. 1993: 6D.

2. Jeanne Achterberg, *Imagery in Healing: Shamanism and Modern Medicine* (Boston: New Science Library, 1985).

3. George Goodheart, *Healers on Healing*, Richard Carlson and Benjamin Shiel, eds. (Los Angeles: Jeremy P. Tarcher Ltd., 1989), 53.

4. Thirty-eight of the women interviewed rated their mothers 8 or more on a credibility scale of 1 to 10.

5. Evelyn Vaughn, from a lecture at the First Nations Women and Wellness Conference, Vancouver, BC, 10 Feb. 1993.

6. Vaughn.

7. Clerk at the American College of Nurse Midwives, Washington, DC, 29 June 1994.

8. Thirty-eight percent of the women interviewed rated doctors' advice 8 or more on the credibility scale of 1 to 10.

Chapter 8. The Nature of Quacks

1. Stephen Barrett and Gilda Knight, eds., *The Health Robbers: How to Protect Your Money and Your Life* (Washington: George F. Stickly Company, 1976), 76–77.

2. Stephen Barrett and the editors of *Consumer Reports, Health Schemes, Scams and Frauds* (New York: Consumers' Union, 1990,) 71.

3. John Smith, *Women and Doctors* (New York: A Dell Trade, 1992), front page.

4. Barrett, 23–24.

5. Barrett, 209.

6. Barrett, 25

7. Barrett, 13.

8. James Harvey Young, *The Medical Messiahs: A Social History of Health Quackery in Twentieth Century America* (Princeton: Princeton University Press, 1967), 218.

9. Young, 360–389.

10. Singh Bolaria and Harley D. Dickinson, *Sociology of Health Care in Canada* (Toronto: Harcourt Brace Jovanovich, 1988), 537.

11. Bolaria and Dickinson, 537.

Chapter 10. What Women Want from Society

1. Singh B. Bolaria and Harley D. Dickinson, *Sociology of Health Care in Canada* (Toronto: Harcourt Brace Jovanovich, 1988), 121.

2. Madeleine Dion Stout, from a speech given to First Nations Women and Wellness Conference, 13 Feb. 1993.

3. The Boston Women's Health Book Collective, *The New Our Bodies, Ourselves* (New York: A Touchstone Book, 1984, 1992), 656, from National Academy of Sciences, Institute of Medicine, Division of health care services, "Health care in a context of civil rights: A report of a study," No. 1804 (Washington, DC: U.S. Government Printing Office, 1981).

4. The Boston Women's Health Book Collective, 656, from Wornie L. Reed, "Racism and health: The case of black infant mortality." *The Sociology of Health and Illness*, 34–44.

5. The Boston Women's Health Book Collective, 656, from S. Woolhandler et al., "Medical care and mortality: Racial differences in preventable deaths," in Phil Brown, ed., *Perspectives in Medical Sociology* (Belmont, CA: Wadsworth, 1989), 71–81.

6. Mae Cohen, "Health care for women," an address to a conference at University of British Columbia Conference, 16 Oct. 92.

7. "Smelling a rat in medical research," *Globe and Mail*, 22 Mar. 1993: A11, from "The Gender Agenda," *The Economist*, 20 Mar. 1993.

8. I. H. Ullrich, R. A. Yeater, and J. Dalal, "Heart disease in women" *West Virginia Medical Journal* 88(12):552–55, 1992.

9. C. Gustafsson, K. Asplund, M. Britton, B. Norrving, B. Olsson, and L. A. Marke, "Cost effectiveness of primary stroke prevention in atrial fibrillation: Swedish national perspective," *British Medical Journal* 305(6867): 1457–1460, 1992.

10. The Boston Women's Health Book Collective, *The New Our Bodies, Ourselves* (New York: A Touchstone Book, 1992), 631.

11. "Smelling a rat in medical research."

12. Lisa Fitterman, "The doctor is out—of touch," *The Vancouver Sun*, 3 Jul. 1993: A2.

13. The Boston Women's Book Collective, 138.

14. Kathryn Wahamaa, "Collaboration not collusion: A foundation for ending wife assault," Tri-City Task Force on Wife Assault, Ministry of Women's Equality, 1992, 33.

15. Bolaria, 190.

16. Rod Mickleburgh, "Murder trial prompts debate on College of Surgeons' inaction," *Globe and Mail*, 4 Aug. 1993: A1.

17. Mickleburgh, A1.

18. Mickleburgh, A1.

Chapter 11. The Cost of Health Information

1. Linda Hossie, "Young Canadians' deaths among highest in West," *Globe and Mail*, 23 Sept. 1993: A1-A2.

2. Rod Mickleburgh, "User-fee proposals bankrupt, health-care experts say," *Globe and Mail*, 10 Sept. 1993: A1.

3. Personal communication with the clerk at the British Columbia Medical Association office, 24 Jan. 1994.

4. Drew Fagan, "Health care costs eating up GNP," *Globe and Mail*, 25 Apr. 1993: A3, from 1990 statistics from the World Bank.

5. *Statistical Abstract of the United States 1993, The National Data Book*, 113th ed. (Washington DC: U.S. Department of Commerce, Economic and Statistics Administration, Bureau of the Census), 108, from the U.S. Health Care Financing Administration, *Health Care Financing Review*, Winter 1992.

6. John Robert Colombo, ed., *The Canadian Global Almanac, 1994* (Toronto: Macmillan, 1993), 179.

Chapter 12. Healing in Different Cultures

1. Donna J. Haraway, *Simians, Cyborgs and Women: The Reinvention of Nature* (New York: Routledge, 1991), 204.

2. "Northwest Territories," *Pro-Choice News*, Summer 1992, 5.

Chapter 13. Finding Health Information

1. The Alberta/Northwest Territories Network of Immigrant Women, "Multicultural health for immigrant women—A dialogue," a report of proceedings from a one-day workshop organized by the ANNIW, Multicultural Health Committee, Calgary, 28 March 1992, 1.
2. The Alberta/Northwest Territories Network of Immigrant Women, 4.
3. Rod Mickleburgh, "Breast cancer victims given voice," *Globe and Mail*, 16 Nov. 1993: A4.

Chapter 15. Some Examples of Close-to-Ideal Centers

1. The Women's Community Advisory Committee and the Grace Hospital Board Planning Committee, *Woman and Health: Sharing the Vision* (The Grace Hospital, May 1992, 3,4.
2. MCMC University, "One team, one school of thought," handout from the Mid-Columbia Medical Center, The Dalles, Oregon.

Chapter 16. What One Woman Can Do

1. The Boston Women's Health Book Collective, *The New Our Bodies, Ourselves* (New York: A Touchstone Book, 1992), 684.

Chapter 17. The Next Generation

1. Sandy Friedman, therapist, Boundary Health Unit, Surrey, BC, personal communication, 8 July 1994.
2. Lyn Mikel Brown and Carol Gilligan, *Meeting at the Crossroads: Women's Psychology and Girls' Development* (Cambridge: Harvard University Press, 1992), 215.

Resources

American Foundation for Alternative Health Care, Research and Development

25 Lanfield Ave.
Monticello, NY 12701
914-794-8181

American Foundation of Traditional Chinese Medicine

505 Beach St.
San Francisco, CA 94133
415-776-0502

American Cancer Society

1599 Clifton Rd. NE
Atlanta, GA 30329
1-800-ACS-2345

American Chiropractic Association

1701 Clarendon Blvd.
Arlington, VA 22209
703-276-8800

The American College of Nurse-Midwives
1522 K St. NW, Suite 1120
Washington, DC 20005
202-347-5445

American Diabetes Association
Box 25757
1660 Duke St.
Alexandria, VA 22314
1-800-ADA-DISC

Alzheimer's Association
919 N. Michigan Ave., Suite 1000
Chicago, IL 60611
1-800-272-3900

Autism Society of America
7910 Woodmont Ave., Suite 650
Bethesda, MD 20814
1-800-3-AUTISM

Center for Medical Consumers and Health Care Information
237 Thompson St.
New York, NY 10012
212-647-7105

Federation of Feminists Health Center
633 E. 11th Ave.
Eugene, OR 97401
503-344-0966

Frontier Nursing Service
Wendover, KY 41775
606-672-2317

Hospice Association of America

519 C St. NE
Washington, DC 20002
202-573-8484

International Association of Cancer Victors and Friends

7740 W. Manchester Ave., No. 110
Playa Del Fey, CA 90293
310-822-5032

International Women's Health Coalition

24 E. 21st St., 5th Floor
New York, NY 10010
212-979-8500

Mid-Columbia Medical Center

1700 E. 19th St.
The Dalles, OR 97058
503-296-7592

National Alliance of Breast Cancer Organizations (NABCO)

1100 Avenue of the Americas
New York, NY 10036
212-719-0154

National Black Women's Health Project

1237 Ralph David Albernathy Blvd. SW
Atlanta, GA 30310
1-800-ASK-BWHP

National Cancer Institute

Cancer Information Service
Building 31, Room 10A18
Bethesda, MD 20892
1-800-422-6237

National Hospice Organization
1901 North Moore St., Suite 901
Arlington, VA 22209
1-800-658-8898

National Women's Health Resource Center
2440 M St., Suite 325
Washington, DC 20037
202-293-6045

National Women's Health Network
1325 G St. NW
Washington, DC 20005
202-347-1140

Native Women's Health Network
1325 G St. NW
Washington DC 20005
202-347-1140

Planned Parenthood Federation
(*Look in your local phone book for the number nearest you.*)

Society for the Right to Die
250 W. 57th St.
New York, NY 10107
212-246-6973

St. Charles Medical Center
2500 NE Neff Rd.
Bend, OR 97701
503-382-432

In Canada

Congress of Black Women of Canada

Ontario Region
756 Ossington Ave., No. 6
Toronto, Ontario M6G 3T9
416-269-4245

Immigrant Association of Canada

Box 1515, Station B
Ottawa, Ontario K1P 4R4
613-267-1269

Immigrant Women's Association

(By province in the *Directory of Associations in Canada*.)

Native Women's Association of Canada

9 Melrose Ave.
Ottawa, Ontario K1Y 1T8
613-722-3033

Planned Parenthood Federation of Canada

1 Nicolas St., Suite 430
Ottawa, Ontario K1N 7B7
613-238-4474

Toronto Women's Health Network

1884 Davenport Rd.
Toronto, Ontario M6N 4Y2
416-392-0898

Vancouver Women's Health Collective

1675 W. 8th St.
Vancouver, British Columbia V6J 1V2
604-736-4234

Women's Health Clinic

419 Graham Ave., 3rd Floor
Winnipeg, Manitoba R3C 0M3
204-947-1517

Women's Health Education Network

Box 99
Dearborn, Nova Scotia B0M 1T0

Women's Health Resources

The Salvation Army Grace Hospital
1402 8th Ave., NW
Calgary, Alberta T2N 1B9
403-282-9152

Yellowknife Women's Centre

Box 2645
Yellowknife, Northwest Territories X1A 2P9
403-920-6177

In Other Countries

Institute for Complementary Medicine

Box 194
London, England SR16 1Q2

British Acupuncture Association and Register

34 Alderney St.
Westminster
London, England SW1V 4EU

FINRRAGE (Feminist International Network of Resistance to
    Reproductive and Genetic Engineering)

Box 583
London, England NW3 1RQ

Healthsharing Women
318 Little Bourke St., 5th Floor
Melbourne, Australia 3000

Nurses' and Midwives' Central Clearing House
Box 346
Bristol, England BS99 7FB

The Nursing Adviser
Scottish Health Service Centre
Crewe Road South
Edinburgh, Scotland EH4 2LF

Women's Global Network for Reproductive Rights
NZ Voorburgwal 32
1012RZ Amsterdam, The Netherlands

Women's Health Information Resource Collective Inc.
Box 187
North Carlton
Victoria, Australia 3054

Directories

There are many associations that give information on thousands of conditions and diseases. You can go to the reference section of your library and ask:

For the United States

Encyclopedia of Associations, 28th ed., Peggy Kneffel Daniels and Carol A. Schwartz, eds., Gale Research Inc., Detroit, 1993.

For Canada

Directory of Associations in Canada, Repertoire des Associations du Canada, Micromedia Ltd., Toronto, 1993.

For Other Countries

Encylopedia of International Organizations 1993, 27th ed., Linda Irvine, ed., Gale Research Inc., Detroit, 1993.

Bibliography

Books

Achterberg, Jeanne. *Imagery in Healing: Shamanism and Modern Medicine*. Boston: New Science Library, 1985.

Adamson, Nancy, Linda Briskin, and Margaret McPhail. *Feminist Organizing for Change: The Contemporary Women's Movement in Canada*. Toronto: Oxford University Press, 1988.

Altman, Nathaniel. *Everybody's Guide to Chiropractic Health Care*. Los Angeles: Jeremy P. Tarcher, 1990.

Armstrong, David, and Elizabeth Metzger Armstrong. *The Great American Medicine Show: Being an Illustrated History of Hucksters, Healers, Health Evangelists and Heros from Plymouth Rock to the Present*. New York: Prentice Hall, 1991.

Barrett, Stephen, and the editors of *Consumer Reports. Health Schemes, Scams and Frauds*. New York: Consumer's Union, 1990.

Barrett, Stephen, and Gilda Knight, eds. *Health Robbers: How to Protect Your Money and Your Life*. Philadelphia: Stickley, 1976.

Blake, Catriona. *The Charge of the Parasols: Women's Entry to the Medical Profession*. London: The Women's Press, 1990.

Bolaria, B. Singh, and Harley D. Dickinson. *Sociology of Health Care in Canada*. Toronto: Harcourt Brace Jovanovich, 1988.

The Boston Women's Health Book Collective. *The New Our Bodies, Ourselves*. New York: A Touchstone Book, 1984, 1992.

Boyd, Peggy. *The Silent Women*. Reading: Addison-Wesley, 1984.

Brown, Catrina, and Karin Jasper, eds. *Consuming Passions: Feminist Approaches to Weight Preoccupation and Eating Disorders*. Toronto: Second Story Press, 1993.

Camp, John. *Magic, Myth and Medicine*. New York: Taplinger Publishing, 1974.

Carlson, Richard, and Benjamin Shield, eds. *Healers on Healing*. Los Angeles: Jeremy P. Tarcher, 1989.

Chicago, Judy. *The Dinner Party: A Symbol of Our Heritage*. New York: Anchor Books, 1979.

Chisman, Forest P., and associates. *Leadership for Literacy: The Agenda for the 1990s*. San Francisco: Jossey-Bass Publishers, 1990.

Chopra, Deepak. *Perfect Health: The Complete Mind/Body Guide*. New York: Harmony, 1990.

Canadian Research Institute for the Advancement of Women. *Learning from Diversity*. Ottawa: CRIAW, 1992.

Crook, Marion. *The Body Image Trap: Understanding and Rejecting Body Image Myths*. North Vancouver: Self-Counsel Press, 1991.

Crook, Marion. *Looking Good: Teenagers and Eating Disorders*. Toronto: NC Press, 1992.

Crook, Marion. *Please Listen to Me*. North Vancouver: Self-Counsel Press, 1992.

Crook, Marion. *Teenagers Talk about Suicide*. Toronto: NC Press, 1990.

Eisler, Riane. *The Chalice and the Blade: Our History, Our Future*. San Francisco: Harper, 1987.

Faludi, Susan. *Backlash: The Undeclared War against American Women*. New York: Anchor Books, 1991.

Franklin, Ursula. *The Real World of Technology*. Concord: Anansi, 1990.

Gatchel, Robert J., and Andrew Baum. *An Introduction to Health Psychology*. Reading: Addison-Wesley, 1983.

Gilligan, Carol, and Lyn Mikel Brown. *Meeting at the Crossroads: Women's Psychology and Girls' Development*. Cambridge: Harvard University Press, 1992.

Goodheart, George. *Healers on Healing*. Richard Carlson and Benjamin Shiel, eds. Los Angeles: Jeremy P. Tarcher, 1989.

Greer, Germaine. *The Change: Women, Aging and the Menopause.* Toronto: Alfred A. Knopf, 1991.

Haraway, Donna J. *Simians, Cyborgs and Women: The Reinvention of Nature.* New York: Routledge, 1991.

Heilbrun, Carolyn G. *Reinventing Womanhood.* New York: Norton, 1979.

Heilbrun, Carolyn G. *Writing a Woman's Life.* New York: Ballantine Books, 1988.

Holbrook, Stewart. *The Golden Age of Quackery.* New York: Macmillan, 1959.

Huard, Pierre, and Ming Wong. *Chinese Medicine.* New York: McGraw-Hill, World University Library, 1968.

Hurd-Mead, Kate Campbell. *The History of Women in Medicine: From Earliest Times to the Beginning of the Nineteenth Century.* Haddan: The Haddan Press, 1938.

Illich, Ivan. *Medical Nemesis: The Expropriation of Health.* New York: Pantheon Books, 1975.

Kleinman, Arthur. *The Illness Narratives: Suffering, Healing and the Human Condition.* New York: Basic Books, 1988.

Krippner, Stanley, and Alberto Villoldo. *The Realms of Healing.* Millbrae: Celestial Arts, 1976.

Mackie, Marlene. *Gender Relations in Canada: Further Explorations.* Toronto: Butterworths, 1991.

McDonnell, Kathleen. *Adverse Effects: Women and the Pharmaceutical Industry.* Toronto: The Women's Press, 1986.

National Council of Jewish Women of Canada. *Health Education and Learning Project (H.E.L.P.).* Winnipeg: National Council of Jewish Women, 1993.

Roberts, Nancy. *Breaking All the Rules: Feeling Good and Looking Great No Matter What Your Size.* New York: Viking Penguin, 1985.

Rousseau, David, W. J. Rea, and Jean Enwright. *Your Home, Your Health and Well-Being: What You Can Do to Design or Renovate Your House or Apartment to Be Free of Outdoor AND Indoor Pollution.* Vancouver: Hartley & Marks, 1988, 1989.

Showalter, Elaine. *The Female Malady: Women, Madness and English Culture.* New York: Penguin Books, 1987.

Siegel, Bernie. *Love, Medicine and Miracles.* New York: Harper & Row, 1986.

Smith, John M. *Women and Doctors*. New York: Dell, 1992.

Steinem, Gloria. *Revolution from Within: A Book of Self-Esteem*. Boston: Little, Brown and Company, 1992.

Taylor, Robert L. *Health Fact, Health Fiction: Getting Through the Media Maze*. Dallas: Taylor Publishing, 1990.

The Traditional Knowledge Working Group. *Report of the Traditional Knowledge Working Group*. Yellowknife: Northwest Territories Culture and Communications, 1991.

Vithoulkas, George. *A New Model of Health and Disease*. Berkeley: Health and Habitat and North Atlantic Books, 1991.

Waler, Barbara. *The Woman's Encyclopedia of Myths and Secrets*. San Francisco: Harper, 1983.

Weatherford, Jack. *Native Roots: How the Indians Enriched America*. New York: Fawcett Columbine, 1991.

Young, James Harvey. *The Medical Messiahs: A Social History of Health Quackery in Twentieth Century America*. Princeton: Princeton University Press, 1967.

Periodicals

The Alberta/Northwest Territories Network of Immigrant Women. "Multicultural health for immigrant women: A dialogue." A report of proceedings from a one-day workshop organized by the ANNIW Multicultural Health Committee, Calgary, Alberta, 28 Mar. 1992.

Bird, Florence, Jacques Henripin, John P. Humphrey, Lola M. Lange, Jeanne Lapointe, Elsie Gregory MacGill, and Doris Ogilvie. "The report on the Royal Commission on the Status of Women in Canada." Secretary of State Department, 28 Sept. 1970.

Browne, H., and G. Isaacs. "The Frontier Nursing Service." *American Journal of Obstetrics and Gynecology* 123, 1976.

Durand, A. Mark. "The safety of home birth: The farm study." *American Journal of Public Health* 82(3), March 1992.

Editorial. "Towards a more inclusive model of women's health." *American Journal of Public Health* 83(1), Jan. 1993.

Fagan, Drew. "Health-care costs eating up Canada's GDP" (From World Bank statistics). *Globe and Mail* 25 Aug. 1993.

Frontier School of Midwifery and Family Nursing. "Community based nurse-midwifery education program." *Frontier Nursing Service* 1993.

Gittelsoha, Alan M., Jane Halpern, and Ricardo L. Sanches. "Income, race and surgery in Maryland." *American Journal of Public Health* 81(11), Nov. 1991.

Graveley, Elaine A., and John H. Littlefield. "A cost-effectiveness analysis of three staffing models of the delivery of low-risk prenatal care." *American Journal of Public Health* 82(2), Feb. 1992.

Hossie, Linda. "Young Canadian deaths among highest in West." *Globe and Mail* 23 Sept. 1993.

Kassulla, D., K. Stenner-Day, M. Coory, I. Ring, "Information-seeking behaviour and sources of health information associated with risk factor states in an analysis of three Queensland electorates." *Australian Journal of Public Health* 1993 Mar. 17(1), 51–57.

Levy, B. F. Wilkinson, and W. Marine. "Reducing neonatal mortality rate with nurse-midwives." *American Journal of Obstetrics and Gynecology* 109, 1971.

Mathey, Jeannett. "The cancer that needn't have been." *Globe and Mail* 20 Apr. 1993.

McBeuth, Wm. H. "Health for all: A public health vision." *American Journal of Public Health* 81(12), Dec. 1991.

Metropolitan Life Insurance Company. "Report on the FNS of Hyden, KY," 1932.

Mickleburgh, Rod. "Murder trial prompts debate on College of Surgeons' inaction." *Globe and Mail* 4 Aug. 1993.

Mickleburgh, Rod. "Breast cancer victims given voice." *Globe and Mail* 16 Nov. 1993.

Michielutte, P., J. Bahnson, M. B. Dignon, E. M. Schroeder, "The use of illustrations and narrative text style to improve readability of a health education brochure." *Journal of Cancer Education* 7(3): 251–60, 1992.

Miller, Leslie. "Alternatives meet the mainstream." *USA Today* 22 Jul. 1993.

Miller, Marilyn Suzanne. "Cancer for Christmas." *Globe and Mail* 15 Jan. 1993.

MCMC University. *One Team, One School of Thought.* Handout from the Mid-Columbia Medical Center, The Dalles, Oregon.

Midwives Association of British Columbia. "Information package." *Midwives Association of British Columbia* 1993.

Moyers, Bill. "The cures within: An interview with Candace Pert." *Globe and Mail: Body and Soul.* From Public Affairs Television and David Brubin Productions Inc., Toronto: Doubleday, Spring 1993.

Pro-Choice News. Northwest Territories, Summer 1992.

Shah, P. M., B. J. Selwyn, K. Shah, and V. Kumar. "Evaluation of the home-based maternal record: A WHO collaborative study." *Bulletin of the World Health Agency* 71(S), 1993.

"Sixty-seventh annual report of the Frontier Nursing Service Inc. for the Fiscal Year of May 1, 1991 to April 30, 1992. *Quarterly Bulletin of Frontier Nursing Service* 68, Summer 1992.

Slome, C., H. Wetherbee, M. Daly, K. Christensen, M. Meglen, and H. Theide. "Effectiveness of certified nurse-midwives." *American Journal of Obstetrics and Gynecology* 124, 1976.

"Smelling a rat in medical research." *Globe and Mail* (From "The Gender Agenda," *The Economist,* 20 Mar. 93) 22 Mar. 1993.

Smith, Vivian. "Unwilling to keep taking it like a man." *Globe and Mail* [Toronto] 27 Apr. 1993.

"Social justice and family therapy." *Dulwich Centre Newsletter.* New Zealand, Lower Hutt: No. 1, 1990.

"Social studies: Violence against women." *Globe and Mail* [Toronto] 18 Jan. 1993.

Statistics Canada. *Adult Literacy in Canada: Results of a National Study.* Cat. #89–525E.

Steele, E. "Report on the four thousand confinements of the Frontier Nursing Service." *Quarterly Bulletin of Frontier Nursing Service* 16.

"Summary of the first 10,000 confinement records of the Frontier Nursing Service." *Quarterly Bulletin of Frontier Nursing Service* 33, Spring 1958.

Taylor, Paul. *Globe and Mail* 28 Oct. 1991.

Traditional Knowledge Working Group. "Report of traditional knowledge working group." Yellowknife: Department of Culture and Communications, 1991.

Ullrich, I. H., R. A. Yeater, and J. Dalal. "Heart disease in women." *West Virginia Medical Journal* 88:12, 1992.

Women's Community Advisory Committee and the Grace Hospital Board Planning Committee. *Women and Health: Sharing the Vision.* Calgary: May 1992.

Other

Bartlett, Judith, G. From a lecture at the First Nations Women and Wellness Conference. Vancouver: 10 Feb. 1993.

Cohen, May. "Health care for women." An address to a conference at the University of British Columbia, 16 Oct. 1992.

St. Charles Medical Center. "Endometriosis treatment program." St. Charles Medical Center brochures, 1993.

Tudiver, Sari. "Manitoba Voices: A Qualitative Study of Women's Experiences with Technology in Pregnancy." In: *Prenatal Diagnosis: Background and Impact on Individuals,* Volume 12, Research Volumes. Royal Commission on New Reproductive Technologies, Ministry of Supply and Services: Ottawa, Canada, 1993.

Vaughn, Evelyn. From a lecture at the First Nations Women and Wellness Conference. Vancouver: 10 Feb. 1993.

Index